THE SUPPORTIVE STATE

D1566294

Praise for *The Supportive State*

"*The Supportive State* is a groundbreaking analysis of how to rethink the relationship between the state and the family. Maxine Eichner carefully examines a series of issues, ranging from marriage to foster care to teen abortion to children's rights, as she develops her theory of the supportive state. The book makes a significant contribution to liberal political theory and to our understandings of the family, while also offering concrete suggestions on how the state should promote family flourishing."

—Naomi Cahn,
Professor of Law, The George Washington University Law School
and co-author of *Red Families v. Blue Families*

"*The Supportive State* makes a splendid contribution to contemporary discussions of families and public policy. She argues rigorously for state support of caregiving relationships (involving children, family members, the elderly, the disabled, and others). In the course of her discussion, Maxine Eichner offers stimulating reflections on same-sex marriage, welfare reform, parental and community control over school curricula, and other pressing concerns involving families and the state. Eichner's compelling vision and clear writing invite readers to examine their own views about public responsibility for the caregiving that sustains both families and civil society."

—Mary Shanley,
Professor of Political Science, Vassar College

"Debates over marriage, the family, and family values have been a staple feature of political rhetoric for the last several decades, and show no sign of ceasing. As patterns of family life in the United States have undergone dramatic change, family law continues to undergo dramatic evolution. Legal and political theory—as well as public policy—are slowly beginning to address the family as a vital political and social institution. It is important that these debates and this evolution be informed by concern for the relevant political goods and principles that Maxine Eichner elaborates in *The Supportive State*."

—Linda C. McClain,
Professor of Law, Boston University School of Law

THE SUPPORTIVE STATE

*Families, Government, and America's
Political Ideals*

MAXINE EICHNER

OXFORD
UNIVERSITY PRESS

OXFORD
UNIVERSITY PRESS

Oxford University Press is a department of the University of Oxford.
It furthers the University's objective of excellence in research, scholarship,
and education by publishing worldwide.

Oxford   New York

Auckland   Cape Town   Dar es Salaam   Hong Kong   Karachi
Kuala Lumpur   Madrid   Melbourne   Mexico City   Nairobi
New Delhi   Shanghai   Taipei   Toronto

With offices in

Argentina   Austria   Brazil   Chile   Czech Republic   France   Greece
Guatemala   Hungary   Italy   Japan   Poland   Portugal   Singapore
South Korea   Switzerland   Thailand   Turkey   Ukraine   Vietnam

Oxford is a registered trade mark of Oxford University Press
in the UK and certain other countries.

Published in the United States of America by
Oxford University Press
198 Madison Avenue, New York, NY 10016

© Oxford University Press 2010

First issued as an Oxford University Press paperback, 2013.

Library of Congress Cataloging-in-Publication Data
Eichner, Maxine.
The supportive state : families, government, and America's
political ideals / Maxine Eichner.
p. cm.
Includes bibliographical references and index.
ISBN: 978-0-19-534321-2 (hardcover); 978-0-19-993594-9 (paperback)
1. Family policy—United States. 2. Families—United States.
I. Title.
HQ536.E35 2010
306.850973—dc22   2009046432

1 3 5 7 9 8 6 4 2

For Hannah, Abe, and Eli, who both inspired this book and delayed its completion considerably, and for Eric, who, among many other things, is my first, last, and best reader.

ACKNOWLEDGMENTS

I am resisting beginning with "it takes a village" clichés (well, only partially resisting), but the fact is, my debts are many. This has been a book very long in the making, and I owe many people gratitude for help along the way.

A few scholars encouraged me to go forward at the early stages of this project, including Kathryn Abrams, Michael Lienesch, Hiroshi Motomura, Elizabeth Scott, Mary ("Molly") Shanley, and Thomas Spragens. I am grateful for both their encouragement and their advice. Tom also generously spent a number of lunches hashing through liberal theory with me, which were extremely helpful. Mike pushed me to make this a far more rigorous, and better, book than it would have been otherwise.

Other scholars and colleagues provided me with helpful comments at critical times (and, occasionally, critical comments at helpful times), including Kerry Abrams, Jane Aiken, Katharine Bartlett, Susan Bickford, Curtis Bridgeman, Naomi Cahn, June Carbone, Jennifer Collins, Pamela Conover, Adrienne Davis, Joanna Grossman, Melissa Jacoby, Margaret Johnson, Alicia Kelly, Joseph Kennedy, Michael Klarman, Holning Lau, Steven Leonard, William Marshall, Linda McClain, Eric Muller, Gene Nichol, Angela Onwuachi-Willig, Ziggy Rifkind-Fish, Maria Savasta-Kennedy, Carisa Showden, Jana Singer, Mark Weisburd, and Deborah Weissman. In addition, I owe a large intellectual debt of gratitude to Martha Fineman and Thomas Spragens; without Martha's work on dependency and Tom's on civic liberalism, this book could not have been written.

Three excellent colleagues and friends, Clare Huntington, Molly Shanley, and Jeffrey Spinner-Halev, read the entire draft of this book and gave me detailed and helpful comments, for which they have my undying gratitude. In addition, Denise Powers, with whom I was lucky to become friends years ago in graduate school, applied her extraordinary skills as a copy editor to this manuscript before its submission to Oxford University Press. My editor, David McBride, at Oxford University Press, guided me through the publication process with wisdom, grace, and the patience of Job.

Here at UNC, I am indebted to the law librarians, particularly Jim Sherwood and Julie Kimbrough, for their excellent research. I also have several years of research assistants to thank, particularly Cameron Contizano, Caitlin Cullitan, Jerry Dowless, Kristen Formanek, Blake Huffman, Ian Keith, Molly Maynard, Carolyn Pratt, Dan Rose, and Angie Spong. Special thanks are due to Molly and Angie for seeing me through the final crunch to finish this book. In addition, I owe many thanks to Kim Price and Mika Chance for their help in typing the manuscript. I am also grateful for grants and fellowships that helped me along the way from the Miller Center of Public Affairs, the Carolina Women's Center, and UNC School of Law.

Finally, I am fortunate to come from a large and wonderful family whose members were enormously patient during the long time it took me to complete this (only toward the end were there much-deserved jibes about the never-finished book), and supported me through its writing. I thank Vicky and Arthur Eichner, Jane and Adam Stein, June Eichner and Barry Elman, Faith and Jeff Adler, Gerda Stein and Roberto Quercia, Josh and Anna Stein, Robert Eichner, April Terlizzi, and all their children for bearing with me through this. This book is dedicated to Hannah, Abe, and Eli Stein Eichner, and to Eric Stein, for teaching me over and over again the joys that families can bring, and the important role that they play in giving meaning to human lives.

CONTENTS

THE SUPPORTIVE STATE

Introduction

Most of us spend the majority of our lives in long-term relationships with others whom we consider family. These relationships have a fundamental influence on us from our day of birth, and are central to our emotional and moral commitments. They profoundly affect the way we live our lives on a daily basis. In addition, they serve an important role in meeting the dependency needs that must be met for citizens themselves and our society to flourish. It is through these relationships that we largely rear our children; handle much of the caretaking for sick, disabled, and elderly adults; and generally manage other issues of dependency, including financial dependency.

What role should the state play with respect to these critical ties among citizens? Until now, the set of beliefs and assumptions that has animated American political thought and public policy has had little to say about the inevitability of dependency in human lives and the important role families serve in dealing with dependency. These beliefs and assumptions generally derive from the dominant tradition of political thought in the United States, namely, that of liberal democracy.[1] Liberalism, particularly in its American incarnations, has largely conceived of citizens as able, autonomous adults, and has focused on them as individuals rather than as members of families. Conceiving of citizens in this manner has served valuable functions: It has helped ground the liberal moral ideal that all citizens should be treated as free and equal. It has also justified the important notion that citizens have an entitlement to rights that the state should safeguard.

However, although the liberal conception of humans as able, autonomous adults is an important moral ideal, it is still only a moral ideal. It is not, as it is often treated, an adequate ontological understanding of the human condition. The conception of citizens as able adults freezes citizens at one point in time in the human life cycle, and even then it exaggerates their independence from one another.[2] In reality, citizens spend most of their lives dependent on one another to some greater or lesser degree. Citizens are born completely dependent and live in near total dependence on others for roughly the first decade of their lives. They spend their next decade requiring considerable assistance from others, although generally to a decreasing extent. During these first two decades, and often longer, they require a number of things to become healthy, flourishing adults and contributing members of the polity. For one thing, they require significant caretaking, which, for young children, involves a wide array of tasks. They must be supervised to ensure they are safe, played with, interacted with, fed, bathed, changed, put to bed, picked up when they are crying, and taken to the doctor when they are sick, among a hundred other activities. In addition to caretaking, children require certain things to foster the human development it takes for them to become sound adults and good citizens. During the course of youth, they must learn to perform for themselves many of the tasks that adults have performed for them. They must also develop deep and stable attachments with at least a few others, receive moral guidance, learn social skills, acquire an education and skills to support themselves when they reach adulthood, and develop citizenship skills. Meeting human development needs, like meeting caretaking needs, requires a considerable investment of time, attention, and resources.

Some small but significant number of citizens will never achieve a substantial degree of independence from the caretaking of others because of physical or mental disabilities. Most others will enter an adulthood in which they are largely, although never completely, independent. When it comes to dependency issues, no adult is an island; virtually all adults have some periods in which they require significant caretaking because of physical or mental illness, and most have intermittent periods of such dependence.[3] Further, a considerable portion of adults will experience serious disabling conditions that will leave them dependent for long periods of time, if not permanently.[4] And as they age and approach the end of life, most adults will become increasingly dependent on others for care.[5] Not only does all this mean that most people spend a good deal of their lives dependent on others, it also means that many citizens—particularly women and minorities—spend a good part of their adult lives engaged in caretaking for children or ill or aging adults.[6]

Focusing on the dependency of the human condition makes the picture of what citizens need from their government more complex than dominant versions of liberal democratic theory would have it. These versions conceive the state's role in terms of ensuring citizens' freedom to pursue their own life plans and, often, ensuring at least some measure of equality. Conceiving the state's role in this manner is a natural outgrowth of conceiving of citizens as able adults; given this conception of citizens, the appropriate role for the state is to ensure that their individual rights are respected. Further, if adults are conceived as capable and autonomous, the respect for human dignity that grounds liberalism requires, above all, ensuring their freedom and equality. Once the human life cycle is introduced into this picture, however, the importance of caretaking and human development come to the fore as every bit as important to the liberal democratic project as safeguarding the mainstream liberal goods of freedom and equality. The importance of caretaking and human development, in turn, calls attention to the role of the family, which, in our society, has been the institution largely responsible for performing these functions.

To the scant extent liberal theory has attended to families, it has generally conceived of them as if, like the adults that head them, they properly are and should be autonomous. The goal of public policy, in this view, is to keep the family as free as possible from state intervention. Moreover, insofar as dependency needs of children arise, this theory contends that the autonomous adults who head families should properly deal with them, without action by the state. This view of family autonomy, however, like the view of individual autonomy, is a gross oversimplification.[7] In truth, the ways in which families function are always deeply and inextricably intertwined with government policy.[8] To mention just a few examples, child-labor laws keep children financially dependent on their parents; equal employment legislation has encouraged women's movement into the labor market and out of the home; and Social Security survivors' benefits influence some recipients not to marry. Most importantly, for the purposes of this book, law and public policy affect families' ability to deal with dependency needs. Because of this, and the critical role that sound families play in the lives of flourishing citizens and a flourishing society, the family-state relationship must occupy a central position in liberal democratic theory. The tasks of integrating dependency and the role that families play in dealing with it into liberal democratic theory, and considering the role that the state should play with respect to American families, are the subjects of this book.

Although this book seeks to put families in appropriate perspective as a matter of theory, the current neglect of dependency and families in dominant versions of liberalism has had far more than theoretical consequences in the United States. Political theory never translates seamlessly into public policy; there are always gaps and discontinuities. With that said, the theoretical tenets that have obscured the importance of families have prevented the formulation of coherent law and public policy regarding families in the United States. This has resulted in government policies that fall far short of achieving goods that we, as a nation, should care a great deal about.

At the top of this list of goods is the welfare of children. Contemporary liberal democracy's focus on protecting the rights and liberties of able adults, and its expectation that children's dependency issues will be dealt with solely by families headed by these adults, has made it difficult to formulate policies that adequately support children's well-being. The result is that the poverty rate among children in the United States is among the highest in the industrialized world, with 22 percent of all children and 39.1 percent of African-American children living below the poverty threshold. Although other relatively wealthy nations, such as France, Ireland, New Zealand, and the United Kingdom, have higher child-poverty rates than the United States before government aid, the United States' government-aid policies are much less ambitious than these, and its child-poverty rates are, therefore, substantially higher.[9]

The lack of a well-thought-out theory of dependency in combination with the assumption of family autonomy has also resulted in laws that inadequately support families in ensuring that children receive the caretaking they need to flourish. The influx of women into the workforce during the past two generations has created a situation in which the citizens who had been largely responsible for raising children now have significant other demands on their time. Between 1975 and 2008, the percentage of women in the workforce with children under the age of six years grew from 39 percent to 63 percent.[10] Women with children between the ages of six and seventeen increased their participation in the workforce from 55 percent in 1975 to 75 percent in 2008.[11] Seventy percent of families are now headed either by two working parents or by an unmarried working parent.[12] Yet the United States has implemented very few policies to help families ameliorate the conflicts between work and family.[13] The result is that, on average, U.S. families work significantly more hours than they have in the past,[14] and far longer hours than parents work in other industrialized countries.[15] Meanwhile, younger children are placed in day care settings that are largely unregulated and generally not developmentally enriching.[16] Many older children, in turn, come home to empty, unsupervised homes.[17]

Among the many disadvantages for children caused by the extended hours that parents work is the negative impact it has on their relationship with their parents. A recent UNICEF report ranked the United States twenty-third out of twenty-five member countries of the Organization for Economic Cooperation and Development (OECD) in terms of the percentage of teens who eat dinner with their parents several times a week, an indicator of parental-child interaction that UNICEF found to be an important determinant in children's well-being.[18] Both this indicator and the U.S. child-poverty rates, among other factors, contributed to that same report ranking the well-being of children in the United States as second to last overall among OECD nations measured, twentieth of the twenty-one countries ranked, when all areas of children's well-being were measured.[19]

These blind spots regarding dependency also perpetuate gender inequality. As I noted earlier, they weaken the justification for the state to provide protection for working parents as well as for the many workers who care for sick or aging family members. Faced with jobs that do not accommodate caregiving, it is generally women who step off the career track and either leave the paid workplace or choose non-demanding "mommy-track" jobs so that they will have adequate time for this caregiving.[20] They do so at a substantial economic cost. A growing body of evidence suggests that the reduction in women's pay caused by childrearing is the primary factor in women's continued economic inequality with men in the United States.[21] Those women who are childless, by one calculation, earn 90 percent as much as men do; mothers, however, earn only 70 percent as much as men.[22] This wage gap does not appear to be diminishing over time. Researchers considering it concluded that "children decrease women's wages significantly, and this penalty has been quite stable."[23] These inequalities in pay cause women to have less decision-making power within marriages, less future earning power in the case of divorce, and lower pensions in the case of their husbands' deaths. Moreover, it is women's child-care responsibilities that are the biggest continuing factor in the feminization of poverty.[24]

Yet the lack of attention to dependency and to the important role that the state can play in supporting families dealing with dependency issues has effects that extend still more broadly. The failure to support workers who have caretaking responsibilities puts the great number of families with significant dependency responsibilities in a significant bind for time. The influx of women into the workforce in the last four decades has caused families to add 10–29 hours per week working outside the home.[25] In an attempt to preserve family time, American parents have responded by spending significantly fewer hours socializing with friends and engaging in community activities than they once did. This has caused their social circles to narrow dramatically and the broader social networks in neighborhoods and communities to shrink.[26] Not only does this affect the quality of lives of those adults whose social circles have narrowed, but also the well-being of communities, which lack the benefits of engaged citizens. Further, the weakening of social ties among citizens negatively affects levels of civic trust in society, which is important for a democracy to function well.[27]

Among the many other effects of liberalism's blindness to dependency, in combination with its myth of family autonomy, is that it leaves social programs that address dependency vulnerable to the criticism that they are inimical to our way of life. These programs are derided as "creeping socialism" or the rise of the "nanny state." Even their supporters find them difficult to justify, since they have no coherent ideological structure within the dominant liberal understanding of the world on which to hang them.[28] The result is that public policies that address issues of dependency and families are generally patchwork rather than coherently laid out, and they are particularly vulnerable to the political vagaries of the time. This explains the drastic swings of policy regarding both welfare and foster care in the 1990s, as well as the extended debates regarding the propriety of single-parent families in that era.

The absence of a well-developed liberal theory regarding families also leaves questions unresolved about the legitimacy of particular family forms. The heated and rapidly-changing battle now being waged over same-sex marriage in the United States is a case in point. The recent admission of same-sex couples into the institution of marriage, first in Massachusetts, then in California (albeit temporarily), and in Connecticut, Iowa, Vermont, New

Hampshire, and New York, represents a seismic shift in family law in these states.[29] Yet the majority of states have enshrined rejection of same-sex marriage explicitly into state law, many in their state constitutions.[30] The federal government has done the same for federal law.[31] This polarization between the states over same-sex marriage has shed a strong light on the ways that, even in the absence of a coherent theory of the family-state relationship, state power in the United States has routinely favored some families over others. Federal law and the law in most states currently grant hundreds, if not thousands, of privileges to those families deemed to warrant it—generally heterosexual marital families.[32] Yet these privileges are accorded with few coherent ideological underpinnings to justify them.

Same-sex marriage presents the most volatile and visible, but not the only, pressing issue with respect to how the state should deal with different types of families. The high contemporary divorce rates,[33] the increasing visibility of same-sex relationships,[34] the mushrooming rates of single-parent families,[35] and the growing number of couples who cohabit without being married[36] challenge conventional understandings that families necessarily take any pre-given form, removed from political and social circumstances. Today, fewer than one in four U.S. households consist of a husband, wife, and children, down from 44 percent in 1960.[37] That number drops to fewer than 10 percent for households in which both parents live with their biological children and the wife does not work outside the home.[38] The lack of a nuanced theory of the state's relationship to families has exacerbated the polarized debates taking place about nontraditional families, and has led to inconsistent public policies that apply to them.

Liberalism's problematic relationship with families and dependency has not been lost on legal and political theorists in recent years. In the past decade or so, the legal, political, and social developments surrounding families have spurred a long-overdue conversation regarding the family-state relationship.[39] Feminists, communitarians, and queer theorists have all pointed out liberal theory's shortcomings with respect to families. The great majority of this still relatively new discussion has consisted of critique of liberal theories and the policies derived from them. There has been much less focus on reconstructing the relationship between families and the state in a more productive manner. Moreover, those theorists who have sought to develop a new vision have generally called for the abandonment of liberal principles and the adoption of some other theoretical framework.

This book takes a different tack. It develops a normative account of the family-state relationship that is liberal in nature, at least if the term *liberal* is construed expansively. I use the term here in the broad sense of liberalism as a theory of the state that is committed to the equal dignity of all human beings, the importance of limits on government, considerable respect for individuals' own views of how to live their lives, and the view that legitimate government is grounded in the consent of the people.[40] Although this definition of liberalism is more expansive than some liberals would have it, it comports with earlier understandings of this line of thought. Conceived in this way, in my view, liberalism is a tradition worth preserving so long as it is amended to accommodate the recognition of dependency and the role of families. Staying within the liberal tradition also has the virtue of not foreclosing the possibility of political relevance. For better or worse, our political tradition is overwhelmingly liberal. A theory of dependency that can be squared with this tradition has a greater chance of being implemented than one that radically departs from it.

The theory I develop, however, rejects the more limited recent understanding of liberalism as a theory that requires the state to be neutral on all visions of the good life, and dedicated above all to furthering individual justice (generally described, depending on the theorist, in terms of some optimal mix of liberty and equality). That understanding, most prominently associated with John Rawls,[41] has come under fire by liberal revisionists in the last decades, who argue that a liberal polity must strive to further a broader range of goods and purposes than the individualistic versions of justice that have been associated with it in contemporary liberal theory.[42] Some of these revisionists call themselves "civic liberals," to signal their views that a healthy, liberal democracy demands that the state seek to promote the values of community and civic virtues, in addition to the standard liberal goods. I agree with the view that liberalism needs to achieve greater moral complexity than it has demonstrated in recent years,[43] but I think these liberal revisionists have not cast their nets widely enough. Specifically, given the significant role that dependency plays in the human condition, the state must seek to expand its purposes to support caretaking and human development. This places me in the company of those feminists who have argued that the liberal state must recognize the virtue of care.[44] Among the most important means to support caretaking and human development, I contend, is through supporting families. Support for families is necessary to further the value of human dignity, which gives liberal democracy much of its normative appeal. Once we recognize the dependency of the human condition, supporting caretaking and human development becomes necessary so that citizens can lead full, dignified lives, both individually and collectively.

The account developed in this book not only seeks to draw on liberal principles, but democratic principles as well. Although I generally treat liberalism and democracy as if they walk hand-in-hand on issues of family and state, the fact that the two are so often linked can sometimes obscure the tension between the two concepts.[45] Those who stress the *liberal* in liberal democracy see the point of that form of government as being the preservation of individual rights to allow citizens to live their lives as they choose. Those who stress the *democratic* aspects, in contrast, focus on the exercise of collective self-government as individual citizens join together to create a political community that together determines its way of life. Families play an important role at the juncture between these two conceptions, not only serving as the emotional center of many citizens' life plans, but also serving a key role in developing the traits and virtues necessary for the collective self-rule on which democracy depends.

To be viable, a theory of liberal democracy must recognize both the private and public aspects of the family. To do so, it must stitch together the dominant liberal purposes of the state in safeguarding liberty and equality with support for caretaking and human development. This theory must also take into account the complex ways that families affect the goods necessary for democracy, including a sense of community among citizens, and the presence of civic virtues in the citizenry. It is only by considering this richer range of goods and principles, and by seeking more nuanced approaches that ameliorate the inevitable tensions among them, that the appropriate relationship between families and the state can be brought into focus.

My argument that the state has an integral role in supporting families puts me in conflict with a number of scholars and commentators across the political spectrum. In contrast with some conservatives, I reject the idea that state support for families leads to dysfunctional dependency. In fact, in my view, supporting families is as central to a sound polity as developing a competent police force to ensure citizens' safety. I am, however, more willing to require that families bear significant financial responsibility, as well as other forms of responsibility, for caretaking and human development functions than some of my colleagues on the left.[46] And, in contrast to other colleagues on the left who argue that state support for some forms of families is both narrow-minded and discriminatory and seek instead the repeal of privileges, I take the position that the state has good reasons to privilege and support particular family relationships.[47]

When it comes to determining which relationships should receive state support, I define the field expansively, in contrast to those on the right and in the middle of the political spectrum. A wide range of long-term relationships can foster the caretaking and human development necessary for a flourishing citizenry, and are, therefore, good candidates for state support. As a result, I take issue with those who argue that there is some sort of "natural" family out there that is the only sort that the state should privilege,[48] and with those who contend that the state should support only heterosexual marriage because it is the best environment in which to raise children.[49]

But why start with considering families at all when thinking about how society should deal with issues of dependency? The longer answer to this question, laid out in the course of this book, is that families properly form a vital part of the caretaking networks necessary for flourishing citizens and a flourishing society, even if they should never be taken for the whole of such caretaking networks. The shorter answer to this question is that it is because families—defined broadly—currently constitute a key institution responsible for dealing with dependency issues. Perhaps if we were constructing society from the ground up, we might decide to deal with these issues another way—say, through relegating all care work to the state. As Justice McReynolds said of Plato's idea that children should be removed from their parents and raised communally, "Although such measures have been deliberately approved by men of great genius, their ideas touching the relation between individual and State were wholly different from those upon which our institutions rest."[50] Political theory that seeks to design social institutions from the ground up risks irrelevancy. As Ian Shapiro counsels, humans "seldom design institutions afresh;" instead, they redesign existing institutions.[51] The important question, then, is how to persuade people to redesign them in ways that more closely accord with our best political ideals. To answer that question, I assume that at least some significant part of the work of caretaking and fostering human development will continue to occur within intimate caretaking relationships with those whom we consider "family." This does not exclude, however, considering the extent to which other institutions should take up some of the responsibility for these tasks; indeed, this book calls for some redistribution of this responsibility.

A normatively compelling vision of the family-state relationship must pay specific attention to promoting conditions in which families will flourish, rather than just taking such conditions for granted. Healthy families, in this view, are an achievement to be pursued rather than an inevitability. Yet such a vision must also avoid looking at families through rose-colored glasses; an adequate theory of the family-state relationship must keep in mind both the persistent inequalities within many relationships sanctioned by the state as "families" and the recognition that families sometime function in ways not conducive to the welfare of their members or the polity. A realistic yet productive set of family policies built on these theoretical premises can be achieved without bankrupting the country, ignoring principles of fairness to those who are not members of families, or undermining the responsibility and autonomy of the adults who head families. Accomplishing these ends, however, requires nuanced policies that are capable of harmonizing the tension among the diverse array of goods for which a liberal democracy should strive.

During the course of this book, I develop my supportive-state model to demonstrate how the United States should organize its family-state relations and reconcile the tensions among these important goods. Contrary to the view that currently underlies public policy, state support should be seen as appropriate not only after families "fail," in the sense that the state deems them to have inadequately accomplished their caretaking or human development functions, but should be considered an integral part of the state's responsibilities. Yet the state's responsibility to families does not usurp the responsibility of family members, themselves, for the welfare of children and for other dependency needs of their members. Instead, families appropriately bear responsibility for the day-to-day caring for (or arranging the care for) children and for meeting other dependency needs. Meanwhile, the state bears the responsibility for structuring societal institutions in ways that help families meet their caretaking needs and promote adequate human development. At a minimum, the state must arrange institutions in such a way that family members can, through exercising diligent, but not Herculean, efforts meet the basic physical, mental, and emotional needs of children and other dependents without being impoverished or having their emotional well-being threatened. In other words, the state should assume the responsibility for ensuring that the "rules of the game" facilitate caretaking and human development. Central to accomplishing this task is supporting families. The supportive-state model in this way undergirds families while still allowing them freedom to pursue their own visions of the good life, as well as the visions of the individuals within them. Further, it does so in a manner gently designed to ensure that families are a part of the larger community, rather than a barrier from it. Although I develop my account within the context of the United States, many of the principles developed will be applicable to other liberal democracies.

To consider these issues, my plan is straightforward. Chapter 1 considers the ideological stumbling blocks that have prevented an adequate conceptualization of the family-state relationship in both theory and public policy in the United States. The first part of the chapter uses the work of John Rawls to consider the absence of families in contemporary liberal theory, and to explore the specific assumptions that are responsible for this elision. I focus on Rawls's work for this purpose because it has set the agenda for liberal theory since the 1970s. The second part of the chapter then demonstrates that many of these same assumptions about the family-state relationship permeate both law and public policy. To illustrate this, I consider the way that the intersection between work and family is constructed in United States law. Although there is often considerable distance between dominant tenets of political theory in the academy and the public policy that is actually enacted, I show that there is considerable overlap between them when it comes to work-family law. These tenets, I argue, create a problematic platform on which to construct an adequate family-state relationship.

Chapter 2 considers how liberal democratic theory would change if we took seriously the role of dependency in the human life cycle, and the role of families in dealing with dependency. This chapter begins by demonstrating that although certain features of liberalism make it more difficult to focus on families than do other theories of government, there is nothing intrinsic to liberalism that precludes a nuanced treatment of the subject. From there, it takes a closer look at how families should be conceptualized as a theoretical matter, and then lays out a version of the family-state relationship that is more conducive to important liberal democratic goods. In my supportive-state model, family members bear the primary responsibility for caring for or arranging the care for other family members with dependency needs. The state, though, has a corresponding responsibility to facilitate this caretaking, and to organize other social institutions to support families in this fundamental task. In the final sections of the chapter, I consider what role the current concept of family privacy should play in the supportive state.

Chapter 3 develops the supportive-state model in the context of caretaker-dependent, or "vertical" relationships. I consider the state's responsibility vis-à-vis families for citizens who are substantially dependent on others, including children, the aged, and those with significant disabilities. To what extent is the welfare of dependents the state's responsibility, and to what extent is it their families'? It is this issue that underlies contentious policy debates concerning welfare reform, foster care, and family leave. I explain how the supportive-state model helps resolve these conflicts.

Chapter 4 then considers the stance that the state should adopt with respect to relationships among adults, or "horizontal" relationships. In contrast to most caretaker-dependent relationships discussed in the previous chapter, adults in a liberal polity can generally order their own affairs. Should the state, therefore, distance itself from these relationships? It is on this issue that current debates over same-sex marriage, calls for the state to disestablish civil marriage, and proposals to encourage two-parent families hinge. I demonstrate that here, too, the supportive-state model helps to strike an acceptable balance among the important goods and principles at stake.

Finally, Chapter 5 considers how the state should protect children's interests in a framework that both respects the value of family privacy, but also recognizes that families are seldom perfect and that sometimes these imperfections redound to children's detriment. The mainstream view that underlies contemporary theory and public policy has been to affirm the doctrine of family privacy and to preclude state action to support children's welfare until families fail to safeguard this welfare. At that point, coercive intervention in families is deemed appropriate. The supportive state does better, I argue, in supporting families in the ordinary course of events. Doing so will many times keep families from reaching the point of crisis and coercive intervention. At the same time, because of children's necessary dependence on their parents, the state generally does better to protect children's welfare by assisting parents, rather than giving children rights that can be exercised against their parents. Yet while the supportive state gives considerable weight to the good of family privacy, it considers it as one of a range of goods that must be supported in a flourishing society, rather than a complete trump to state action. The supportive state therefore seeks nuanced ways to respect family privacy to the extent possible while still safeguarding important liberal democratic norms.

ON TERMINOLOGY AND METHODOLOGY

Before I begin my discussion, let me clarify the key terms associated with this project, specifically my use of the terms *family* and *state*—neither of which is self-explanatory. With regard to the former, the issue of which intimate relationships are and should be considered families is deeply contested in our society. Instead of assuming that there is any clear, nonpolitical answer to the question, my project takes as a starting point the view that what counts as a family is inherently intertwined with politics and power. My use of the term is not meant to elide this definitional issue, but rather to explore it. In doing so, I seek to consider which relationships are now embedded in our legal understanding of the term *family* and which are excluded, to consider how these inclusions and exclusions affect the construction of the family-state relationship, and to think through which forms of associations should be recognized as families in a liberal democratic polity.

On a related issue, in writing this book, I considered adopting the plural form of *families*, and, thus, *families-state relationship* to denominate the relationship between intimate associations and the state. Using this somewhat more cumbersome terminology would avoid the mistaken impression that there is any unitary entity that can be identified as a family. However, I have chosen to rely on the singular form, *family,* for the sake of simplicity and clarity. In doing so, I ask the reader to keep in mind that the critical caretaking relationships that sustain us, and on which a viable liberal democracy depends, come in a number of shapes and sizes.

My use of the term *state* also requires some elaboration. As a number of theorists have pointed out,[52] the term is often used, yet rarely pinned down. Moreover, it runs the risk of oversimplifying a complex array of relations, structures, and institutions. That said, I use the term in the sense that it has generally been used in the liberal tradition, to invoke the set of government institutions that have a monopoly on legal authority (in this project, specifically executive, legislative, and judicial authority). The state can use its authority in a broad variety of ways when it comes to families. It can go so far as to put the coercive force of criminal law behind its determinations of appropriate family forms, as every state now does in prohibiting polygamous marriage. The state can also regulate families through civil law by, for example, enacting statutes that determine who can enter and exit marriage and parental relationships, and on what terms. Moving one step further from coercive power, the state can also act by providing subsidies to particular families or particular activities, such as when the federal tax code provides tax deductions for children or child care. The state can also affect family behavior by influencing the shape and function of the surrounding society, for example, through regulating and subsidizing day care, or through zoning that discourages sprawl and, therefore, reduces parents' commuting times. Still further from the coercive end of the spectrum, the state may use its power to educate or persuade citizens— for example through exposing younger citizens to examples of gender-neutral roles. Finally, government officials can also use their offices as a bully pulpit to exhort citizens about how families should function, as when Barack Obama urged African Americans to adopt more responsible models of fatherhood. In our federal system, as the examples above suggest, both the federal and state governments can exercise this authority when it comes to families.

Turning briefly to an issue of methodology, this project seeks to consider how families relate to the complex ideals and purposes that should motivate the liberal democratic project. It probably goes without saying (but, just in case): Since my method is not to deduce conclusions from claimed fundamental moral principles as, for example, John Rawls sought to do in his earlier work, my arguments will succeed or fail to the extent I convince the reader of the normative attractiveness of my proposal. As Thomas Spragens says of a similar project: "It should be obvious, then, that no one can reasonably pretend to have any knock-down arguments in this particular universe of discourse."[53] My hope, however, is still to convince the reader that the vision of the family-state relationship that I propose is far better for children, for adults, and for the polity itself than either the existing, dominant vision or its current contenders. Both theoretical and practical considerations make state support for families an imperative for a just and flourishing political order.

CHAPTER 1

The Family-State Relationship in Contemporary Political Theory and Public Policy

What responsibilities does the state have to families, and how should it treat them? These questions have seldom been asked in the liberal political theory that has dominated in the United States. That theory's attention to individuals has largely occluded consideration of families, and its conceptualization of individuals as autonomous and able has prevented focus on the dependency needs that families serve. Outside of political theory, however, families have not been so easily ignored. In fact, when it comes to political discourse in the real world, families get talked about quite a bit. Politicians vie for the label of pro-family and spend a good deal of time talking about how they will help families. Laws are titled in a manner designed to show heightened awareness of families, including Temporary Assistance for Needy Families, the Family and Medical Leave Act, and the Adoption and Safe Families Act, to name just a few.

On the surface, then, there seems little relationship between political theory and public policy on these issues. On closer look, however, there are considerable similarities between the two that this chapter explores. In the first part of this chapter, I focus on the way that contemporary political theory conceptualizes families and their relationship to the state. I use John Rawls's work as my example because of the tremendous influence it has had on contemporary political theory. Rawls is widely credited with reinvigorating normative political theory from its period of dormancy after World War II through his publication in 1971 of *A Theory of Justice*.[1] His magnum opus has had such vast influence because it provided a powerful moral defense of liberal democracy, rescuing it from the then-dominant view that this form of government was simply the better alternative to anarchy or civil war. Rawls's justification of liberal democracy and his framework for assessing the legitimacy of social and political institutions continue to cast a long shadow both inside and outside the academy.[2]

By considering *A Theory of Justice* and some of Rawls's later work, I explore why the treatment of families has been so inadequate in contemporary political theory. Some of the features of Rawls's theory that have set the agenda for contemporary liberal democratic theory—its focus on justice defined in terms of liberty and equality, to the exclusion of other goods such as caretaking and human development; its failure to conceptualize the dependency inevitable in the human condition; and its attempt to keep the state neutral with respect to citizens' conceptions of the good—obscure attention to families. Furthermore, even when Rawls focuses on families, other elements of his theory produce a stunted conception of the ways that the family-state relationship should be constructed.

In the second part of the chapter, I show that the same theoretical tenets that prevent adequate conceptualization of the family-state relationship in political theory are replicated in current law and public policy. Using as an example the way that the intersection of work and family is treated in American law, I show that its conceptualization of the family-state relationship demonstrates many of the same incoherencies that occur in Rawlsian political theory. Here, too, the intersection between work and family is generally conceived in terms of individual rights that are framed in terms of liberty and equality; human dependency is conceptualized narrowly when it is considered at all; and the state is not deemed appropriately to help families in meeting dependency needs. The result is a version of the family-state relationship that fails to support goods that are critical to the flourishing of American citizens and their communities.

THE FAMILY-STATE RELATIONSHIP IN CONTEMPORARY POLITICAL THEORY: JOHN RAWLS

In his groundbreaking work, *A Theory of Justice,* John Rawls sought to set out the principles that should guide a just society. Rawls stated that he was limiting his theory's focus to principles of justice rather than to other principles that might guide a polity, such as achieving happiness, virtue, or human development, because "[j]ustice is the first virtue of social institutions, as truth is of systems of thought."[3] Rawls used his now-famous hypothetical construct, which he called the "original position," to derive the principles to which he argued free and equal citizens would consent.[4] On the basis of this construct, Rawls asserted that citizens would arrive at two principles of justice that should guide the organization of society and the distribution of its resources. The first, which takes lexical priority over the second, pertains to liberty: Each person should be guaranteed such liberty as is consistent with a like liberty for all. The second pertains to equality: Social and economic inequality should be to the greatest benefit of the least advantaged, and offices should be open to all under conditions of fair (instead of merely formal) equality of opportunity.[5]

As Rawls explained it, these principles of justice do not apply to every interaction between citizens, but govern only "the basic structure of society, or more exactly, the way in which the major social institutions distribute fundamental rights and duties and determine the division of advantages from social cooperation."[6] Among the major social institutions that fall into this category, Rawls listed competitive markets, private property in the means of production, and, most importantly for the subject at hand, families.[7] Rawls then spent the majority of the book exploring how these principles would apply to these social institutions.

Despite Rawls's categorization of the family as part of the basic structure in the early part of the book, throughout the rest of the book he largely ignored families, mentioning them only in a few contexts, and then only in passing.[8] When he did mention them, it was generally to point out their problematic effects for his principles of justice. For example, Rawls described families' implications for the equal opportunity guaranteed by his second principle. In Rawls's words:

> [T]he principle of fair opportunity can be only imperfectly carried out, at least as long as the institution of the family exists. The extent to which natural capacities develop and reach fruition is affected by all kinds of social conditions and class attitudes. Even the willingness to make an effort, to try, and so to be deserving in the ordinary sense is itself dependent upon happy family and social circumstances.[9]

Although these observations might have invited an examination of the institution of families and even, perhaps, consideration of how the state might support families to encourage the development of these natural capacities, Rawls never took up these subjects. Instead, he simply asserted that it would be unfair to reward or penalize the differences caused by different family circumstances, and these differences should, therefore, be deemed irrelevant for purposes of receiving societal benefits.[10]

The only time that Rawls recognized any positive role that families play with respect to justice is in the less-widely read Part III of *A Theory of Justice*. At this point, Rawls linked children's development of a sense of justice to the existence of a particular kind of relationship between children and their parents that includes love and guidance. Rawls treated children's development of a sense of justice in families, however, as if it occurred in a black box—as if a family's ability to develop this sense in its young is unaffected by its social, political, and economic context. His discussion of how the state should organize society to justly distribute collective resources, therefore, never reached the issue of what families need to thrive.

The Features of Rawls's Theory That Obscure Attention to Families

In *Justice, Gender, and the Family,* Susan Moller Okin called attention to the absence of families in Rawls's work.[11] She argued that Rawls's account of the development of children's sense of justice depends on the internal justice of the family but that, inexplicably, Rawls failed to consider whether the heterosexual family is, in fact, just with respect to gender.[12] Okin contended that Rawls's theory has great potential for feminism, but only if it is applied to families. I want to build on Okin's critique to some extent, but to depart from this last conclusion. While Okin's basic contention that Rawls should have considered families is correct, this omission seems more explicable to me than to Okin. As I argue, particular features of Rawls's theory made it almost inevitable that he would largely ignore families.

Focus on Individual Justice (Framed in Terms of Liberty and Equality)

First and foremost, by confining his theory of state action to the good of justice,[13] Rawls obscures much of the relevance of families to liberal democracies and their citizenries. The purpose of a theory of justice, Rawls tells us, is to answer the question of how the fruits of social cooperation, which he defines in terms of fundamental rights, duties, and goods, should be distributed within society.[14] Rawls then defines his two principles of justice in terms of guarantees of individual liberty and equality.[15] This narrow framing of the purposes of government, and the narrow spectrum of goods on which he focuses, largely miss what families bring to a liberal democracy. Under Rawls's lens, the important roles that families serve in caretaking and human development are irrelevant insofar as they cannot be related to justice.

Not only does this framing cause Rawls to miss the goods of caretaking and human development that families contribute, it also causes families to appear mainly as a problem for Rawls's theory. In spite of the valuable functions that families serve, they tend to be an obstacle to equality, since, as Rawls notes, they often lead to unequal distributions of wealth, capacities, effort, and character.[16] Because of this, the likely result of focusing only on justice framed with significant reference to equality is to conclude that the family as an institution should be eliminated. Indeed, Rawls gestures toward this conclusion, stating that in this inquiry he would "assume that the basic structure of a well-ordered society includes the family in some form," while noting that "in a broader inquiry the institution of the family might be questioned, and other arrangements might indeed prove to be preferable...."[17] Rather than determining that a theory that cannot recognize the goods that families can contribute is focused too narrowly, Rawls avoids the issue by simply assuming families' existence.

It should be mentioned that the difficulty with Rawls's theory in conceptualizing families cannot be obviated simply by adding the goods of caretaking and human development to the other goods considered in his theory. This is because the manner in which Rawls develops his principles of justice precludes any meaningful compromise between justice and other principles. Rawls does not define justice in terms of a basic institutional threshold that a well-ordered, free society should meet, for example, by ensuring that all citizens have voting rights, that the rule of law applies to all, and that all have fair access to courts. Conceiving of justice in this way would allow the remaining societal resources to be used to pursue other goods and aspirations once these prerequisites of justice had been satisfied. In contrast, Rawls's principles of justice dictate the way in which *all* rights, responsibilities, and goods that are part of the basic structure are distributed. Only in the situation in which alternative schemes are equal from the perspective of distributive justice, but produce different consequences for other goods, can such goods be considered.[18] Where there are two possible distribution schemes, the first of which is high on justice and low on caretaking, as against the second, which is almost as high on justice but far higher on caretaking, Rawls's theory requires that the first be chosen. There is a strong argument to be made, however, that a theory that would select a society that is distributively just, based on Rawls's criteria, but whose citizens are stupid, ill, and unhappy, is flawed in fundamental ways.

Furthermore, even if we incorporated the missing goods of caretaking and human development into Rawls's theory, and, therefore, allowed it to grasp the value that families contribute, Rawls's theory would give us no way to choose among these goods and the liberty and equality considered by his theory. Part of the beauty of Rawls's theory is that it presents principles of justice against which we can measure different social programs. Yet it is only by limiting the goods to equality and liberty that Rawls can assign his principles of justice a determinate lexical priority. Were the range of goods in his theory broadened to include caregiving and human development, his theory would provide us with no direction regarding how to assess trade-offs among the various goods. To what extent should the state support families in order to foster human development if to do so would create more inequality? Rawls's principles do not allow us a means to answer this question.

Failure to Focus on Human Dependency

It is not simply Rawls's focus on justice that renders families invisible; his conception of the human condition does so as well. Certainly there is no problem with Rawls modeling his theory (and his conception of persons in the original position) on the moral ideal of persons as free and equal citizens who cooperate with one another on the basis of reciprocity and mutual respect.[19] Yet Rawls sometimes seems to mistake this moral ideal for an account of the human condition. In doing so, he frames a theory that largely ignores the dependency that is an inevitable part of human lives.[20] This, in turn, ultimately diverts attention from the primary institution in which dependency is managed within our society—families. Indeed, Rawls's framing of the central project of society as how to divide basic social goods among citizens, rather than how to bring sound citizens into existence and nurture their development, bespeaks a view of humanity in which dependency is a relatively minor concern.[21]

As relevant as dependency issues are for goods aside from justice, they also have important implications for social justice, which Rawls neglects. The failure to consider dependency's relationship to justice leaves open the not-unlikely possibility that the dependency work necessary in any society will be accomplished through exploitation.[22] In the United States, as elsewhere, a disproportionate amount of dependency work has been and continues to be performed by women.[23] Much of that work is unpaid. Moreover, disproportionately more of the burden of care work for family members falls on minority and low-income families, who cannot afford to pay others for care work or for residential care-work options.[24] This care work can exact a tremendous toll in terms of lost wages, stress, and foregone educational and job opportunities.[25] Further, even dependency work that is remunerated is generally poorly paid, and is disproportionately performed by African-American and other minority women.[26] It is only by recognizing that dependency is an inherent part of the human condition that a state committed to justice can properly ensure that care work is accomplished in a just manner.

State Neutrality

Rawls's efforts to keep the state neutral with respect to citizens' visions of the good life also limits his theory's capacity to deal with families. In Rawls's view, the liberal state rests on an idea of "equality between human beings as moral persons, as creatures having a conception of their good and capable of a sense of justice.... Systems of ends are not ranked in value."[27] Rawls's concern that the state not be used as an instrument to support some views of what constitutes a valuable life over other views leads him to argue that citizens are entitled to the same distribution of primary goods no matter what plan of life they enact or activities they undertake.

Under this doctrine of neutrality, the liberal state should respond the same whether or not citizens develop family ties with others. Furthermore, the state should not privilege citizens' activities of caretaking over other activities. The same resources are entitled to a citizen whether they are caring for children or playing video games, since, in this view, what is important is citizens having the opportunity to choose whatever life plan they wish, free from interference of the state. This logic precludes the state from recognizing the importance of caretaking and the other work that families perform. To the extent that state support for families is necessary for them to perform caretaking well, it means that the liberal state will not be able to further those practices necessary for a flourishing society.

Assumptions about Families That Distort the
Family-State Relationship

Not only does liberal theory incorporate tenets that obscure the importance of families, even when families are considered, other assumptions distort the way in which the family-state relationship is constructed. Rawls's later work provides a good example of these assumptions. In a 1997 article titled "The Idea of Public Reason Revisited,"[28] more than 25 years after the publication of *A Theory of Justice,* Rawls apologized to feminist critics who had taken him to task for his earlier failure to discuss families, claiming that it "was a fault of mine and not of political liberalism itself."[29] Rawls's attempt to discuss the application of his theory of justice to families, while well intentioned, reveals further problems that this mode of theorizing has in constructing an adequate theory of the family-state relationship.

In "The Idea of Public Reason Revisited," Rawls developed his claim from *A Theory of Justice* that families are part of the basic structure of society, since they have the function of perpetuating society and culture from one generation to the next. In his words:

> [R]eproductive labor is socially necessary labor. Accepting this, a central role of the family is to arrange in a reasonable and effective way the raising of and caring for children, ensuring their moral development and education into the wider culture.... The family must ensure the nurturing and development of such citizens in appropriate numbers to maintain an enduring society.[30]

Rawls explicitly recognized here what he had not focused on in his earlier work: that families serve important caretaking and human development functions that are not captured by the principles of justice. Because of these important functions, Rawls stated, the necessity of family structures

> limit[s] all arrangements of the basic structure, including efforts to achieve equality of opportunity. The family imposes constraints on ways in which this goal can be achieved, and the principles of justice are stated to try to take these constraints into account.[31]

Rawls then took up the problem posed by feminist critics of whether the state should take action to assure that labor within the family is not assigned based on gender. In answer to this question, Rawls announced that "[w]e wouldn't want political principles of justice...to apply directly to the internal life of the family" to ensure equal distribution of caretaking between the sexes; instead the state should seek to guarantee simply the "basic rights and liberties, and the freedom and opportunities, of all its members."[32] To support this assertion, Rawls likened the family to other voluntary associations such as private universities and churches which, he contended, need not be constrained by principles of justice internally, so long as they do not hinder these principles from operating outside these associations.[33] For example,

> [c]hurches cannot practice effective intolerance, since, as the principles of justice require, public law does not recognize heresy and apostasy as crimes, and members of churches are always at liberty to leave their faith. Thus, although the principles of justice do not apply directly to the internal life of churches, they do protect the rights and liberties of their members by the constraints to which all churches and associations are subject.[34]

Based on this internal-external dichotomy, Rawls counseled that the state should not seek to interfere with the gendered division of labor within marriage. He stated that:

> Some want a society in which division of labor by gender is reduced to a minimum. But for political liberalism, this cannot mean that such division is forbidden. One cannot propose that equal division of labor in the family be simply mandated, or its absence in some way penalized at law for those who do not adopt it. This is ruled out because the division of labor in question is connected with basic liberties, including the freedom of religion. Thus, to try to minimize gendered division of labor means, in political liberalism, to try to reach a social condition in which the remaining division of labor is voluntary. This allows in principle that considerable gendered division of labor may persist. It is only involuntary division of labor that is to be reduced to zero.[35]

Instead of seeking to minimize the gendered division of labor during the marriage, Rawls stated the principles of justice should instead properly be applied at the end of a marriage to ensure that women are justly compensated for child rearing. This means that "the government would appear to have no interest in the particular form of family life, or of relations among the sexes, except insofar as that form or those relations in some way affect the orderly reproduction of society over time."[36]

Despite Rawls's attempt to use "The Idea of Public Reason Revisited" to at last remedy his previous inattention to families, his effort demonstrates the difficulties his theory has in grappling with this institution. Although Rawls finally recognized the important role families play in caretaking and human development, he still had no way to recognize these goods in his theory of justice. How did he deal with this quandary? Only by violating his own principles of justice by declaring an exception to them: Families, rather than being constrained by the principles of justice, "limit all arrangements of the basic structure, including efforts to achieve equality of opportunity," and impose "constraints on ways in which [equality of opportunity] can be achieved."[37] In other words, in a rather extraordinary departure from his theory, because of the importance of caretaking and human development, and families' role in furthering them, Rawls declared that families will limit the workings of the principles of justice, rather than vice versa. Faced with an institution that contributes other important goods, Rawls's theory has no way to integrate these other goods or to weigh them against the dictates of justice except to invent a post hoc exception to his principles of justice.[38] Once Rawls posited that the existence of families must be assumed, however, he could then frame the issue in terms of the goods his theory can cognize: the relevant question for the state with respect to families thus becomes how it should balance the goods relevant to his conception of justice—equality and autonomy—by determining the extent to which the state should intervene when family members have worked out a gendered division among themselves. In this discussion, two new assumptions about families emerge that compound the problems Rawls's theory has in grappling with the family-state relationship.

The Public-Private Split: Families as Possessing Pristine Internal Dynamics

To begin with, Rawls conceptualized a world with a firm demarcation between the public and private realms. In keeping with the idea of a state neutral on citizens' conceptions of the good life, he conceived of families as possessing an internal realm that is and should be left immune from the power of the state, and which operates in some natural, pre-political way that would be adulterated if the state were to intercede. State action, he asserted, must "leave room for a free and flourishing internal life" of the family.[39] This conception of the family-state relationship might be graphically depicted by drawing a circle on a sheet of paper. It is only at the circumference of the circle—the interface between families and the state—that the state may regulate. Everything within the circle is the family's private realm, which should be left to the family's own "natural" functioning, and in which the state should play no part. In Rawls's words, "[a]t some point society has to rely on the natural affection and goodwill of mature family members."[40] In theorizing the relationship in this manner, however, Rawls misstated the relationship between families and the state. In today's complex society, there is no way to separate out any "natural" function of the family that somehow stands apart from state action.[41] Instead, how families function is inextricably intertwined with both law and social policy.[42]

By the same token, Rawls presented a peculiarly simplistic account of the workings of individual choice and decision-making within families. In Rawls's view, decisions made by families can be ascribed to the individuals who compose them; these choices are either voluntary or they are not, with no grey area between these two poles. In this conception, social constraints, cultural roles, religion, and interpersonal dynamics are treated as part of the black box of the familial sphere with which the state should not interfere; decisions motivated by these factors are considered unproblematically voluntary. Rawls's analysis, therefore, skates over difficult questions about what it means for a choice to be "voluntary" in a society that still sends strong cultural and religious messages about gender roles. In a similar vein, Rawls's treats fulfilling moral responsibilities as simply one of many voluntary choices that citizens may make; in this regard, a citizen's decision to care for an elderly relative is treated much the same as a citizen's decision to choose vanilla over chocolate ice cream. Finally, Rawls's assumption that the individual's "choice" ends the state's responsibility overlooks the ways in which public systems can influence private choices. It also ignores the possibility that the state may and should have some responsibility to support particular activities, such as caretaking for children, even though children may be deemed a "choice."

Families as Flourishing Autonomously

On a related note, Rawls assumed that families generally will flourish, so long as they remain unimpeded by the state. Although he recognized that the state must impose certain constraints on families, for instance to prevent cases of abuse and neglect, Rawls assumed that the optimal posture for the state regarding families is hands off in order to allow families' "natural affection and goodwill" to take hold.[43] This is in accord with Rawls's treatment of children's development of a sense of justice in *A Theory of Justice,* where he assumed that families' ability to develop this sense in its young is unaffected by their resources and surroundings. This assumption misses the ways in which families' ability to flourish and to produce sound, healthy future citizens are affected by economic, social, and political resources.

In sum, several features of Rawls's theory prevent the development of a family-state relationship that adequately serves the interests of the United States and its citizens. Some of these features—the focus on individual justice, the failure to focus on human dependency, and the view that the state should remain neutral—turn attention away from families. Other features—the view that families should function in ways unadulterated by state action and the assumption that families will flourish if they are left alone are simply inadequate to account for the reality of the family-state relationship.

THE FAMILY-STATE RELATIONSHIP IN U.S. LAW: THE INTERSECTION BETWEEN WORK AND FAMILY

At first glance, American political rhetoric and public policy have little in common with the marginalized position of families in academic political theory. Political rhetoric often focuses on families—some would say even obsesses about them. Newspapers, public opinion polls, and political speeches all proclaim that Americans strongly support children and families, and believe in the importance of strong families and good parenting. This intense focus, however, has resulted in startlingly little real support for families in many areas of law. Interestingly, the disjuncture between rhetoric and public policy is at least partly the product of the same set of faulty assumptions that underlie contemporary liberal theory. Here again, these assumptions prevent formulation of a coherent set of supports for families.

The legal protections offered to parents when their family responsibilities conflict with work provide a particularly important example of the dysfunctional way that the family-state relationship is constructed in U.S. law. The conflict between family and work responsibilities is a significant issue for American families today. In 1930, only a minority of children lived in families in which both parents had jobs; roughly 55 percent lived with a father who worked for pay and a mother who was the homemaker.[44] Today, however, a family with a breadwinner and a homemaker is the exception: As I noted earlier, 70 percent of children live with two parents who both work or a single parent who works.[45] The current workforce includes roughly 94 percent of fathers and 70 percent of mothers with children under eighteen.[46] Moreover, roughly 15 percent of workers are actively involved in providing care for an older family member or friend.[47] A large portion of the care needed by children and aging citizens used to be provided by women without paid jobs. As mothers moved into the workplace, however, few institutional changes were made in the United States to enable families to care for their children and senior citizens. In fact, a comparison of policies in 173 countries found that when it came to parental leave protections in the workplace, the United States came in dead last, tied with only three other countries: Liberia, Papua New Guinea, and Swaziland.[48]

Why does U.S. law have such difficulty protecting families when it comes to work responsibilities? Because the same problematic assumptions that are embodied in political theory are also present in U.S. law. These assumptions—that individual liberty and equality are the goods appropriately cognized by law; that dependency is not a condition that law needs to recognize; that the state should be neutral on issues of family; and that the state should not adulterate families' internal dynamics—prevent development of policies that effectively support families.

Employees whose work and family responsibilities conflict have generally sought protection under two different statutes: Title VII of the Civil Rights Act of 1964,[49] and the Family and Medical Leave Act of 1993 ("FMLA").[50] On their face, these two statutes are very different: Title VII is concerned with eliminating employment discrimination from the workplace, while the FMLA provides protection for employees requiring time off from work to attend to serious family needs. Yet both share a particular, narrow interpretation of what is at stake and what the state's role should be when it comes to employees' family responsibilities.

Work and Family Protections under Title VII

The Family and Medical Leave Act provides the only federal statutory protection that explicitly protects U.S. workers from adverse employment actions based on caregiving responsibilities. Because of the limited scope of the FMLA, however, employees seeking protection for family responsibilities have generally litigated their claims under Title VII. Title VII makes it unlawful for an employer "to fail or refuse to hire or to discharge any individual, or otherwise to discriminate against any individual...because of...sex."[51] To state a claim under Title VII for protection for caregiving responsibilities, employees must, therefore, show that an adverse employment action for care giving was linked to sex discrimination in some way.

As courts have interpreted Title VII's prohibition on sex discrimination in the context of caretaking, employees who are terminated for caregiving responsibilities must generally demonstrate that a similarly situated employee of the opposite sex was treated differently. Title VII has, therefore, been most helpful to those workers willing to meet the demands of their job, but who are falsely stereotyped as unwilling or uninterested based on their caretaking responsibilities. It is less helpful to the many workers whose jobs are structured in a manner unsuited to caretaking responsibilities who seek to accommodate the demands of their job to caretaking demands. Thus, in *Chi v. Age Group,*[52] the court held that a plaintiff had not stated a violation of Title VII when she asserted that she was terminated for her refusal to work long hours in order to care for her children. The court stated that the plaintiff's allegations failed because she had not linked this to sex discrimination, for example, through showing that a similarly situated man who refused to work long hours had not been fired. According to the court, the plaintiff's termination because of her refusal to work late so she could care for children was not only insufficient to state a claim as a matter of law, her refusal to stay late demonstrated that she was unqualified for the job, and, therefore, ineligible for relief under Title VII.[53] Likewise, the court in *Guglietta v. Meredith Corporation,*[54] held that plaintiff had no legitimate claim when she was terminated for refusing to change her work hours to an early-morning schedule because she lacked child care during those hours. In dismissing the case, the court held that the employer had no duty to make an "affirmative accommodation" for her child-care needs.

Despite strong evidence that women's unequal caretaking responsibilities are the largest continuing obstacle to sex equality,[55] the only place in which Title VII provides any explicit protection for childbearing or rearing is in the Pregnancy Discrimination Act ("PDA"), an amendment to Title VII that forbids employers from discriminating based on pregnancy or childbirth. The PDA provides that "women affected by pregnancy, childbirth, or related medical conditions shall be treated the same for all employment-related pur-poses...as other persons not so affected but similar in their ability or inability to work."[56] To succeed on PDA claims, women need to show that they were, in fact, treated differently from others who were similarly able or unable to work. Those whose abilities are truly limited by their pregnancy or childbirth, however, are not protected by the PDA if others who are similarly unable to work would not be accommodated.[57] As under Title VII generally, this means that the PDA is most helpful to women in the narrow slice of cases in which pregnant women can work but are falsely stereotyped to be incapable of work-ing. In cases in which women truly have difficulty with established work requirements because of their pregnancy, however, they generally remain unprotected.

The Supreme Court case of *International Union, UAW v. Johnson Controls, Inc.,* demonstrates the problematic way that Title VII constructs the intersec-tion between work and family.[58] In that case, employees of defendant Johnson Controls, a battery manufacturer, challenged a company policy excluding all women from jobs involving actual or potential exposure to lead, except those whose infertility had been medically documented. The company had instituted the policy to respond to the risks of fetal hazards caused by lead exposure. Plaintiffs claimed that the policy violated Title VII's prohibition on actions that discriminated based on sex. The employer, in response, argued that although its exclusionary policy treated women differently from men, the policy was lawful because it fell under Title VII's bona fide occupational qual-ification (BFOQ) exception. That exception permits employment practices that discriminate based on sex if they are "reasonably necessary to the normal operation of that particular business or enterprise."[59]

In ruling for the plaintiffs, the United States Supreme Court declared that the BFOQ exception applied only to a worker's ability or inability to perform the job in question and could therefore not take into account possible harm to the fetus from lead exposure. According to the Court: "[e]mployment late in pregnancy often imposes risks on the unborn child,...but Congress indi-cated that the employer may take into account only the woman's ability to get her job done."[60] The "welfare of the next generation"[61] could not be cog-nized within this framework: "No one can disregard the possibility of injury to future children; the BFOQ, however, is not so broad that it transforms this deep social concern into an essential aspect of battery making."[62] Having discarded the welfare of children, and the public's own interest in children's welfare from the statute's consideration, the Court cast the issue in terms of parental autonomy, declaring the employer's policy unlawful, because "[d]ecisions about the welfare of future children must be left to the parents who conceive, bear, support, and raise them."[63]

Johnson Controls illustrates many of the difficulties that Title VII's framework has in grasping what is at stake in the intersection between work and family, and the way this framework excludes or distorts a number of important goods. In this analysis, autonomy and equality emerge as the only relevant interests, dependency issues are discarded as irrelevant, and the state is seen to be properly neutral with respect to citizens' life choices. In these ways, the antidiscrimination analysis shares many features with Rawlsian liberal theory. I discuss each of these features in turn.

Focus on Individual Justice (Framed in Terms of Liberty and Equality)

As the analysis in *Johnson Controls* illustrates, Title VII is an antidiscrimination law that is constructed to further individual justice. Like Rawlsian liberal theory, it casts the relevant issues in terms of those goods considered relevant to justice—liberty and equality. In this framing, employers' liberty interests, conceived in terms of their right to run their businesses as they choose, are pitted against employees' own interests in liberty and sex equality. As with contemporary liberal theory, important goods outside this limited range are excluded—including the welfare of children and parents, the development of future citizens of the polity, and the well-being of families.[64]

In a society in which there is considerable unease about the value of sex equality in some political quarters but a relatively clear political consensus about the importance of families, it is somewhat ironic that plaintiffs seeking protection for caregiving must phrase their claims in terms of sex discrimination to succeed. Yet that is precisely what Title VII demands. In this regard, Title VII protects the employee against adverse employment actions taken because of the employee's family responsibilities only if these adverse actions can be linked to sex discrimination, and, therefore, to the good of sex equality. Further, the employee's family responsibilities are neither protected nor encouraged in themselves: the interests of the employee are protected only *as an employee* when her job has been adversely affected by family responsibilities (assuming they can be linked to sex discrimination). The law is not triggered when the employee/parent's family responsibilities have been or will be adversely affected by work responsibilities. If all women employees could be convinced to ignore their caretaking responsibilities, and simply attend to work responsibilities, the conditions of Title VII would be satisfied.

Further, the *Johnson Controls* Court construes even the goods this approach can cognize in a particular, contestable way. The Court conceives the autonomy of employees in the same way that Rawlsian liberal theory does—to require simply a zone of non-interference around parents' choices. This conception fails to recognize the ways in which parents' autonomy can be constricted by this reading: by failing to allow employers to take into account children's welfare, it forces parents to take this consideration into account purely privately. Parents must therefore decide between two unpalatable outcomes: On the one hand, they can choose their job and, therefore, economic security for their children, in which case they may not have an adequate opportunity to parent (or, in the case of fetal hazards, a healthy child to parent); on the other, they can choose to ensure their child is adequately parented and healthy, but may not be able to afford to rear them.

In addition, in limiting the antidiscrimination inquiry to securing women equal terms and conditions of employment with men, the *Johnson Controls* Court ultimately undercuts the goal of substantive sex equality. Requiring only that women be treated the same as men, without requiring accommodations for pregnancy and caretaking, requires women to choose between the welfare of their children and future children and a job that does not take this welfare into account. Thus, while *Johnson Controls* may in theory seem a victory for women,[65] the Court's blinkered definition of women's interest in equality ultimately runs the risk of forcing women who want to bear and rear children out of the workplace.

This is not to say that *Johnson Controls* was wrongly decided, given the limited framework of inquiry provided by antidiscrimination law. It is instead to say that a broader framework than Title VII's individual-justice paradigm is required to reconcile the range of important interests at stake. Under the paradigm applied here, employers are required to allow women to stay in jobs that pose fetal hazards so long as these jobs are open to men, but may not consider a wider range of interests. Under a broader framework, the state might require that other interests be considered in addition to sex equality, including the welfare of children and future children. Doing so might have resulted in other solutions that better accommodated this broader range of goods, such as requiring that the employer make job structures safe for pregnant employees or, alternatively, offer women and men seeking to have children the opportunity to transfer into safer jobs with equal pay.

Failure to Focus on Human Dependency

By virtue of its limited goal of eliminating discrimination in the workplace, Title VII cannot grasp the centrality of dependency to human lives. Except for its recognition of the disability that may occur during pregnancy, the Act provides no recognition of dependency. And even the recognition of dependency of pregnant workers is considerably limited. A pregnancy-related condition is limited to "incapacitating conditions for which medical care or treatment is usual and normal."[66] Thus, moderate levels of morning sickness that do not rise to the level of clinical dehydration are not covered. Further, the Act provides no protection for childrearing. As the House Report for the Pregnancy Discrimination Act states, "if a woman wants to stay home to take care of the child, no benefits must be paid because this is not a medically determined condition related to pregnancy."[67]

The Seventh Circuit Court of Appeals' decision in *Troupe v. May Department Stores*[68] underscores the thin protection that the PDA offers to protect pregnant women. In that case, the plaintiff, a department store salesperson who became pregnant, was placed on probation for repeated tardiness caused by severe morning sickness. She was subsequently fired from work the day before she was scheduled to begin maternity leave. Judge Posner, of the Seventh Circuit, rejected the claim that Title VII prevented her termination for tardiness on account of pregnancy:

> Her lawyer argues with great vigor that she should not be blamed—that she was genuinely ill, had a doctor's excuse, etc. That would be pertinent if Troupe were arguing that the Pregnancy Discrimination Act requires an employer to treat an employee afflicted by morning sickness better than the employer would treat an employee who was equally tardy for some other health reason. This is rightly not argued. If an employee who (like Troupe) does not have an employment contract cannot work because of illness, nothing in Title VII requires the employer to keep the employee on the payroll.[69]

All that is required by Title VII, in other words, is blindness to the fact of an employee's pregnancy. There is no requirement affirmatively to accommodate any disability that attends it.

Judge Posner went on to declare that even if the department store had fired the plaintiff because it did not believe that she would return from maternity leave, this, too, would be lawful. According to Posner, that would constitute a rational financial reason to want to fire an employee, rather than the animus against pregnancy prohibited by Title VII. The point, for Judge Posner, is that Title VII offers no substantive protection for pregnant employees in the workforce. In Posner's words,

> The Pregnancy Discrimination Act does not, despite the urgings of feminist scholars,...require employers to offer maternity leave or take other steps to make it easier for pregnant women to work—to make it as easy, say, as it is for their spouses to continue working during pregnancy. Employers can treat

pregnant women as badly as they treat similarly affected but nonpregnant employees, even to the point of 'conditioning the availability of an employment benefit on an employee's decision to return to work after the end of the medical disability that pregnancy causes.'[70]

Title VII, then, is not a tool to protect the welfare of mother and fetus, or even generally to facilitate sex equality or women's substantive inclusion in the workplace. Instead, its function is merely to rid the workforce of irrational animus against pregnant women.

With regard to children's dependency, as well, Title VII provides no guarantee of protection for caregiving or human development. Instead, it provides only the same level of protection for these activities that it provides to other ways in which women may be disadvantaged relative to men (or vice versa). In other words, treating family responsibilities within an antidiscrimination framework requires no substantive support or accommodation for caretaking on its own merits. Indeed, the affirmative reasons to support caretaking and human development—because of their centrality to human dignity, to children's flourishing, and to a healthy polity—cannot be comprehended within an antidiscrimination rationale.

State Neutrality

The limits of state action under Title VII's paradigm closely tracks the model of legitimacy set out in the Rawlsian framework of individual justice. In Title VII's paradigm, it is appropriate for the state to act to enforce individual rights, defined in terms of autonomy and equality. Seeking to further goods aside from these, however, is seen as inappropriate state intervention. The state, in this view, simply provides a neutral framework of rights, defined in terms of fair procedures, in which individuals can choose their own valued ends. In this conception of neutrality (which, as I discuss in Chapter 2, is actually not neutral at all), state protection for citizens' rights is justified based on the importance of preserving citizens' liberty and equality. It neither imposes a substantive vision of the good life nor privileges some versions of the good life over others. Under this conception of government neutrality, the issue of how work could be structured to best realize goods, such as promoting the welfare of workers, their children, and aging parents, is not open for consideration.

Likewise, within this neutral framework, citizens may choose particular ways of life or to participate in particular activities, but the state may not give them extra resources on this basis. Instead, decisions by individuals are treated as a matter of individual choice, which is their own private affair. In this view, caregiving becomes a choice of family members that the neutral state may neither support nor punish. Recall the Supreme Court's discussion of these issues in *Johnson Controls:* The Court announced that employers could not consider the health of unborn children because "[d]ecisions about the welfare of future children must be left to the parents who conceive, bear, support, and raise them."[71]

The Public-Private Split: Families as Possessing Pristine Internal Dynamics

The demarcation drawn between the public and private realms in Title VII jurisprudence also echoes Rawls's conception. In both, the state's role is to stay out of the private realm, leaving its dynamics unadulterated. Individual choice, in this view, as in the Rawlsian framework, must be treated as completely voluntary and therefore left both unhindered and unaided by the state. Thus in *Maganuco v. Leyden Community High School District 212*,[72] the court construed the plaintiff's claim as "dependent not on the biological fact that pregnancy and childbirth cause some period of disability, but on a ... schoolteacher's choice to forego returning to work in favor of spending time at home with her newborn child."[73] The court then used the parenting-as-choice construction to deny legal protection to the plaintiff on the ground that she could have "chosen" not to parent.[74]

To the extent that this framework acknowledges the dependency of the human condition, it sees this dependency as an inappropriate concern of the state. Instead, dependency is properly confined within families, where the autonomous adults who head these families will properly manage it. From this perspective derives a conception of the state's responsibility conceived in terms of protecting individual rights from incursions by others rather than as supporting caretaking. This perspective is furthered by conceiving of children as a product of individual choice that excuses social support, and hence as just one more expression of adults' autonomy. In this framework, we have far less difficulty conceiving of children as falling within a parent's personal sphere of autonomy—and thus allowing parents the right to be free of interference in order to raise children as they see fit—than recognizing how the state might actively support parents in caring for children.

The conceptual demarcation between the public and private realms bolsters the idea that the state should not properly concern itself with caretaking and human development. Two distinct aspects of this dichotomy hinder protection of parenting in the employment context. First, the realm of work is seen as "public," in contrast to the "private" domestic realm. The activities associated with each sphere are then considered properly confined to that sphere. Activities such as child care that are associated with the private realm are, in this view, bracketed from consideration in the public realm of work. For this reason, while the workplace is considered an appropriate place for some social policies, including those that protect the welfare of workers by requiring employers to pay into the workers' compensation and unemployment compensation systems, laws providing for leave due to pregnancy, childbearing, or child rearing are seen as inappropriate "social engineering." This ideology forces parenting issues out of the workplace and the economic realm, and leaves many full-time jobs with structures inconsistent with parenting. In this conceptualization, it is only in the private realm of the family that the activity of care is valued.[75]

The implications for women's equality of this public/private dichotomy have been explored by a number of feminist writers.[76] They note that not only are certain activities and qualities traditionally associated with women located within the private realm, but that women, themselves, tend to be associated with this sphere. Indeed, the maintenance of this dichotomy depends on a gendered structure of society—the public world can exclude the domestic only because women are left in the private realm to focus on necessities such as rearing children and caring for aging family members. Because of this formulation, those women who do enter civil society must do so on socially "male" terms as liberal subjects who can separate themselves from the demands of the private realm. The task is often an impossible one for women, insofar as family demands can be confined to the domestic realm only if women stay there in order to meet them.

A second aspect of the liberal demarcation between "public" and "private" also undercuts support for working parents. In this conception, while the workplace is public when defined against the domestic realm, it is private when contrasted with the public realm of government. While the first aspect of the public/private dichotomy holds that the workplace should not accommodate family responsibilities because these responsibilities are private, the second view then allows workplace policies that fail to accommodate caretaking to appear nonpolitical, as merely the private, individual decisions of employers.[77] Thus, in the area in which work and family issues intersect, parenting issues are, first, bracketed as domestic and therefore inappropriate for intervention in the work sphere and, second, bracketed as altogether nonpolitical because they intersect with the economic system. The neutral state, concerned with enforcing individual rights, should have little to do with either.

The Family and Medical Leave Act

The only federal law regulating the intersection between work and family that protects caretaking responsibilities in their own right is the Family and Medical Leave Act. The FMLA, in this and in other respects, moves past the blinkered vision that Title VII constructs of work-and-family law. It specifically recognizes the importance of families, and protects caretaking alongside other important goods. The preamble to the FMLA affirms the importance of the "development of children and the family unit;" the interests of "fathers and mothers [to] be able to participate in early child rearing" without being forced "to choose between job security and parenting;" the national interest in preserving "family integrity;" and the goal of equal opportunity for men and women.[78] In addition, the FMLA sets a solid floor beneath which positive protection for caretaking may not fall: Covered employees are entitled to up to 12 weeks of aggregated annual leave, after which their jobs are guaranteed back to them.[79] In the narrow range of cases in which the FMLA applies, there is no question that it performs an important function.[80]

Yet the support for caretaking actually afforded by the FMLA is miniscule compared to the total level of caretaking needs in society. Because the statute applies only to employees who work for companies with 50 or more employees, and employees must satisfy particular prerequisites,[81] only roughly 50 percent of the workforce is covered.[82] The rest of the workforce—roughly 65 million employees—is not eligible for leave. Moreover, the FMLA simply guarantees that workers can return to their jobs after the leave; it provides for no wage replacement.[83] As a result, the vast majority of covered employees—by one count, 78 percent—cannot afford to make use of the benefit.[84] Only three states have thus far moved toward filling this void in parental protections by providing workers with paid leave for family medical emergencies.[85] In addition, as I describe below, the FMLA still incorporates problematic assumptions about the family-state relationship.

Dependency as an Aberrant Condition

While the FMLA recognizes dependency as a human condition, it does so in an extremely circumscribed way. The FMLA defines the conditions that give rise to leave in a manner that excludes most of the caretaking that family members require. Parents may obtain leave to care for children only for circumstances involving the birth or adoption of a child, or for situations involving a severe medical emergency. Parents who need time for care giving in other circumstances are left to fend for themselves.[86] As pointedly stated by the district court in *Kelley v. Crosfield Catalysts*:

> The Act clearly does not provide qualified leave for every family emergency. A call from a police station or from school authorities, a minor ailment that keeps a child home from school with no help immediately available, or a personal crisis in the life of a child or a parent may cause a severe conflict for an employee between work and family responsibilities. None is covered by the FMLA. The legislative history makes it clear that the Act is intended to reach four situations: to provide leave relating to the birth of a child or to the adoption or initial foster care of a child…, to care for a seriously ill child, spouse, or parent, or to attend to the employee's own serious health condition. The statute provides minimal protection in those circumstances.[87]

The FMLA's scope also excludes most of the care that aging adults need. Much of the help that senior citizens require involves relatively mundane situations: ensuring that they get to necessary places when they no longer drive, making sure that they have adequate groceries, helping them prepare meals, picking up the antacid pills they need from the drugstore. Yet because the FMLA limits leave to serious health issues requiring medical care, none of these activities are covered by the FMLA.

The problem with the FMLA in the context of elder care is brought home in the case of *Pang v. Beverly Hospital*.[88] In that case, the plaintiff sued her former employer under the FMLA for her termination for taking leave to help her mother move to an apartment. The move was motivated by Pang's mother's age and medical problems, which included high blood pressure, arthritis, circulatory problems, and a heart condition. She had also suffered a stroke some years before that left her with balance problems, and she had a separate condition that left her unable to use one arm. These conditions made it difficult for her to remain in her two-story home. The plaintiff agreed to help her move since her mother was unable to pack her belongings without assistance. When the plaintiff notified her employer that she was taking leave, however, she was fired on the ground that she was abandoning her job.

The California Court of Appeals affirmed the trial court's dismissal on the grounds that the plaintiff's aid to her mother was not covered by statute. According to the court, "Pang's admissions make clear that she was not there to directly, or even indirectly, provide or participate in medical care for her mother. Instead, she was there to help pack her mother's belongings."[89] The court continued,

> We sympathize with Pang's argument that her mother was moving on account of and in order to accommodate her various medical conditions. Even so, she was not being placed in a nursing home and was not moving as part of a change in her care.... The two-story home, with its flight of stairs and yardwork, had simply become too much for the mother to handle, prompting her move to an apartment. This did not involve a change in [medical] care. Instead, the move was designed so Pang's mother could continue in a living situation without care and treatment.[90]

Families as Flourishing Autonomously

In keeping with the FMLA's grudging recognition of dependency, the Act is still largely premised on a model of family autonomy. In limiting the events eligible for leave to the birth or adoption of a child or the serious illness of dependents, and in confining its protection to a period of twelve weeks, the FMLA assumes that the majority of dependency needs in society are properly met by families without state support. The FMLA takes no account of the fact that it requires far more than twelve weeks to raise a child or to care for aging parents, that most parents and adult children will be working during that time, and that the majority of caretaking will be performed under conditions not triggered by the medical requirements of the FMLA. In the normal situation, it tells us, aside from major life events and emergencies, there is no need for the state to play a role in supporting families. State support of families, in this view, is residual in the sense that it should only occur on the rare occasions that families properly exhaust their own resources.

The assumption that families should properly be autonomous that underlies the FMLA is reinforced by a strand of thought that has received far more traction in public discourse than in academic theorizing. This strand counterposes the properly autonomous family against the threat of dependency, which is conceived broadly in terms of families receiving many types of public support.[91] This threat of dependency justifies public support as a necessary evil only when the perceived "normal" state of familial autonomy has broken down, and then only until the crisis can be overcome. The dichotomy drawn between autonomy and dependence (viewed in terms of public support) limits state support for families to conditions of emergency and breakdown. It therefore forecloses examination of the rationales for the state to support caretaking in the ordinary course of the lives of parents and children.

The assumption that families should properly function without support from the state, combined with the perceived threat of dependency, limits assistance for caretaking in the FMLA to crisis situations. The recognition of the government's role in supporting caretaking is so grudging that it occurs only at the margins, in situations in which a concrete, tangible need can be verified by a health-care professional. In keeping with the view that state action should be confined to extraordinary events, the more mundane needs of children—the need to feed them, supervise them, play with them, teach them—are invisible under these standards, as are the caretaking needs of elderly family members.

In sum, the FMLA is a sign of movement toward a recognition of the broader interests at stake in the family-state relationship, particularly when this Act is compared with both Rawlsian theory and Title VII. In its recognition of the fact of dependency, the importance of caretaking, and the link between caretaking and families, the FMLA makes significant gains. Yet this departure from Rawlsian liberal theory is still relatively limited, and the protections it offers significantly circumscribed.

Consequences of the Current Framework

Taken together, Title VII and the FMLA embody a number of tenets of liberal political theory that hinder adequate work-and-family protections. The dominance of the individual justice framework limits the relevant goods to autonomy and equality, and ensures that on the rare occasions that other goods are considered, the recognition is halting. The pervasive marginalization of dependency impedes any significant support for caretaking and human development. Moreover, the view that the state should properly remain aloof from issues other than protecting rights combines with the belief that families should be autonomous to ensure that any support for caretaking will occur only in the extraordinary situation.

The result of these tenets is a work-and-family law that provides few protections to the many families who need it. The consequence of the current law's failure to ameliorate conflicts between family and work is that families are left to deal with these issues on a private basis. Faced by job structures that do not accommodate caretaking, and laws that offer them no recourse, American families deal with these issues in a variety of ways. In many families, both parents plunge into a labor market that demands long hours, and consequently send their children out to paid childcare. In others, one parent—generally the woman—detaches herself from full participation in the labor market. In still others, parents take on jobs with nonstandard hours to ensure that children have a caretaker at home. Each of these alternatives, however, imposes large costs on both families and important public goods.

Working Parents

In most families with children in the United States, all parents—both parents in two-parent families or the only parent in single-parent families—work full time.[92] Many parents are no doubt spurred to do so by the significant reduction in wages and benefits that part-time work pays.[93] In doing so, they enter a workforce that keeps substantially longer hours than other wealthy industrialized countries. For most of the twentieth century, the United States fell roughly in the middle of industrialized countries when it came to average total working hours.[94] During the last three decades, though, other countries have, through work-week regulation or strong labor unions, funneled increases in productivity into dramatically reduced work hours; in contrast, the United States has reduced work hours only very slightly.[95] The 1,966 hours that the average American worker works annually amounts to roughly ten more weeks a year of work than Swedish workers (1,552 hours), and significantly more hours than France (1,656), Germany (1,560), Canada (1,732 hours), and the United Kingdom (1,731). This means that even in the countries at the higher end of the scale, Canada and the United Kingdom, full-time employees work roughly the equivalent of six fewer weeks a year than their American counterparts.[96]

The lack of regulation of workplace hours in the United States means that American parents work substantially longer hours than parents in other countries. American parents in two-earner families together spend an average of 80 hours a week at their jobs, compared to 71 hours for dual-earner couples in the United Kingdom, and 69 hours per week in Sweden.[97] Particularly remarkable is the high percentages of American couples working very long hours. Almost two-thirds of American dual-earner couples with children report joint work weeks of 80 hours or more.[98] A study by Janet Gornick and Marcia Meyers that compared the United States with 11 other relatively similar countries showed that, except for Canada, no more than one-third of couples in the other countries spent this much time in the workplace.[99] What is more, in the United States, 13 percent of dual-earner couples with children work more than one hundred hours a week.[100] Working long hours is more common at the upper echelons of careers, but by no means limited to them. According to a study by Jerry Jacobs and Janet Gerson, male workers with college degrees worked 46 hours a week on average; but those with high-school degrees worked only a slightly reduced 43 hours weekly.[101]

The long hours required of employees means that many workers deal with the conflict between work and family by placing their children in some form of paid caretaking, often for many hours. More than three-quarters of preschool-age children with working mothers are cared for by someone other than their parents; roughly half of these children are in non-parental care settings for more than 35 hours a week.[102] This is true even for young children: Two-thirds of children under age one whose mothers work are cared for outside the home; the same is true for three-quarters of two- and three-year old children.[103] For school-aged children ages six to twelve whose mothers work, almost half spend an average of 12.5 hours a week in non-parental care beyond what they spend in school.[104] Moreover, while their parents work, 5 percent of six- to nine-year olds are latch-key kids with no parent at home for some time each week, as are 23 percent of ten- to eleven-year olds, and almost 50 percent of twelve-year olds and older children.[105]

These child-care arrangements do not serve most children well. Although children who attend good quality day care generally fare as well as those who are cared for by a parent, most day care in the United States' lightly regulated system is not good quality.[106] More than half of day-care facilities provide care that is poor to mediocre. Only roughly one in seven provides care that has been deemed developmentally enriching.[107] This poor care is related to the inability or unwillingness to pay the costs of hiring qualified professionals to fill these positions. As Janet Gornick and Marcia Meyers note, "the average earnings of workers in child-care centers are about the same as—and those of family child-care providers are barely half of—the wages earned by parking-lot attendants." As they also point out, in addition to the harms this system causes to children, it creates the impoverishment of a large group of American workers.[108] The system also fails to serve older children well, as they are often left home in the afternoon without supervision. Studies suggest that juvenile crime, drugs, sex, and other risky behavior increase dramatically during unsupervised afternoon hours.[109]

This system also creates a precarious financial situation for many families with young children. Most care arrangement by nonparents are market based. The average cost of child care across all families with children in care in 2000 was $286 a month, or 9 percent of the entire household earnings; for lower income families, this percentage is appreciably higher.[110] Given that most families with young children are headed by adults near the beginning of their working lives with little savings, these are difficult costs to bear. The lack of subsidization in child care contributes to the high child poverty rates in the United States.

Partial or Complete Separation from the Workforce

Faced with jobs that do not accommodate caregiving, many parents with young children step off the career track and either leave the paid workplace or choose nondemanding mommy-track jobs so that they will have more time for child care. While this may be the best decision they can make among the available options for their families, there are several critical disadvantages to this strategy for important public goods. One of these goods is sex equality. For a complicated array of reasons in our gender-structured society, it is generally women who are the ones who step down from full attachment in the labor market. Moreover, stepping down even a little from full-bore involvement in the labor market results in a huge hit to women's economic equality.[111] And many women move not simply to less-demanding full-time jobs, but from full-time to part-time jobs, which generally pay far less than proportional pay or benefits to full-time jobs.[112]

The difficulty in combining caretaking with the long hours required of most full-time jobs poses an especially heavy burden on single-parent families. Because they have no other parent at home to share breadwinning and caretaking responsibilities, the heads of these families, usually single mothers, must choose between a job that adequately supports their family and assurance that their children receive adequate parenting. The difficulty that single parents have in holding demanding full-time jobs as a primary caretaker leads a considerable number of them into mommy-track jobs. The lower pay in these jobs, combined with the lack of child-care subsidies in the United States, the absence of paid leave on the birth of a child, and the high costs of child care not only perpetuates sex inequality, it also redounds to children's detriment, contributing to the United States' 21.9 percent poverty rate for children.[113] This is a substantially higher rate than in many other European countries; for example, only 2–4 percent of children in the Nordic countries are poor.[114] Chronic poverty for children jeopardizes not

only their present well-being but, also, their future prospects. It puts children at risk of lower cognitive development, poor school achievement, and
early childbearing.[115]

Working Nonstandard Hours

Some dual-parent families deal with the work-family conflict by having one
parent switch to a job schedule with nonstandard hours so that they can care
for children during regular working hours. According to Harriet Presser, in
35 percent of dual-earning couples with children under age five, and 31 percent of couples with children under fourteen, at least one parent works nonstandard hours or weekends. Although many parents say they do so because
their jobs in the service economy require it, 35 percent of mothers working
nonstandard hours said that they did so primarily because of caretaking for
children; another 9 percent said that they did so in order to care for another
family member.[116]

Such "split-shift" or "tag-team" parenting, however, imposes considerable
costs on these families. Working nonstandard hours is associated with a number of medical risks, and significantly increases the risk of marital dissolution.[117]
Married men who work at night are six times more likely to get divorced than
those who work days; married women who work nights are three times more
likely to get divorced than their counterparts who work days. Finally, mount-
ing evidence suggests that children whose parents work nonstandard hours have
lower achievement at school and are far more likely to be disciplined at school.[118]

The Cost of These Choices

What we have, then, is a system in which American families must deal privately with a labor market that remains structured in a manner inconsistent
with caretaking. Under this system, workers with caretaking responsibilities
must choose between a set of alternatives that all have significant drawbacks
for important goods: They may accept jobs with high time demands, and out-
source the caretaking to lightly-regulated paid caretakers—often at high cost
to children; they may accept part-time or lower-paying jobs that accommodate caretaking, at a significant cost to the family's financial well-being and
to sex equality; or they may accept jobs with nonstandard hours, which can
avoid the need for paid child care, but at a high cost to children and marriages.
The result is a system that leaves families with children in financially precarious situations, which has poor outcomes for children and their parents, and
which takes a heavy toll on sex equality.

The cost to important public goods does not end with this list, however.
One more important public good that suffers from the current system is civic

involvement. As Robert Putnam has shown, vigorous democracies depend on a flourishing civil society composed of citizens who are involved in the community.[119] This involvement creates ties among citizens that increase social trust and norms of reciprocity, which are crucial to a well-functioning democracy. The current system, however, jeopardizes healthy levels of civic involvement and citizens' ties. As mothers have moved into the workplace and the overall hours that American families work have risen, parents have struggled to ensure parenting time with their children in the hours they are not working.[120] What has been sacrificed from their schedules is the time that citizens used to spend in civic associations and socializing with friends.[121] Given the importance of ties among citizens in creating the civic trust that a democracy requires, these findings are disturbing for the nation's future. The choice between alternatives that impose such stark costs is not inevitable. Most European countries have developed a shared system of public and private responsibility that ameliorates the conflicts among these goods and helps shield families from having to make such tragic choices. In comparison, the United States has done little to set up such institutional structures.

CONCLUSION

Particular tenets embodied in both contemporary liberal theory and in United States law cast families in a distorted light and have produced a narrow, pinched version of a family-state relationship. Some tenets—that the state should properly attend to individual justice, liberty, and equality to the exclusion of other goods; that citizens should be conceptualized absent their dependency needs; and that the state should be neutral with respect to citizens' choices—obscure attention to families. Other tenets— that the state should allow families to function pristinely in the private realm, and that families are properly autonomous—prevent adequate conceptualization of the family-state relationship even after families are taken into account. The inadequate conception of the family-state relationship that has resulted takes a great toll on a number of goods that we as a society should care a great deal about, including children's welfare, sex equality, and civic involvement. Given the important role that families play in citizens' lives, as well as in a flourishing polity, there is a critical need for liberal theory and United States public policy to address these shortcomings. It is to these issues that I now turn.

CHAPTER 2

Theorizing the Supportive State

John Rawls's work is part of a line of liberal political theory that extends back for more than three centuries. In paying little attention to the issue of families, Rawls's work is hardly atypical; except when families were used as a foil to develop contrasting principles that should apply to the political realm (which was deemed not to include the family),[1] there has been little attention to families in this tradition. Some of the explanation for families' absence is intrinsic to liberalism itself. One of the demarcations between the medieval political thought that preceded liberalism, on the one hand, and the liberal tradition, on the other, was liberalism's adoption of methodological individualism, which embodied the view that individuals rather than communities or families are the relevant unit for political theory. Further, what was relevant about individuals for purposes of liberal theory was no longer their position in the social network, including their familial position. Instead, each individual possessed their own, inviolable human dignity that entitled them to rights such as liberty and equality.[2]

Liberalism's emphasis on the individual as an individual did not require ignoring individuals' social and familial ties, but it at least kept attention elsewhere. Moreover, the efforts of liberals to carve out a sphere of individual liberty for citizens also drew attention away from families, since families were perceived as quintessentially part of the private realm from which the state should be removed. So although it was not inevitable that theorists in this tradition would depict the subjects of political theory as autonomous adults, conceived apart from their families, neither was it completely the product of chance. As the conservative critic of Thomas Hobbes, William Lucy wrote more than three hundred years ago: "Methinks that he discourses of Men as if they were...born out of the earth, come up like Seeds, without any relation one to the other.... [By nature a human is] made a poor helpless Child who confides and trusts in his Parents, and submits to them."[3]

Yet there is nothing intrinsic to liberalism, itself, that precludes an adequate theorization of families. Indeed, the classical liberal theory developed by early liberals contained several features that allowed fuller consideration of families than contemporary versions of liberalism. First, it embodied a greater moral complexity than does Rawlsian liberalism. Although the protection of rights and liberty was the primary focus of classical liberalism, civic virtues and human development still played a crucial role in it.[4] Early liberals' understanding of human institutions as tools that could be used to foster virtue in citizens also allowed focusing on the role that families might play in this process. Although it is certainly true that classical liberals saw human nature as less malleable than the line of continental European theorists stretching from Rousseau to Marx, they were still considerably more likely to view institutions as helping to shape citizens than contemporary liberals, who tend to see them simply as vehicles to distribute societal goods and privileges. For example, Locke saw the law not simply as a tool to arbitrate among individual rights: "For law, in its true notion, is not so much the limitation as the direction of a free and intelligent agent to his proper interest, and prescribes no farther than is for the general good of those under that law."[5] Law here does more than carve out zones of individual liberty—it actively attempts to move citizens toward a flourishing community.

John Stuart Mill's work demonstrates the rich theorizations of families and the family-state relationship possible in liberal theory. Mill, despite penning what has remained the most enduring defense of liberty in the liberal tradition, still recognized the important link between sound citizens and good polities. "If we ask ourselves on what causes and conditions good government in all its senses, from the humblest to the most exalted, depends, we find that the principal of them, the one which transcends all others, is the qualities of the human beings composing the society over which government is exercised."[6] He recognized, as well, that good citizens do not spring up fully formed like mushrooms. In fact, Mill's *Considerations on Representative Government* is essentially a long discourse about how political institutions could be used to contribute to the human development of citizens.[7] The recognition of the link between flourishing citizens and a flourishing society led him to emphasize the connection between the interests of a society and the human development of its citizens:

> [T]he existing generation is master both of the training and the entire circumstances of the generation to come; it cannot indeed make them perfectly wise and good, because it is itself so lamentably deficient in goodness and wisdom; and its best efforts are not always, in individual cases, its most successful ones; but it is perfectly well able to make the rising generation, as a whole, as good as, and a little better than, itself. If society lets any considerable number of its members grow up mere children, incapable of being acted on by rational consideration of distant motives, society has itself to blame for the consequences.[8]

Mill recognized here that dependent children become good citizens only with appropriate rearing. This, combined with his attention to the inevitable fact of interdependence of citizens, caused him to posit a societal responsibility for child rearing. This is not simply to ensure basic human survival: the interdependence of citizens is so great, he says, that society must aim instead to foster "goodness and wisdom."

Mill's discussion here has much in common with what is commonly identified with republican theorists or modern-day communitarians: an emphasis on virtue, and a focus on the way that institutions can instill it. Yet Mill also recognized the limits to virtue: He did not rely on it to ground citizens' responsibility to the next generation; instead, he relied on the collective benefits for society if the next generation is well raised. At the same time, Mill's recognition of societal interdependence did not diminish his emphasis on individual liberty and responsibility: He expected that parents would assume primary responsibility for the task of child rearing, but recognized that society and the state also have some role to play.

What is more, Mill recognized the importance of the liberal good of equality in this mix.[9] In applying it to the sexes, Mill used the tools and concepts of liberal theory to gain a critical perspective on the family as an institution, an inquiry that other liberal theorists, both then and now, have largely avoided. Specifically, because families are a training ground for democratic citizenship, Mill argued that they must reflect the principles of equality and justice on which a democracy is founded. He, therefore, condemned the inequality of women in the current family structure as inhibiting the development of children's democratic character.[10]

In sum, although there are some features of liberal theory that put stumbling blocks in the path of theorizing the place of families in the political order, there is nothing inherent in liberalism that precludes it. In fact, particular features of classical liberalism that have been lost from later theory provide fertile ground for theorizing the family-state relationship. These include the focus on a broad range of goods in addition to liberty and equality, a clearer recognition of dependency in at least some quarters, and a greater recognition of the interdependence between individuals and society. Finally, early liberalism's recognition that good government requires particular virtues opens the door wide for consideration of the role that families play in fostering these qualities. A renewed liberalism capable of grasping the place of families in the political order must recover these features.

RETHINKING FUNDAMENTALS OF CONTEMPORARY LIBERAL THEORY

The able and autonomous adult that has been the subject of liberal theory is, at its best, an incomplete description. If we recognize that humans are necessarily dependent to varying degrees during the course of their lives, the subjects of liberal theory change substantially. The central questions asked of political theory must also be amended: No longer is it sufficient simply to ask what a just distribution of societal goods among citizens would be, or how we should best organize society to protect citizens' rights. We must also ask how we can bring into being, care for, and develop the faculties and virtues of sound citizens.

Put another way, the liberal tradition has been built on a vision of human dignity premised on able, autonomous adults.[11] What such citizens are due by virtue of their dignity is protection of their individual rights to liberty and equality with others. To ensure these, central liberal institutions provide for sovereignty of the people; a limited state; and the security of its citizens. It is based on such a conception of the "natural dignity of man" that Thomas Paine argued for individual rights and freedom from patriarchy.[12] Once we adjust the image of citizens to account for the dependency in the human life cycle, however, respect for human dignity entails more than just protecting citizens' individual rights: The importance of caretaking and human development come to the fore as every bit as important to human dignity as safeguarding citizens' liberty and security. This, in turn, focuses attention on families as a central liberal institution. This change of focus, however, requires revising fundamental tenets of liberal theory.

Reconceptualizing the Subjects of Political Theory to Recognize the Fact of Dependency

An adequate political theory of the family-state relationship must begin by recognizing the inevitability of the condition of dependency during the course of citizens' lives.[13] Putting dependency in its proper perspective requires transforming the conception of the individual who is the subject of liberal theory. The able adult of our tradition of liberal theory must be put in context: This description applies to citizens for only a limited part of their lives, and, even then, it is an idealized description. A better theory would conceptualize citizens as existing somewhere on a spectrum between complete autonomy and complete dependence, with their exact position changing over the course of the human life cycle, and contingent on their individual situation. This conception owns up to the fact that dependency is an inevitable condition in all human lives. It does not disavow the ways in which humans can be autonomous, but makes it clear that this autonomy will never be complete. It also focuses attention on the fact that humans do not emerge with their faculties, personalities, and desires fully formed, as liberal political theory sometimes takes them. Instead, their identities develop within the social world, and within the web of institutions in which they are raised. This, in turn, requires expanding the questions we ask of political theory to include how we as a society can best bring into being, care for, and develop the faculties of sound citizens.

Reconceptualizing Important Societal Goods— Supplementing Freedom and Equality with Caretaking and Human Development

Reframing liberal theory to recognize the fact of dependency makes it clear that the standard goods of liberty and equality recognized by contemporary liberal theory are not adequate to support human dignity. The dependency inherent in the human condition requires that caretaking and human development be added to this list.[14] Not only does this reconception of liberal theory require that liberty and equality share the marquee of important liberal values with these new contenders, it also necessarily reorients how both of these heretofore dominant liberal values should be conceived. This recognition requires discarding the idea of complete liberty as both an impossible and unpalatable goal; dependency will always be a part of life to be managed in any human society committed to the dignity of its citizens.[15]

Yet the ideal of liberty need not be abandoned altogether: We should still hold tight to the belief in liberty, more precisely termed "autonomy," that is central to the liberal project, which is the belief that humans should be able to plan and pursue their own course in life.[16] Recognition of the fact of dependency in human lives, and a focus on the human life cycle, however, make it clear that autonomy is not a condition that can simply be assumed and respected by the state through defending an individual's freedom to be left alone. Instead, it is an accomplishment that can only be achieved through complex systems of nurturance. Without caretaking and adequate development of their capabilities, individuals could not become the (largely) autonomous citizens whose choices are worthy of respect.

The recognition of dependency in the human condition also has significant consequences for equality, the good generally given second billing behind liberty in our tradition of liberal thought. The care work that dependency necessitates has profound implications for gender, economic, and racial equality. The failure to recognize dependency as an integral issue for political theory has led to the exploitation and inequality of those who perform dependency work.[17] Putting dependency in proper theoretical perspective therefore requires thinking through how a society distributes its care work, and the benefits and burdens that accompany it.

Adding caretaking and human development to the aspirations of a liberal democracy not only transforms liberal theory, it also, necessarily but unfortunately, complicates it. Contemporary liberalism already embodies an unsettled internal tension between liberty and equality, which is responsible for the conflict between libertarians and progressives. Adding caretaking and human development to this list increases the chances that the relevant goods that the state needs to balance will conflict in any particular situation. The situation becomes still more complicated because, as civic liberals have correctly argued, the goods of civic virtue and community must also be considered in this mix. Yet an adequate liberal democratic theory has no alternative but to embrace this larger list of goods since they are all fundamental to a healthy polity. A theory that eliminates these other goods in order to produce determinative results attains predictive power at the cost of both normative accuracy and persuasiveness.[18] Rather than artificially restricting the important goods at stake, what is called for is a more nuanced theory and more nuanced public policies that carefully calibrate this mix of goods, and, as far as possible, ameliorate the tension among them.[19] Where this tension cannot be resolved through carefully-crafted policies, hard choices must be made among this expanded list of goods. At least a revised vision of the family-state relationship can do so explicitly and thoughtfully, rather than by ignoring the existence of important goods.

Broadening the aspirations of liberal democracy comports with recent critiques of liberal theory from communitarians, civic liberals, and feminist theorists. These critics point out the paucity of goods valued in Rawlsian liberal theory. Feminists argue that contemporary liberal theory's obsessive focus on freedom rests on a gendered view of the world: Communities have survived and flourished only because women attended to caretaking and human development at a far more fundamental level than is accounted for by liberal conceptions of choice and the free pursuit of ends.[20] As Susan Moller Okin pointed out, the emphasis on the freedom of liberal subjects rests "on the often unstated assumption of women's unpaid reproductive and domestic work, their dependence and subordination within the family, and their exclusion from most spheres of life."[21] In a related vein, communitarians and civic liberals correctly point out that liberal theory's focus on freedom obscures the need to develop civic virtues and a sense of community that are necessary for the collective self-government of a liberal democracy, which, in turn, is necessary to sustain the freedom of citizens.[22]

Insofar as feminist and communitarian critics seek to discredit mainstream liberalism's valuing of justice and freedom, rather than put them in perspective among other important goods, however, they throw the baby out with the bathwater, missing what is so valuable about the liberal democratic project. This is the case when Michael Sandel criticizes the Supreme Court's rationale for supporting abortion as a fundamental right in *Thornburgh v. American College of Obstetricians & Gynecologists*.[23] In that case, the Court defended women's right to abortion on the ground that "[f]ew decisions are…more properly private, or more basic to individual dignity and autonomy, than a woman's decision... whether to end her pregnancy. A woman's right to make that choice freely is fundamental."[24] Sandel argues that this rationale demonstrates the Supreme Court's problematic view that what makes people human is their capacity to live autonomously, in the sense of choosing their lives and relationships for themselves.[25] In doing so, however, he mistakenly conflates the legitimate normative claim that the Supreme Court did make—that individuals have an important right to determine their own future—with the inaccurate ontological claim that the Court did not assert—that individuals are radically unencumbered by their ties and commitments.[26] Conflating the two claims causes Sandel to seek to jettison one of liberalism's most valuable tenets—that each person's views about how to live their own life should be taken seriously.

The same is true for the feminist conversation about the relationship between justice and care. Feminists who have criticized liberalism for its focus on justice to the exclusion of care certainly have valid cause for grievance. Yet the best of this work recognizes that what is called for is not to reject the goods associated with justice entirely, but rather to develop a political ethic that reconciles them with goods such as caretaking.[27] An exclusive focus on the value of care that is not balanced by a focus on justice runs the risk of perpetuating women's roles as the helpmates of others without independent claims to be subjects in their own right.[28]

In sum, while recognizing the value of individual liberty and equality, a revised version of liberalism must also recognize their limits. It must take account of the facts that individuals are never completely autonomous; that even individuals who are autonomous in the sense of being self-governing are made, not born; that for a liberal democratic society to flourish, its citizens need caretaking, and must come to possess particular capabilities and virtues. This calls for a liberal democratic theory both more capacious and more nuanced than existing contenders, and with a longer list of social goods that it must seek to further. This list should be expanded to include not only the civic virtues and sense of community sought by communitarians and civic liberals, but also caretaking and human development.

Rethinking the Role of the State—from Neutrality to Support for Caretaking and Human Development

The Rawlsian view of the role of the state in liberal theory was that it should be neutral with respect to different ways of life. As Ronald Dworkin expressed this view: The state "must be neutral on... the question of the good life [and] political decisions must be, so far as is possible, independent of any particular conception of the good life, or of what gives value to life."[29] William Galston aptly summarizes this view of the liberal state as "presid[ing] benignly over [different ways of life], intervening only to adjudicate conflict, to prevent any particular way of life from tyrannizing over others, and to ensure that all adhere to the principles that constitute society's basic structure."[30]

Both communitarians and feminists have demonstrated that what was taken by these Rawlsian liberal theorists to be neutral actually embodies a particular conception of the good life premised on autonomy and individual choice.[31] Adapting liberal theory to recognize citizens' dependency needs points out further difficulties with the Rawlsian view of the state's role. If we conceive of citizens as able, autonomous adults, the state best respects their dignity by constructing a private realm that is off-limits for state action, and by limiting the role of the state to enforcing individual rights. Incorporating dependency into our understanding of human relations, however, transforms the focus of the liberal project: Respect for human dignity now demands more than the protection of individual rights and freedom. It also requires that the state actively support individuals in receiving the caretaking and conditions for human development necessary for them to become responsible, self-directing citizens. This responsibility of the state to support caretaking and human development becomes every bit as fundamental as its responsibility to establish an adequate police force in order to safeguard citizens' individual rights.

Transforming the conception of the state's role from neutral protector of individual rights to active supporter of caretaking and human development does not mean the state should abandon its commitment to neutrality entirely, but that it must transform this commitment. As Rawls recognized in his later work, his earlier commitment to keeping the state neutral with respect to citizens' visions of the good life was somewhat too constraining: certainly a liberal state must be able to distinguish between good citizens and psychopaths. He, therefore, asserted in this later work that the liberal state need be neutral only in the less restrictive sense that it may not be used to impose any particular vision on its citizens based only on some citizens' personal philosophies of right and wrong, which Rawls referred to as "comprehensive" views of the world. In this more permissive view of the state's proper role, state action must be neutral only in the sense that it can be justified in a manner that citizens with a broad range of world views can accept—what Rawls called "public reason."[32] The requirement of public reason posits that state action is supportable only insofar as it is grounded on a set of public ideals and principles—a sort of public morality.[33] Although "the Bible told me so," may explain one person's motivation for rearing children in a particular manner, it is not a sufficient reason to ground state action in a nation that respects pluralism and is committed to considerable individual autonomy. The state's support for caretaking and human development is eminently defensible under the standard of public reason. Recognizing the fact of dependency as an inevitable feature in human life, and the interplay of this dependency with the respect for human dignity that is central to liberalism, gives the state strong public reason to act to support these goods.

In sum, focusing on dependency complicates the state's role in a liberal polity. No longer can the state be seen as simply protecting individual rights. Instead, the state has a responsibility to support specific goods, including caretaking and human development. Focusing on how to support these goods leads ineluctably to consideration of the family-state relationship.

RETHINKING THE STATE'S RELATIONSHIP WITH FAMILIES: THE SUPPORTIVE STATE

Mainstream contemporary liberal theory pays little attention to the institution of the family because citizens are taken as autonomous and able. Families, in its view, exist in the private realm, and are only relevant to the public discussion in the limited ways that they affect freedom and equality. Once we take into account the fact of dependency, and we focus on citizens during the course of the human life cycle, however, the role of families in caretaking and human development becomes a central subject for political theory. In the discussion that follows, I consider how families should be theorized in a revised liberal theory. I then turn to consider how the relationship between families and the state should be conceptualized.

Theorizing Families

Whereas Rawlsian liberal theory paid little attention to families and to how they manage to produce the citizens who become the subjects of liberal theory, a revised liberal theory must do better. It must attend to how families are organized, how they function, and what their benefits and risks are to both society and their own members. Specifically, there are three tenets that a revised theory should incorporate.

The Issue of What Constitutes a "Family" Is a Political Question

The issue of what constitutes a family is not a pre-political question that can be determined based on science or nature, but is instead heavily freighted with legal and political determinations.[34] On this issue, Rawls had it right: He recognized early on in A *Theory of Justice* that families are a political institution, rather than a natural entity, and that their existence and form are subject to political authority. Despite some conservatives, such as former Senator Rick Santorum, arguing that there is a "natural family,"[35] the institutions in which children have been raised, and in which other care work has been accomplished, have varied considerably over time and place. A vast body of work by anthropologists and social historians demonstrates that the family that seems natural in our culture—the heterosexual nuclear family unit headed by a man and woman, who are monogamous, dwell in their own private home, and are emotionally committed to themselves and their children—"is so far from being 'natural' that it has hardly ever existed outside of Western Europe and North America after the Protestant Reformation."[36]

At the most basic level, the very determination of whether a particular group of citizens constitutes a family is determined by state action. In Martha Nussbaum's words:

> People associate in many ways, live together, love each other, have children. Which of these will get the name "family" is a legal and political matter, never one to be decided simply by the parties themselves. The state constitutes the family structure through its laws, defining which groups of people can count as families, defining the privileges and rights of family members, defining what marriage and divorce are, what legitimacy and parental responsibility are, and so forth. This difference makes a difference: The state is present in the family from the start, in a way that is less clearly the case with the religious body or the university; it is the state that says what this thing *is* and controls how one becomes a member of it.[37]

Without state recognition and sanction, not only would no legal privileges and protections attach to particular relationships, they would not be understood as "families" in the same way. This point has been dramatically illustrated in recent years in the battle over what kind of state recognition should be accorded to same-sex relationships. For many gay and lesbian rights advocates, state recognition of same-sex relationships as civil unions is a valuable and important step on the road to equality. Civil-union status accords official recognition of these relationships, as well as the same package of rights and benefits that accompany marriage. With that said, the reason that these unions have also been palatable to some same-sex marriage opponents, and the reason that many same-sex rights advocates argue that civil unions are insufficient, is precisely because of the significance invested in the state attaching a different label than "marriage" to such unions. Although civil unions accord same-sex couples the same legal rights accorded married couples, the status itself is infused with a very different set of social meanings than is the status of marriage.

Of course, the notion that families are political entities can easily be reduced to absurdity. Certainly, even in the absence of state sanction, people would still engage in relationships of affection and caretaking. Yet, as Hendrik Hartzog points out in the context of discussing marriage in the nineteenth century, the legal components of such relationships are constitutive:

> A marriage was both legally constituted and private. Law was not everything in a marriage. Love, lust, hatred, duty, friendship, respect, affection, abandonment, commitment, greed, and self-sacrifice, all the feelings and practices that made up a nineteenth-century marriage, were not primarily legal. But law was always there as well. Law was there when a marriage began; it was there when it ended. And in between: law was there when a husband and wife struggled or negotiated over the terms of power between them; law was there when a married couple constructed or reconstructed a relationship with a world of others—including children, parents, and third party creditors; law was there when husbands or wives thought about themselves as husbands or wives; law was also there when those same husbands or wives denied or repressed their identities as husbands and wives.[38]

The Way Families Function Cannot Be Isolated from Their Political, Economic, and Social Contexts

Just as there is no natural, pre-political family, there are no natural, pre-political ways in which families function. In today's complex society, the ways in which families function are always deeply and inextricably intertwined with government policy.[39] The state is not only involved in determining what constitutes a family and when family relationships are dissolved, it is also involved directly and indirectly in a multitude of other ways. For example, it reinforces parents' authority over children by subjecting the children to court supervision should they disobey their parents; by preventing other adults from caring for them; by allowing parents to have considerable power over whether children are institutionalized for mental-health reasons; and by child-labor laws that limit children's ability to live independently. As Frances Olsen points out, these policies generally go unrecognized as intervention by family privacy advocates only because they are so accepted that they are taken as inevitable.[40]

And there are many other ways that state regulation and public policy affect family life. Some of these ways are more obvious: For example, the relaxation of divorce laws affects whether and which families stay together. Others are less obvious: For example, the state's regulation of other institutions outside the family deeply and profoundly affects the lives of families. The provision and mandating of education shaped and continue to shape the lives of children and affect parents' control over them. Equal employment legislation for women encouraged women's movement out of the household and into the labor market.[41] Equal employment laws likely also contributed to the increase in divorces, as women in unhappy marriages began to have more financial wherewithal to divorce their husbands.[42] Laws governing the availability of health insurance for employees' family members influence which family members work.[43] And United States welfare policy was, as Alice Kessler-Harris has demonstrated, constructed deliberately on a model that pitted work and family in mortal conflict, having considerable implications for the ways in which families function.[44]

By the same token, the care that children receive from parents is inextricably intertwined with state policies. Parental care takes place in a matrix of constraints and entitlements that affect a parent's ability and opportunity to parent. The existence or nonexistence of minimum wage laws, union rights to bargain, and overtime provisions affect parents' ability to meet the financial needs of their children.[45] Welfare-reform laws requiring recipients to work in order to receive welfare subsidies affect parents' ability to care for their children.[46] The scope of family-leave laws affects parents' opportunities to stay home with their children.[47] The stability and security of a parent's job affects stress levels in the household, which also affect the quality of parenting. State support for and subsidizing of drug-treatment programs makes it easier or harder for parents to deal with drug addictions that can impair their ability to care for their children.

Along these same lines, the ways in which families function are intricately interlinked with economic and social conditions, which are also influenced by public policy. This tenet is dramatically illustrated by Friedrich Engels's description of working-class families in his account of factory life in Manchester, England in 1844. In that account, the grueling demands of the workplace drained families of their nurturing function, as men, women, and children worked from early morning to late at night. In this society, infants were left alone all day in their parents' unheated flats. The children they became were never properly socialized. In short, the pressure of economics suffocated feelings of love and affection, eviscerated caretaking, and led to the breakdown of the family.[48] A more modern, if somewhat less dramatic, example is illustrated by the "Barriers to Marriage Among Fragile Families" study, which found that the poor job prospects of unmarried fathers reduced the chances of marriage between unmarried parents, because marriage was unlikely to improve the economic status of the family and both partners viewed the "father as having a steady job" to be an important factor in marital stability.[49] The point is also made by contemporary studies that demonstrate the link between domestic violence in families and the surrounding economic and social circumstances.[50] These examples suggest that families need certain preconditions to produce and sustain sound, healthy citizens.

In these circumstances, the family has no "natural" baseline of functioning that it can be left to "apart from" the state and public policy, and that would be adulterated if the state were to intercede, as Rawls posits. Nor does the modern administrative state have a neutral, isolated position it can assume while leaving families autonomously to deal with their own affairs, as work-and-family law suggests. Instead, the state is always and continually influencing how families conduct their affairs. The issue is not whether state policy will influence families, but whether it will be formulated with this inevitable influence in mind. When it comes to the ways families function, no family is an island.

Families Are Always Imperfect, and Sometimes Very Imperfect

Families, even at their best, are imperfect. Sometimes families operate in ways that are unfair to individual members. For example, in some relationships, one party's desires might be realized while another's might continually be postponed. Sometimes they pass illiberal or undemocratic norms on to the next generation, for example, when parents pass on sexist or racist beliefs to their children. At their worst, they are downright abusive or oppressive. For instance, at least 653,000 citizens were harmed or killed by intimate partner violence in the United States in 2008.[51] The year before, an estimated 794,000 children were confirmed by social service agencies to be victims of abuse or neglect, while an estimated 1,760 children died due to child abuse or neglect.[52]

Any adequate theory of the family-state relationship must contend with these flaws and risks. Just as the framers of the Constitution sought to deal with the inevitability of human corruption in government and to construct institutions that minimized the effects of human frailties, so must a theory of the family-state relationship contend with the large and small ways that families can and do go awry. In fact, there are particular reasons to be specially concerned about the misuse of power in families, because this is often the place where vulnerable individuals are the most vulnerable.

The importance of this tenet to developing an adequate theory of the family-state relationship cannot be overstated. Too many accounts that discuss the critical role that families play in a sound society view this institution through rose-colored glasses. Thus, Rick Santorum touts the virtues of the traditional family without once mentioning the possibility of domestic violence or abuse within families. By the same token, Santorum never mentions the sex inequality that is common within heterosexual families, except to criticize the "radical feminists" who promote the ideal of equal opportunity for women.[53]

The fact of imperfection and risk of abuse are not, however, reasons for the state to seek to discourage families, given that we have no other credible alternative for meeting the considerable amount of caretaking and human development needs that exist in our society. Instead, they require that the state seek ways to reduce the risks that can occur in families. One important way the state should guard against some risks is to build some redundancy into the institutions responsible for human development. Doing so would ensure, for example, to that if children do not get some of the assistance they need at home, they can receive it elsewhere, such as at school. The state should also develop other caretaking institutions aside from families, including day-care centers and elder-care programs, to ease the stress on family caretakers. Finally, an adequate theory of the family-state relationship must set standards for determining when to intervene to protect family members in cases in which its prevention efforts fail and significant risks to family members come to pass.

Theorizing the Relationship between Families and the State

We come, then, to the issue of how to theorize the relationship between families and the state. I have argued already that the state has a responsibility to support caretaking and human development. To what extent should this affect the way it constructs its relationship with families? In a liberal democracy, we expect citizens to do the things they reasonably can do for themselves. Does this mean, then, that the responsibility for dealing with dependency should fall in the first instance to family members, and only to the state if families fail? Rawlsian liberal theory and a good deal of public policy presume this. In this view, families are properly autonomous, providing for the needs of their members without state support.[54] As I have already suggested, however, in our world, the situation is more complicated than this version of family autonomy would have it.

Certainly when it comes to ensuring that family members receive caretaking, there are good reasons to expect that family members will shoulder much of the responsibility to provide or coordinate this care. Where children and spouses are concerned, doing so holds citizens accountable for obligations they have assumed. Citizens who have children should be responsible for their decision to do so, and should be expected to plan carefully and budget wisely for them, as well as to care for them. Where family members beyond children and spouses are concerned, holding citizens accountable for shouldering some responsibility for family members is still generally consistent with the idea that society should recognize "nested obligations" among citizens. As explained by Eva Feder Kittay, moral obligations toward others are appropriately created not only by agreement of the parties, but also on a more broadly based sense of reciprocity, in which the caretaking actions of one person toward another within a network of care obligates the second person to care for others within that network of care. Thus, we may care for an elderly aunt because we were once cared for by family members and will likely be again, and we should ensure this same caretaking to others.[55] Expecting that some portion of the responsibility for caretaking should rest with family members is also in accord with the moral precept that those who are best positioned to care for the vulnerable should have the responsibility to do so.[56] In many cases, family members will be in the best position to care for other family members, both because they know the needs of their family members best and because they are most motivated to act in their interests because of their emotional bond with them.

Yet the view that family members should bear responsibility for other family members does not exempt the state from responsibility for its citizens' dependency needs, as well. In fact, there is little controversy over the proposition that the state bears some responsibility for dependent citizens. For example, few would argue that the state has no duty to remove children who are the victims of serious abuse from their homes. Instead, the controversy is not about *whether* the state has a duty, but about *when* that duty of the state is triggered. Opponents of state support argue that the state's duty is "residual," in the sense that it should be triggered only *after* families fail in some serious way.[57] The abuse example is, therefore, uncontroversial in terms of state action because the parents have failed to keep their child safe. The theoretical tenets embedded in current child-welfare law and in a broad array of public policies adopt this residual view of the state's responsibility.

Residual responsibility involves a type of apportionment of responsibility that Robert Goodin, in his schematization of the division of moral responsibility for vulnerable persons, refers to as "disjunctive." The defining feature of disjunctive responsibility is that, if A is vulnerable to B or to C or to D, then "any one of them could provide the needed assistance; and if any one of them does, none of the others need to."[58] The paradigm case of this type of responsibility is that of the drowning child at the crowded (but unguarded) beach: Any one of the bystanders could effect a rescue, and if any one does, the others need not. In the case of disjunctive responsibility, a particular person (for example, the nearest adult) may have a moral obligation to aid the vulnerable person before others attempt a rescue; this primary responsibility does not let all others off the hook, however. Once it becomes clear that the person with primary responsibility is not going to act, responsibility devolves on others. This, in essence, is the theory proposed by those who advocate only a residual role for the state: Parents are supposed to have primary responsibility for children's welfare; this duty devolves to the state only if parents fail in their responsibility.

But a disjunctive division of responsibility is not the only possible division of responsibility. As Goodin counsels, when it comes to the division of moral responsibility for vulnerable persons, responsibility can also be divided in a "conjunctive" way, so that several persons—or, in this case, family members and the state—have a responsibility to ensure caretaking for societal dependents jointly.[59] The paradigm case for a conjunctive division of responsibility is a person trapped in a burning house. Not only does the firefighter who helps her out of the window have an obligation to do so; so do the firefighters who hold the trampoline below; and so does the emergency medical technician who provides emergency medical aid. To spin this out still further, the firefighter also requires training from others to be able to do her job well, as well as sufficient equipment. The fact that one actor bears responsibility to act therefore does not preclude concurrent responsibility on the part of others.

So which type of responsibility, disjunctive or conjunctive, should we associate with the state's duty to meet citizens' dependency needs vis-à-vis families? As I argued earlier,[60] the intricate interconnections between families and the state make it conceptually inaccurate to conceive of a family acting *before* the state steps in. Instead, state action always and already affects families' capacity to deal with dependency issues. In addition, families and the state are not similarly situated when it comes to dealing with dependency needs. Families are better suited to performing the hands-on care and arranging of care for those with such needs, yet are less well suited to arranging institutions to support care. In contrast, the state is uniquely suited to ensuring that dependency needs are accommodated at an institutional level by establishing relevant laws and regulations. In this situation, it makes far more sense to conceive of the state's and families' responsibility as conjunctive.

Returning to the example of the child drowning near multiple adult bystanders makes it clear why the model of disjunctive responsibility is a poor fit to the situation of responsibility for dependents. First, the actors at issue—families and the state—do not act independently of one another when it comes to caretaking, as they do in the drowning example. Instead, institutions structured directly and indirectly by the state profoundly affect families' ability to care for their members. The child's best chance for achieving well-being is therefore not for the nearest adult to rescue the child single-handedly while the state acts just as another bystander. Instead, the child is best served by families and the state acting in conjunction with each other. Put another way, the state's position could be likened to a pilot in a nearby helicopter, who could drop a life preserver near the struggling child that would assist the adult in towing the child back to shore. Seen in this light, the positions of the relevant actors are considerably closer to the situation of conjunctive responsibility that Goodin describes, in which the actors should work together to protect the vulnerable person.

The child drowning example, however, omits some of the strongest reasons in favor of conjunctive state responsibility for children and other dependents. Raising children, caring for dependents, and developing human capabilities are all activities that cannot be wrapped up in seconds or minutes like an ocean rescue. Instead, they are complex tasks that are part of a process that generally takes years. No family can reasonably accomplish all these tasks without some help. During that time, moreover, dependents interact with a number of institutions aside from the family that profoundly influence their development, including schools, day-care centers, the labor market, and the health-care system. By the same token, caretakers interact with a number of institutions, most prominently the labor market, that profoundly influence their ability to meet family members' dependency needs. Given the limits of families in controlling and navigating these other institutions, as well as the unique ability that the state has to exercise influence over these other institutions, there are strong reasons to assign the state responsibility along with parents and other family members.

When it comes to adults who are able to order their own affairs, the state does not have the broad ethical responsibility to protect their welfare that it does for vulnerable dependents. With that said, it is not just children and those with disabilities who need caretaking: All humans need care, even generally healthy adults. And as our society is organized, some large portion of the care that adults need will come, if it comes at all, from other adults with whom we share family relationships. The liberal state's commitment to human dignity therefore also gives it good reason to support stable caretaking relationships among adults.

Determining that the state and families are both conjunctively responsible for meeting dependency needs does not mean that the state's role should be identical to the role of families. Rather, each should bear responsibility for the area in which they have greater competence. This means that families should bear responsibility for the day-to-day caring for (or arranging the care for) children and others with dependency needs. Meanwhile, the state should bear the responsibility for structuring institutions in ways that help families meet their caretaking needs, and that support human development. This includes ensuring that families have safe and affordable caretaking options, as well as structuring other societal institutions, such as schools and communities, in ways that foster children's and other dependents' development and well-being. This division of responsibility recognizes the malleability and contingency of institutional structures. It does not artificially separate state action from the realm of families or presume that completely clear boundaries can even be drawn between them, but it does assume certain spheres of authority will exist between the two. I call this vision of the state's role "the supportive state."

In dividing responsibility in this way, the supportive-state model respects citizens' autonomy by treating them as responsible citizens who are accountable for their choices and relationships with others. The liberal state, in this view, provides a scaffold on which citizens can construct their lives, but it does not plan their lives for them, or absolve them of the responsibility to plan carefully and budget wisely to achieve their goals. Yet it maintains that the meeting of dependency needs that these family members perform should be accomplished within institutional structures that facilitate caretaking and human development, and that it is the state's responsibility to secure such institutional structures. This approach recognizes the fact of dependency, and that the ability of families to nurture their members does not simply exist as a matter of fact, or spring up as a matter of spontaneous generation; instead, it is an achievement to be pursued jointly by both citizens and the state.

This conjunctive responsibility does not mean that the state should scrap the ideal of familial autonomy as a goal; as with individual autonomy, however, the conception of family autonomy must be significantly revised. This revision would recognize the fact of dependency and the consequent need for caretaking and human development that families should provide, but it would also recognize that contemporary families' capacity to do so is intimately related to societal institutions. At the same time, it would also recognize the importance of strong families that have the capacity to make their own decisions, set their own goals, and meet their members' basic dependency needs. Just as I argued that individuals sometimes require government action to become as autonomous as possible, the same is true for families. In this view, capable families that can meet their members' dependency needs are an achievement to be jointly pursued by families and the state, rather than an inevitability. State support should therefore not be seen as inimical to autonomy, but rather as an aid to it when it fosters families' capabilities.

THE SUPPORTIVE STATE AND FAMILY PRIVACY

I have contended that a theory of the family-state relationship should be premised on the understanding that these two entities are more closely interlinked than is generally recognized. In doing so, I have argued against the view that ideal families in a liberal democracy are those that are autonomous, in the sense that they do not require any forms of support from the state. There is, however, another tenet of liberal thought that is closely related to the view that families should be autonomous – the belief in family privacy. The conception that there are some areas of life, particularly those connected with the home, personal relationships, and family, that should be free from state intervention and control is central to liberal democratic thought and jurisprudence, especially in its American incarnations. As Justice Kennedy expressed this view in *Lawrence v. Texas*:[61]

> In our tradition the State is not omnipresent in the home. And there are other spheres of our lives and existence, outside the home, where the State should not be a dominant presence. Freedom extends beyond spatial bounds. Liberty presumes an autonomy of self that includes freedom of thought, belief, expression, and certain intimate conduct.

Indeed, one of the hallmarks of liberalism is the conceptual walls it draws between various realms, which limit the legitimate scope of state action.[62] How should we think about the boundary between family and state in a revised version of liberalism? Put another way, given that the supportive state significantly curtails and revises the notion of family autonomy, should it also restrict or even jettison the tenet of family privacy?

Reconceptualizing Family Privacy

The notion that there can and should be an unbreachable delineation between the public world and the private home is, as I have argued, a myth. In contemporary society, there is simply no possibility of constructing a zone that is completely free of the state's interference, no so-called "normal" operation of a family that stands completely apart from state action. The state is so omnipresent in family formation and functioning that, as Frances Olsen charges, the very concept of state intervention in families is itself incoherent.[63] The role of the state with respect to families may be more or less obvious or more or less coercive, but the state always plays some role within families in contemporary society.

Even if the ideal of a complete separation between public and private were attainable, it would be normatively problematic. Feminist theorists have shown how the strict demarcation between the public and private realms as the boundary for state action has served to perpetuate women's inequality in families and in society.[64] These theorists point out that liberal theory, in walling off families from the reach of the state, have preserved the freedom of some at the cost of the oppression of others.[65] Liberalism's attempts to keep the state out of citizens' private lives is predicated on the view that, in the absence of state action, citizens exercise considerable freedom in this realm. Insofar as inequality and other constraints prevail in this realm, though, keeping the state out simply allows these inequalities and constraints to go unchallenged.[66] For this reason, the doctrine of family privacy has, in Catharine MacKinnon's words, functioned a lot like the "right of men 'to be let alone' to oppress women one at a time."[67]

Despite these ontological and normative problems, there still exists an important concern at the heart of the notion of family privacy that deserves continued respect, which harks back to the central liberal notion of autonomy. The view that dignity for humans requires the ability to to be self-directing, in the sense of making important decisions about the course of their lives, is central to the justification for privacy. As Justice Brennan said in crafting the constitutional doctrine of privacy, "If the right of privacy means anything, it is the right of the individual, married or single, to be free from unwarranted governmental intrusion into matters so fundamentally affecting a person as the decision whether to bear or beget a child."[68] This decisional autonomy must continue to be protected by the supportive state.

While recent liberal theory has generally conceived this decisional autonomy to attach to individuals, there are strong reasons to accord this autonomy to families as well. Doing so comports with the concrete historical concerns that motivated liberalism. The institutional reforms sought by early liberals focused more on loosening a range of social enterprises—conducting business, engaging in worship and religious life, participating in scientific inquiry, educating citizens—from the control of the government and elites than on ensuring the untrammeled freedom of individuals.[69] Ascribing decisional autonomy to families and other associations recognizes the important role that they play in the fabric of the liberal democratic society. Citizens do not live their lives as atomistic individuals who construct institutions from scratch as an exercise of their individual autonomy, as simplistic social contract reasoning might suggest. Instead, they live their lives in and through institutions that organize and give meaning to their lives. Because of this, "an embodied liberty, one that is not merely abstract and hypothetical, is to a greater extent than generally realized a function of flourishing, well institutionalized, and broadly autonomous civic enterprises."[70] It is for these reasons that Tocqueville saw civil associations as an important counterweight to the danger of state power on the one hand and the individualism that pervades American society on the other.[71]

Transmuting the current, blanket conception of family privacy into a zone of protection for families' decisional autonomy shifts the state's role. No longer is the appropriate behavior from the state to withdraw completely from the realm of family life (already an impossible goal); instead it is to ensure that families have the means and wherewithal to make important decisions for themselves. Like the old doctrine of family privacy, some of what this requires on the part of the state is forbearance in directing the decision making of families. Under this revised view, decisions about the way in which individual families function should generally be left to the family itself. Absent compelling reasons, the state should not be able to dictate what occurs in families. Where the state has an important interest in the outcome, however, it may seek to use gentler means to persuade families. For example, though Twinkies may not be a part of a sound diet for children, particularly given the recent obesity epidemic, the state has no business prohibiting parents from serving them for dessert, absent a showing that serving them even occasionally will cause a serious and substantial threat to their children's health. The state, however, may still tax Twinkies to give parents a disincentive to buy and serve them.

Yet support for familial autonomy requires more than the state's forbearing from dictating family decisions. The state must also seek to ensure that families have the wherewithal to exercise this autonomy. Not only does this mean helping ensure that families have the capacity to make important decisions about their family, it also means that families have some reasonable means to effectuate their decisions. While early liberals saw the threat to autonomy as coming from the state, much of today's threats of encroachment on decision making come from the market. The danger is not that the market will coercively compel or prohibit certain types of families or decision making in families, the way the state might prohibit family members from using birth control or prohibit the decision by loved ones to take a family member in a vegetative state off life support. Instead, the threat from the market comes from the risk that families will be so much at its mercy that they cannot exercise meaningful choice with respect to how to accomplish important activities such as caretaking. Rousseau's caution should be taken to heart: That it is essential for democracies "as regards wealth, that no citizen should be rich enough to be able to buy another, and none so poor that he has to sell himself."[72] His injunction should be taken to prohibit not just literal sale into slavery but also the condition in which one is forced to sell the bulk of one's waking hours and to sacrifice the majority of one's family time in order to put food on the table, a roof over the head of family members, and provide medical care if they should get sick.

A revised doctrine of privacy should therefore focus on limiting coercion by the market, as well as creating resources and space to ensure decision-making autonomy for families. Measures that establish an upper limit on mandatory working hours, allow employees paid time off for caretaking, prohibit parents of young children from being fired for refusing to work overtime, and enable workers to work flexible hours are some of the many measures the state can use to prevent this encroachment.[73] These measures allow families the institutional space to make important decisions and to accomplish important tasks without being completely beholden to the market.

Although the rationale of family privacy was long used to justify the state's failure to redress oppression within families, a reformulated doctrine can and must do a better job of reconciling family autonomy with the autonomy interests of family members. In some instances these interests will align. Thus, the demands by mothers on welfare in the 1960s that the state discontinue its midnight searches for men in their homes presented a situation in which individual and family interests in decisional autonomy coincided.[74] Similarly, individual privacy and family privacy interests generally run in tandem when women raise rights to privacy to support their claims for keeping abortion legal.

On other occasions, however, family privacy may collide with the autonomy interests of individual family members. For example, one family member may seek state intervention either to protect themselves or to resolve a disagreement between members. Where coercion exists or there are threats to the safety of one of the members, or where there is criminal or tortious conduct among family members at issue, the doctrine of family privacy must give way: The supportive state values family privacy, but never absolutely. It must therefore yield when the physical or emotional well-being of family members are threatened. By the same token, family privacy cannot stand as a justification where the fundamental rights of a family member are at stake. Thus, the state may not legitimately require a pregnant woman to obtain her husband's consent to get an abortion based on the rationale of family privacy, given that to do so would critically infringe the woman's own fundamental right to privacy. What is more, in a situation in which a husband tries to prevent his wife from aborting a pregnancy, family privacy will not justify the state's failure to intercede in order to allow a wife to obtain an abortion if she seeks the state's assistance.[75]

Short of these instances, however, a revised doctrine of family privacy requires a more nuanced approach. The state's general assumption should be that adults in an intact family will work out decisions among themselves without state intervention.[76] This assumption accords with the American tradition of family privacy and concerns for judicial economy and judicial competence: Courts generally should not have to expend the resources to decide these issues, and are not as well positioned as members of a family to decide them. Even when members of a family disagree about important issues, the general rule should be that they should figure out how to resolve these disputes for themselves. This is the case, for example, where members of a couple disagree about which school in which to enroll their child: They should resolve this dispute privately. Should the parents become so stalemated that they decide to end their relationship, assuming that the parents are awarded joint legal custody, resolution of the school dispute by a court would then be appropriate.

The state's removing itself from these decisions, however, can be justified only if adult family members have a relatively equal say in the decision making. This in turn requires that they have relatively equal power within the relationship, as well as an adequate opportunity to exit it should they wish. To ensure an adequate opportunity to exit for all adult family members, the supportive state must ensure that the costs of the breakup, including any reduction in standard of living, are shared fairly. Although no-fault divorce has, as a legal matter, made access to divorce easier for parties seeking to leave marriages, divorce still has substantial costs that are not imposed equally on the partners. The standard application of alimony and equitable distribution laws in the United States vastly favor the primary breadwinner over the other spouse; financial considerations therefore make it significantly more difficult for spouses who have been primary caretakers—generally women—to leave marriages because of financial constraints.[77] Furthermore, those women who have been homemakers during a marriage return to the workplace at a significant disadvantage because they have invested their human capital in their families, rather than in skills deemed marketable in the workplace. These disparate costs of exit can influence the balance of power within the relationship, because the party who can more easily exit can use this advantage to set the terms of the relationship. The state must therefore alter these terms of exit to ensure that the doctrine of family privacy does not deprive one party to the relationship of his or her voice.

Yet the state cannot rely solely on the equal opportunity to exit to ensure that members of relationships have sufficient autonomy for application of the doctrine of family privacy. Even when the terms of exit are fair, the fact of the matter is that there are many non-legal barriers to exiting relationships. Deep and pervasive cultural and religious norms associated with marriage impose their own restrictions on leaving the union.[78] In addition, bonds of love and affection may impede exit, as may concern for the welfare of children of the relationship. As a consequence, the supportive state's ensuring fair terms of exit is necessary but not sufficient to make upholding family privacy normatively permissible; the state must also seek to support equality within extant relationships.

Currently, the inequalities that are tied to caretaking versus breadwinning roles apply not only when and if a couple separates, but during the marriage, as well. Under common-law property rules that apply in a majority of states, during marriage one partner has no access to property earned by the other partner.[79] In this regime, whoever earns the paycheck is the owner of these funds during the marriage; that person has the exclusive right to control these funds. This means that the primary breadwinner in a family has more power to decide financial issues than does the primary caretaker, and, given the prevailing gender divide with respect to caretaking, that men still have more economic power in relationships than women.[80]

The problematic relationship between family privacy and individual autonomy is dramatically presented in the case of *McGuire v. McGuire,* which was decided in 1953, but is still good law today.[81] In that case, the Nebraska Supreme Court refused the petition of a wife in an ongoing marriage who sought to have the state enforce the legal duty of her husband to support the household adequately. Her husband, a well-to-do farmer, refused to provide the household with such basic items as a bathroom, inside toilet, and kitchen sink, and had not allowed his elderly wife money to buy clothes or any household items besides food in the last several years, although she had met her marital obligations to maintain the household. In ruling that judicial intervention was inappropriate, the court stated that "[t]he living standards of a family are a matter of concern to the household, and not for the courts to determine, even though the husband's attitude toward his wife, according to his wealth and circumstances, leaves little to be said in his behalf."[82] In relying on this rationale, however, the court ignored the fact that the "household's" decision would in actuality be made solely by the husband, since as the breadwinner in a common-law property state, he controlled the purse strings of the household.

The supportive state, in contrast, should decline a family member's request to intervene in an extant relationship based on family privacy only insofar as it ensures that the legal backdrop against which the relationship functions promotes the equalization of the power of those within the relationship.[83] This means the state should move toward extinguishing common-law property rules that give spouses an interest only in property that they earn themselves, and move toward the rule currently applied in community property states, which holds that parties in a marriage jointly own the property earned by either of them during the marriage.[84] While couples should be able to opt out of these default "background rules" as an exercise of their autonomy, the default rule should favor equality of power.[85]

The Supportive State and the Gendered Division of Family Labor

The gendered division of labor that still exists in many heterosexual relationships poses a thorny problem for a liberal democracy insofar as it pits the goods of family privacy and the couple's autonomy, on the one hand, against the state's commitment to sex equality on the other. The traditional liberal view is that the first two values trump in such a case: The state has no business interfering with the gendered structure of labor that occurs in families.[86] If competent adults choose to live their lives a particular way, whether or not this way accords with particular public norms, this view posits, the state has no business interfering with their choice.

Yet the view that the state is completely disinterested in how couples arrange their private lives needs to be complicated by the recognition of several things. First, the simple fact that this gender division occurs in what is generally conceived as the private realm does not mean that it has no wider ramifications for women's position in society. A wealth of evidence demonstrates that women's greater caretaking responsibilities are the largest remaining impediment to their economic equality.[87] This inequality in the economic realm then translates back into the private realm, to increase women's inequality in households still further.[88]

And even assuming, for the purposes of argument, that inequality in the family did not affect women's status outside of it, it simply is not the case that the state has no interest in the gendered division of labor within families. Equality is a virtue that a liberal democracy properly values beyond the public realm. Even if African Americans had equal jobs and equal political rights with whites, the state should be concerned if they were routinely denied admission to a range of social clubs, even if that denial did not translate into inequalities in wealth or public power. The same should be true for women. A caste system within families that is tied to biology and gender should be problematic in a liberal democracy even if it does not infect the public realm.

Furthermore, the view that the gendered divisions of labor in households represent the autonomous desires of citizens also oversimplifies the complicated array of cultural and economic forces responsible for the gendered distribution of care work. It misses the welter of cultural pressures on women to have children and assume the bulk of childrearing responsibilities, and the reciprocal pressures on men to be breadwinners. It also overlooks the way in which the labor market is overwhelmingly constructed without reference to parenting responsibilities. In this market, because most jobs are structured without reference to dependency work, one member of a couple is channeled into the role of the breadwinner, and no longer has adequate time to assume significant household responsibilities. This leaves the other member of the couple to assume more of these responsibilities, thereby loosening his or her attachment to the labor market. In the face of these complicated constraints, the extent to which these arrangements can be considered fully voluntary must be qualified.

In addition, there is a strong argument to be made that the persistence of these roles ultimately restricts women's (and men's) autonomy. The extent to which women (and, again, men) are free to pursue a variety of life choices depends on the extent to which gender roles within the family are loosened or restricted. The liberal state has an interest in preserving a broad range of these choices for citizens.

Where does this leave us? On the one hand, the couple's choices are entitled to respect because of both individual and family autonomy, even if the exercise of autonomy must be recognized as constrained by the caveats discussed earlier. As Martha Nussbaum notes, in a liberal system that values liberty significantly, it would be "an intolerable infringement of liberty for the state to get involved in dictating how people do their dishes."[89] Yet the state still has an important interest in reducing the gendered division of labor because of its interest in sex equality. In the face of these conflicting imperatives, although coercive measures by the state are clearly inappropriate, the state should seek to adopt gentler measures to enourage less gendered divisions of labor.

There are a number of ways that the supportive state can seek to move families in the direction of sex equality that do not involve coercive intervention in families.[90] The state can seek to affect this distribution by, for example, encouraging the equal distribution of child care through laws granting each parent parenting leave that is not cumulative between the parents and that would be lost to the family if both spouses did not take it.[91] It can also require employers to restructure jobs that are currently structured in a manner inconsistent with the exercise of caretaking responsibilities. Mandating that employers adapt such structures would encourage the restructuring of family responsibilities, although it would still allow parents to retain traditional roles if they wished to do so. Finally, it can use public education campaigns to persuade both adults and children to discontinue these gender patterns.[92]

CONCLUSION

Revising political theory to take into account the important role that dependency plays in the lives of citizens transforms this theory in important ways.

It changes the central questions that theory asks from simply considering how resources should be fairly divided among citizens, to how flourishing citizens can best be supported and nurtured. It also expands the goods that the state must take into account to include caretaking and human development. Further, it fundamentally transforms the role of the state. No longer can the state simply protect citizens' individual rights from violation by others; it must instead actively support the expanded list of liberal goods by creating institutions that facilitate caretaking and human development. The result is a more complex version of liberalism that must balance a wider range of goods, but one that is in a better position to bolster human dignity and a flourishing polity than current versions of liberalism. How the supportive state should deal with the complex range of goods implicated in parent-child relationships and other caretaker-dependent relationships is the subject of the next chapter.

CHAPTER 3

The Supportive State and Caretaker-Dependent ("Vertical") Relationships

Accepting the premise that the state has a duty to structure institutions to help meet the dependency needs of citizens, many questions still arise about how to conceptualize the state's relationship with families. Family relationships in which dependency needs are met can generally be grouped into two different categories. In the first, which I call "vertical" relationships, one person is dependent on the other to meet fundamental needs for caretaking and human development. Although the parent-child relationship serves as the paradigm of this type of connection, other relationships, including those between an adult child and their aging parent, also fit into this category. This type of relationship stands in contrast with "horizontal" relationships between generally able adults, in which both persons are interdependent and perform caretaking tasks for one another. In this chapter, I flesh out the supportive-state theory I introduced in the last chapter by specifically addressing vertical relationships. In the next, I move on to consider horizontal relationships.

The issue of the state's responsibility to dependents and their caretakers undergirds some of the most contentious public policy debates in our society, including those concerning welfare reform, foster care, work-and-family legislation, and even Social Security. The theoretical premises that underlie this issue of the state's responsibility, however, have been too little examined. In this chapter, I seek to remedy this oversight.

In the first section, I look at existing accounts of the state's responsibility for the dependency needs of children. Some of these accounts, I demonstrate, place too little responsibility on the state and too heavy a burden on parents; whereas others expect too little of parents and too much of the state. The theory of the supportive state, I show, provides a better way to theorize the contours of families' and the state's responsibilities. It conceives of the state as serving an integral role in supporting families, not simply after they break down, but in the ordinary course of events. In this conception, the state possesses a duty to structure institutions to support children's welfare and development, a duty that exists simultaneously with parents' own responsibility for children. Yet the state's role is a limited one, which provides the institutional scaffolding to support caretaking, while also expecting family members to meet caretaking needs.

In the second section, I further flesh out the details of the supportive state's responsibility with respect to vertical relationships. As I elaborate, the supportive state has the duty to arrange societal institutions in such a way that family members can meet the basic physical, mental, and emotional needs of dependents without impoverishing or exhausting themselves or their financial resources. Although there are a variety of ways that the state could structure institutions toward these ends, the best will further the important good of sex equality alongside those of caretaking and human development.

Finally, in the last section of the chapter, I describe how the state should adjust the model for vertical relationships when it comes to dealing with relationships between family members and their aging relatives. As I discuss, important features of these relationships should lead the state to develop somewhat different models of caretaking for meeting senior citizens' needs. Specifically, the state should seek to encourage a broad range of options for that caretaking that preserves elderly people's self-sufficiency to the extent possible. In such models, caretaking by family members should be both encouraged and supported, but not legally mandated.

EXISTING CONCEPTIONS OF THE STATE'S RESPONSIBILITY FOR PARENT-CHILD RELATIONSHIPS

What responsibility should the state have for the dependency needs of young children? The view that dominates liberal theory and public policy is that of the autonomous family. This view ascribes to parents the responsibility for childrearing, and accords the state residual responsibility only when and if parents fail. The most widely known alternative to this residual view conceives of children as public goods, and argues for broad state responsibility for dependency. Neither of these approaches, however, as I demonstrate here, adequately conceptualizes the role of the state.

The Autonomous Family and Residual State Responsibility

University of Chicago Law School professor Mary Anne Case caused a stir at a feminist legal theory conference when she resisted the notion that the state and employers should support employees with caretaking responsibilities.[1] Case argued that feminists who call for the state to ease mothers' caretaking burdens through subsidizing caretaking and mandating workplace protections for working parents were transferring the burden to the wrong people. She contended that it is the children's fathers, rather than employers, other employees, or the state, who should step in to ease the burden on mothers, since these fathers—like their partners—had chosen to bear and rear the children. To do otherwise, she asserted, would be unfair to those who have decided not to have children so that they would not have to assume these responsibilities. Indeed, Case asserted, policies that support parents in caretaking without similarly supporting other activities that employees sought to engage in amount to "special rights" for parents.[2]

According to Case, the state's responsibility for children should properly be triggered "only after those with an individual responsibility, notably fathers, are forced to kick in their fair share, financially and otherwise."[3] Case likened the situation to one in which polluters who create environmental hazards are primarily liable for cleaning them up, while the state assumes secondary liability, which obligates it to act only if the cleanup is not adequately accomplished by the polluters. While Case opposed support for parenting, she stated that she would "be inclined to look more favorably on the state spending money in monitorable and controlled ways on the child and socially useful things for the child. This spending would not be formulated as payback to the parents but as direct benefit to the children."[4]

Residual views of the state's responsibility for dependency like Case's dominate public policy in the United States. Their basic premise—that parents are properly the ones who are responsible for children, and that the state should step in only as a last resort if and when parents have exhausted themselves and their resources—draws from classical liberal theory: Liberalism's respect for individual autonomy and its emphasis on a limited state are premised on the view that, to the extent possible, citizens can and should plan and bear responsibility for their own actions and their own lives.

There are a number of problems with the notion of residual state responsibility when applied to the issue of dependency and families, however—some of which were discussed in the last chapter. The conception that the state should step in only after families fail inadequately conceptualizes the complex interconnections that exist between the family and the state; there is no neutral position in which the state can locate itself until "after" families fail.[5] Further, Case's argument against accommodation for caretaking is premised on a straitened view of the purposes of a liberal democracy, as well as the principles that should guide it. While she pays lip service to the notion that care could serve as a legitimate public value, Case repeatedly presumes that the preferred principle for state action is a narrowly-conceptualized version of equal treatment, in which the state treats all persons the same, whether they are raising children or performing other activities of choice.[6] The fact of the matter, however, is that although the principle of equal treatment has much to recommend it in a broad variety of situations, it should not and cannot be the only principle that determines the distribution rights and privileges if a liberal democratic polity is to flourish. There are times that the state should legitimately support caregiving over other activities because of the important roles it plays in human dignity, human flourishing, and in the health of the polity. Yet the benefits of such policies should not be as tightly circumscribed to mothers as Case presents them: Dependency is a condition experienced not only by children—humans experience illness and disability at other points of their lives, and protection for caregiving should therefore extend broadly and benefit most citizens over the course of their lives. When the state makes provisions for caretaking, however, it should still heed Case's cautions about overburdening individual employers or employees. To do so, it should seek to spread the costs for supporting fairly by publicly funding the costs of caretaking leaves, for example, and by seeking to ensure that the work of those on leave is distributed equitably. But the term "equitably," as we know from equitable distribution law, does not always mean equally; where caretaking responsibilities are concerned, the state has good grounds to further these responsibilities over other activities.

Moreover, Case's preferred public policy of private responsibility for children overlooks the structural obstacles that families face. The fact of the matter is that there are critical institutional issues related to childcare that are beyond the ability of most parents to negotiate privately. For example, many jobs in the United States are organized in a manner that prevents workers from engaging in significant care work for children.[7] For couples committed to raising children well, the consequence is often that one member of the couple will be forced to detach themselves from full involvement in the labor market. These job structures, therefore, lead to family patterns in which one partner becomes a breadwinner and the other a caretaker, even if the couple would otherwise have chosen a more equal distribution of caretaking roles. Until these job structures change, many of those working fathers who seek to answer Case's call to assume their share of caretaking responsibilities will be stymied from doing so.

In addition, although Case distinguishes between the state's providing benefits directly to children, which she would support to further children's welfare, and the state's providing benefits to the parents of children, which she would oppose on grounds of fairness to those who do not have children, the effect of these two policies on children's welfare cannot be so neatly delineated. Children and other dependents need far more than financial subsidies: They need caretaking to become flourishing adults. Because of this, children's interests can never be neatly disentangled from parents the way that Case suggests. Case's opposition to labor-market accommodation would therefore do more than impose a burden on parents— it would inevitably hurt children.

One last argument that Case makes against state support for childrearing also deserves mention. Both she, as well as Columbia Law School professor Katherine Franke, separately argue against public support for caretaking on

sex equality grounds.[8] Each contends that state support for caretaking will ultimately redound to women's detriment by privileging caretaking and motherhood as against women's other life options. They also contend that this support
reinforces the supposed naturalness and inevitability of women assuming the
role of mothers. Rather than encouraging women to have children by giving
them incentives to do so, these scholars assert, feminists should instead focus on
disrupting the perceived naturalness of the link among women, caretaking, and
motherhood, and should instead seek to promote other life paths for women.

Case and Franke make important points when they argue that the system-
atic equating of women with motherhood is persistent and problematic, and
when they point out that there are other activities that contribute as much to
the public good as bearing and rearing children. However, we have long been
conducting the experiment of denying state support for parenting that Case
and Franke call for, and it has been a dismal failure for sex equality. Roughly 80
percent of women become mothers, at some time during their lives,[9] and confront the profound economic and social disadvantages that currently attend
caretaking responsibilities.[10] If large economic and social costs effectively
deterred women from having children, humanity would currently be threatened with extinction.[11] While the state should unquestionably adopt measures
to increase women's understanding of and ability to withstand the social pressures to reproduce and to ensure there are other life paths open to women, failing to adopt public policy measures that accommodate women's childrearing
responsibilities hurts rather than helps the cause of women's equality.

Children as Public Goods

On the other end of the spectrum from Case and other opponents of state support for parenting, are those who argue that the state owes support to parents
because in rearing children they are creating public goods. Emory Law School
Professor Martha Fineman presents a sophisticated explication of this view.[12]
Fineman, one of the pioneer theorists on the issue of the state's responsibility
for dependency, begins theorizing at the appropriate starting point: the recognition that all humans are dependent at various points in their lives. She then
argues that from this dependency comes an obligation on the part of the state
to support caretaking:

> Individual dependency needs must be met if we, as individuals, are to survive,
> and our aggregate or collective dependency needs must be met if our society is
> to survive and perpetuate itself. The mandate that the state (collective society)
> respond to dependency, therefore, is not a matter of altruism or empathy (which
> are individual responses often resulting in charity), but is a matter that is primary
> and essential because such a response is fundamentally society preserving.[13]

The family, Fineman asserts, should be seen as a dynamic public institution that has been assigned the task of caretaking for the benefit of society as a whole.[14] Although families assume the vast bulk of the burdens of caretaking without compensation, "[c]aretaking labor provides the citizens, the workers, the voters, the consumers, the students, and so on who populate society and its institutions."[15] Thus, according to Fineman, the state and the market currently "free ride" on families' labor by delegating the work of rearing future citizens and workers to families without compensating them for their efforts. This fact creates a collective debt on the part of society to caretakers which, in Fineman's words, "must be recognized, and payment accomplished, through policies and laws that provide both some economic compensation and structural accommodation to caretakers."[16]

Through her insistence that the state take account of dependency, Fineman, unlike Case, puts caretaking in its properly central place in society, and does so in a way that doesn't sacrifice other important goods, such as sex equality. Yet Fineman's contention that parents should be compensated because the state gets some benefit from parents' caretaking efforts—a claim often repeated by those asserting that children are "public goods"—raises some conceptual difficulties. Private citizens produce benefits for society in a wide range of instances without accruing any legal or moral right to compensation. For example, if a violinist were moved to play a beautiful solo in a town square, few of us would believe that the town had an obligation to repay her for the value of the pleasure she created for the townspeople. We would likely still reach the same conclusion even if the music were to draw people into the surrounding cafes, and give the area a significant financial benefit. Some people might be moved to drop a tip into the violinist's hat, but that does not create a debt by the café owners or the town at large.[17] It is not clear why raising children should be treated differently.

The simple fact that society would fall into disrepair without caretaking is not sufficient to hold the state responsible for compensating the caretaking performed by families. As political scientists have sought to show empirically, societies fall into disrepair and democracies become unmanageable when civil society lacks associations among citizens that generate "social capital," or goodwill among individuals.[18] This makes it good policy for the state to encourage such associations. Yet this certainly doesn't give those who participate in such associations, including the now somewhat paradigmatic bowling leagues, a claim to compensation by the state.

Fineman's suggestion that the state and employers "owe" parents support for caretaking because both rely on the caretaking labor that parenting produces raises several other thorny issues. First, it suggests that caretakers deserve subsidies because of the net benefits that children will bring to society. Yet, even if we accept Fineman's contention that children's contributions to society should be credited to their parents, the conclusion that children are a net benefit to society does not necessarily follow. Opponents of state support might argue that the ecological, social, and psychic costs from overcrowding outweigh the benefits of children. Second, if compensation should be awarded based on benefits, to what extent should the enjoyment that parents receive from raising children decrease the state's compensation? Parents have children for many reasons; few of them involve altruism toward society generally.

Further, grounding public support on the assertion that children are a net future asset to society produces some unpalatable results. For example, it opens the door for critics of public support to argue that we could get the same benefits for less money if we imported immigrants rather than supported children.[19] Moreover, if the rationale for giving public support to parents is the expectation that children will grow up to be productive citizens, then might we deny support to parents whose children have disorders like cystic fibrosis that might prevent them from reaching adulthood and repaying taxpayers' investment? The reason that most of us would be horrified by this suggestion is that we conceive public responsibility for caretaking to spring from something other than the likelihood of society receiving a future economic return.

Treating parents as entitled to compensation for bearing and raising children also evades the thorny but important issue of the extent to which we should hold parents themselves responsible for the decision to bear and rear children. Although Case errs in seeing parental responsibility as precluding the state's responsibility to children, it should still certainly be an important factor in defining the contours of the state's responsibility. Under Fineman's public goods rationale, however, it is difficult to see where the state's responsibility to children ends and parents' responsibility begins.

THE SUPPORTIVE STATE'S FRAMEWORK FOR PARENT-CHILD AND OTHER CARETAKER-DEPENDENT RELATIONSHIPS

A better way to conceive of the state's role with respect to dependency is to recognize that liberal democratic theory and the public policy constructed from it, particularly in their American incarnations, have been modeled on a stunted conception of human beings. Once we recognize that humans do not spring up fully formed, as our tradition of political theory suggests, but instead are raised in societies through a process that takes years of time and effort, meeting the caretaking needs of these citizens and developing their faculties become equally critical tasks as protecting citizens' individual rights. Deeming the state to have the responsibility to support caretaking and development accords with treating liberalism as deeply grounded in respect for human dignity.[20] It is because of this fundamental respect for the dignity of human beings that, when we conceive of humans as able adults who have capacity to direct the course of their lives, causes us to value autonomy. Once we recognize the fact of dependency in the human condition, that same respect for human dignity also demands valuing caretaking and human development. The state should support these goods, then, not because families are doing the job the state should be doing, or because the state has assigned this job to families, or because the state could not survive without another generation of citizens. Rather, the state should do so because dealing humanely with dependency is central to the state's mission of supporting the dignity of its citizens, in the same way that respecting citizens' autonomy is central to that mission.

But why can't families deal with dependency issues on their own since, in a liberal democracy, we expect citizens to do the things they can do for themselves. As I described in the last chapter, however, there is no "on-their own" option available. Families and the state are sufficiently interconnected in contemporary society that state policies, regardless of whether they are explicitly formulated with families in mind, profoundly affect families' caretaking abilities. In addition, families and the state are not similarly equipped to deal with the same facets of dependency issues. Families are better suited to performing the hands-on care and the arranging of care for dependents. For example, parents know their children and their needs better than the state does, and parents are generally more motivated to promote their children's welfare because of the emotional bond between them. In contrast, the state is singularly placed to ensure that societal institutions are structured in ways that allow families to meet their caretaking responsibilities. Finally, raising children and caring for dependents are complicated, long-term projects. No family can perform these tasks completely on their own.

In supporting caretaking and human development, the liberal polity not only meets its obligations to its vulnerable citizens, it also looks out for its own interests in ensuring that these young citizens are capable of someday assuming the mantle of self-rule.[21] Recall John Stuart Mill's words: "If society lets any considerable number of its members grow up mere children, incapable of being acted on by rational consideration of distant motives, society has itself to blame for the consequences."[22] In the absence of ensuring that the children who will one day be citizens have an adequate capacity for both self-government and collective self-government, the future of a well-ordered society is dubious.

How far does the supportive state's obligation to support caretaking and human development extend? And how should the state weigh these goods against other goods and purposes of a liberal democracy? Clearly the answer to these questions cannot be determined through a kind of "moral geometry," in which a single, correct answer can be absolutely and firmly calculated once and for all.[23] Nevertheless, some guideposts can at least mark out the parameters of this duty. At a minimum, the supportive state should arrange institutions in such a way that family members can, through exercising diligent but not Herculean efforts, meet the basic physical, mental, and emotional needs of children and other dependents and promote human development while avoiding impoverishment or immiseration. Translated into concrete government policies, this means that the welfare system must be structured in a way that those at the bottom of the economic ladder with dependents receive enough financial assistance so that they can provide them with decent environments that promote basic capabilities. Insofar as they are required by the state's welfare policies to work outside the home, they must also have realistic access to good-quality, affordable day care. Further, the state must regulate the workplace to ensure parents enough time with their children so that they are well parented and supervised, and not so pressed for time or frazzled by time pressures that it interferes with adequate caretaking. In this view, the state shirks its responsibility when it forces parents to choose between working to put food in their children's mouths and ensuring that their children receive adequate caretaking.

By this measure, Rick Santorum's account of welfare reform in 1996 misses the mark in considering the state's responsibilities to families.[24] Santorum states that he is immensely proud of the reform effort for putting large numbers of single mothers back to work.[25] Under the old system, he charges, "AFDC [Aid to Families with Dependent Children] was simply about giving money to poor women with children. In return, people getting welfare had to do—well, nothing."[26] Santorum ignores the work these parents were performing in singlehandedly raising their children; further, he pays no attention to how these children would be cared for once their mothers were required to work in the paid labor market.[27] This omission is especially startling given that pages later he rails against parents in two-parent families who both work: "Children of two parents who are working don't need more *things*. They need *us!*"[28] He then argues that "radical feminists," whom he asserts have convinced women that they should succeed in the workplace, ignore "the essential work women have done in being the primary caregivers of the next generation."[29] An acceptable welfare policy must place the same emphasis on the needs of poor children for caretaking and human development that it does for other children.

The state's threshold level of responsibility for structuring institutions to support caretaking and human development, it should be noted, is not a high one. It simply requires that children and other dependents be afforded decent conditions and sufficient caretaking to meet their basic dependency needs and to promote a minimally-adequate level of human development. A relatively wealthy polity should be able to do far better than simply clear this minimum threshold. With that said, millions of children in the United States are now being raised in conditions that do not meet this standard.[30]

Above the state's threshold level of responsibility, state support is no longer an absolute obligation, but rather needs to be balanced against achieving other important goods. Although caretaking is not normally regarded as a distributive good, in many cases it functions in this way because expenditures to support caretaking require trade-offs with other goods. In weighing this trade-off, the state should consider the importance of sex equality, which is tightly linked to state support of caretaking, and the importance of the soundness of the future citizens to the polity's future—both persuasive reasons for the state to prioritize care work above other uses of the state's resources. With that said, under this rationale, supporting care work beyond the threshold level is important to achieving liberal democratic objectives, but neither an absolute obligation of the state nor a debt that must be paid.

In assessing whether to subsidize over and above this threshold level, a liberal polity can find a common-sense midpoint between, on the one hand, those who argue only for the most minimal state support for dependency, such as Mary Anne Case, and, on the other hand, those who argue the state should devote virtually unlimited funding to its dependents. One such sensible midpoint can be found by recalling the words of John Stuart Mill, quoted in the last chapter, who argued that the existing generation, even though it cannot make the next generation "perfectly wise and good,...is perfectly well able to make the rising generation, as a whole, as good as, and a little better than, itself."[31] Seeking to do a little better for the next generation is a realistic but still ambitious goal that recognizes the importance of caring for dependents yet recognizes that there are other goods that a liberal democracy should also pursue.

Finally, at some point toward the end of the spectrum defined by greater state support, it makes progressively less sense for the state to subsidize higher marginal levels of caretaking instead of other goods. At the upper end of the state-support spectrum, subsidizing more caretaking may actually be counterproductive for both the recipients of care, since it may retard their developing the level of autonomy needed to function well in society, and for the caregivers, who may never get to pursue other courses in life. Although family members may still decide to perform this higher level of caretaking for dependents, they should do so without state subsidization.

At any point below the upper end of the spectrum, the state may legitimately support caretaking over other pursuits of citizens because of its close connection to human dignity. This is not to say that other pursuits are not valuable; indeed, many should also be supported by the state given the availability of resources. This is only to say that there are compelling reasons for the state to support caretaking responsibilities.

The Supportive State and the Intersection between Work and Family

Declaring that the state should support caretaking and human development is only the first step in determining the kind of policies the state should enact.

The vision of social organization that should guide the relationship between caretaking and work must also be determined. All welfare systems rest on an implicit normative vision of social organization.[32] The New Deal era's vision, which dominated for more than three generations and still remains in effect in many policy arenas, was built on the presumption that citizens lived and should live in families comprised of a breadwinner married to a caretaker and their biological or adopted children. According to this vision, the husband's wages supported the family, while the wife's caretaking met the family's dependency needs. The welfare system premised on this normative vision included medical insurance for the family attached to the breadwinner's employment, unemployment insurance that would pay the family's basic needs if the worker lost his job, and worker's compensation that would replace the breadwinner's family wages if he were disabled for some period of time.

Events in recent years have forced at least the partial demise of this "family-wage" model, as policymakers were confronted with the recognition, prompted by the rise of divorce rates and single-parent homes, as well as mothers' movement into the workplace, that it did not match the empirical reality of how most citizens currently live their lives. Yet, the model with which it has been replaced in some policy arenas is a "universal-breadwinner" model, which presumes that every adult should now be a breadwinner.[33] This model takes the job structures developed under the family wage model, which were not designed to accommodate caretaking, and applies them to all adult citizens. The problem, of course, is that it is not clear how caretaking will be accomplished if everyone is now a breadwinner. For example, welfare reform in the 1990s instituted requirements that parent/recipients work substantial hours, regardless of whether they had young children at home.[34] Work-and-family law, too, assumes that legal protection should be accorded employment status, with little protection accorded to parenting. In adopting this new model, current welfare policy fails to give caretaking the support necessary to raise sound children and citizens.

In place of the outmoded family-wage model and the problematic universal-breadwinner model, we need a new welfare-state model that is adapted to the demands of today's families, and which properly supports caretaking. There are two possible visions of social organization on which this model could be premised. First, the state could adopt a normative vision in which citizens with caretaking responsibilities leave the labor market to pursue caretaking. To support these caretakers in the absence of a partner in the labor market, the state, presumably by taxing breadwinners, would directly subsidize caretakers for performing care work. Welfare payments that allow parents to stay at home to take care of children are an example of a public policy that comports with this "direct-subsidy" model. In this approach, as in the family-wage approach, the labor market need not be adapted for caregiving;

instead, caregiving would still be performed largely by family members in private homes. The big difference between the old family-wage model and this new approach is that now caregivers would be subsidized for their work by the state (and, at one more remove, by the citizenry generally) rather than by their husbands.[35] This approach might therefore be envisioned as taking from the family-wage model the presumed picture of a family headed by a breadwinner and caretaker, and replacing the breadwinner's picture with that of the state.

An alternative vision of social organization would be premised on the view that all citizens should be able to incorporate both work and family spheres into their lives. While this approach similarly envisions the state as an integral partner in supporting caretaking, it also calls for the state to structure societal institutions in ways that enable citizens to reconcile the roles of caregiver and breadwinner. In this alternative "public-integration" approach, the state, rather than subsidizing citizens to leave the labor market to deal with caretaking, accommodates societal institutions like the labor market to the demands of caretaking, transforming jobs from their structure of the family-wage model. Granting paid leave for workers to care for very young children and then return to the jobs, flex-time for caretakers, and putting a limit on the number of hours that caretakers (and perhaps other workers) are required to work are three examples of programs that comport with the public integration approach. This model might, therefore, be envisioned as replacing the old picture of the breadwinner-married-to-the-caretaker in the family-wage model with one in which citizens are each, individually, both breadwinners and caretakers.

Of these two visions of the relationship between work and caretaking, the supportive state should adopt a public-integration model of support for care-work for several reasons. The first relates to fulfilling its important commitment to sex equality. Through a complex combination of societal processes and expectations, women in our society continue to assume the majority of caretaking in families, which leaves them socially and financially unequal to men.[36] Repeated experience shows that tasks performed by women tend to retain low status until men assume them.[37] Until more men take on caretaking, it is therefore likely to continue to be seen as low-status "women's work." Because the public-integration approach does not require caregivers to completely drop their work identities, it makes men more likely to engage in care work than in the direct-subsidy approach.

Further, women are more likely to close the financial equality gap with men under the public integration approach. As a practical matter, it is difficult to imagine that even a state that enthusiastically adopts a direct subsidy model will subsidize caretaking to such an extent that caretakers will experience no financial penalties whatsoever compared to their breadwinning counterparts.[38] Even the most generous direct-subsidy proposals generally seek replacement only of wages and benefits for the period of caretaking. As economists have shown, however, time taken out of the job market, even if it results in few lost wages during the leave, generally results in considerably diminished financial prospects for the rest of women's lives.[39] Because of this reality, it is important that both sexes are encouraged to share the burden of care work equally, which would be a more likely result under the public-integration approach.

The public-integration approach is also better equipped to combat the destructive complex of myths about care that pervade United States culture. As Fineman argues, our society loudly trumpets the myth of autonomy. But there is a counternarrative to this myth that also circulates widely, sounded less loudly but still quite audibly, which does more than proclaim the importance of caretaking—it announces it to be women's highest calling.[40] In it, children (in contrast to their complete disappearance in the narrative sounding in autonomy) are presented as society's greatest treasure, deserving and requiring the complete attention of their caretakers to fulfill their potential. This narrative shares with the autonomy myth, however, the view that work should not be reformed to accommodate parenting. According to this view, women must sacrifice their careers as well as years of their lives to fulfill their role as mothers adequately. Those mothers who fail to give their children virtually unlimited care and attention are seen as selfish, and their children doomed to a lifetime of failure.[41]

Any model of state support for carework that takes sex equality into account needs to grapple with the complexity and contradictions of these cultural messages, recognizing the dominance of the autonomy myth, but also the fetishization of care in other strands. The public-integration approach is better suited to deal with this than its direct-subsidy counterpart. Public integration recognizes the importance of care work without presuming that women must withdraw from the rest of the world to be good mothers or caretakers, and at the same time contests the ideology that work and family occupy separate and exclusive spheres. It ensures that paid work and caretaking are not fundamentally incompatible pursuits, given sufficient adjustments to the way in which both the labor market and families operate.

The public-integration approach to state support also ensures that children's needs are met, but not obsessively fixated upon. The approach supports the ability of parents to spend significant amounts of time with their children, but not necessarily every hour of the day, and not to the exclusion of all else. In this model, children would likely spend some time in group-care arrangements, but significantly less time than if they had parents working full-time under the current system. This approach therefore has the virtue of recognizing the importance of parents' relationships with their children and supporting those relationships, while also recognizing the value of children spending time with other adults and children in the community. Children who regularly spend time in group-care arrangements are more likely to form bonds with others and less likely to fall victim to the overappreciated-child syndrome, in which they have difficulty functioning without the intensive amounts of attention with which they have been lavished.[42]

While proposals that would help ameliorate the conflict between work and family tend to be dismissed in the United States as pie in the sky, the fact of the matter, as Janet Gornick and Marcia Meyers demonstrate in their excellent book *Families That Work,* is that a number of other developed countries—particularly Denmark, Finland, Norway, and Sweden, but also France, Belgium, and Canada—are much further along the road to this goal than is the United States.[43] As Gornick and Meyers conclude, "[m]any of the problems besetting American families are less acute in other industrialized countries that have more extensive public policies that help families manage competing demands from the home and the workplace without sacrificing gender equality."[44]

The policy proposals that the state would adopt in a society committed to a public role for supporting caretaking have been well laid out elsewhere;[45] therefore, I won't dwell on them. They include paid maternity leaves and job retention guarantees for women at childbirth, and parental leave rights and benefits during children's first few years to give workers time and opportunity for caregiving while allowing them to resume their jobs. They also include granting parents and other caretakers the rights to some further paid leave in order to deal with short-term needs for care that may arise. The funding for all these leaves would be public, in order to distribute fairly the cost across society and minimize the cost to individual employers. In addition, working-time policies that set the standard workweek below the U.S.'s current standard of 40 hours would help ensure that parents who are employed full time will have adequate time for caregiving.[46] Adequate flex-time policies and regulations that improve the quality and compensation of part-time work would further improve caretakers' circumstances. Finally, the state would provide alternative caretaking arrangements for those with dependency needs at a level of quality that supports their development. These arrangements would include public early-childhood-education and care programs, public schooling that is scheduled in a manner compatible with parents' work schedules, and after-school programs and elder-care programs, either paid for by the state or whose costs are shared between the state and families on a sliding scale basis. Various elements of these policies have been successfully instituted in European countries that have assumed a broader role for the state in supporting caretaking than has the United States.[47]

VARYING THE APPROACH FOR THE ELDERLY

Although the dependency that occurs in elderly citizens raises some of the same issues as those raised by the dependency of children, there are also important differences. For one thing, adults know that they will age and, therefore, generally have the opportunity to plan and save for this stage of life. For another, we expect to mold the moral capacities of children and, accordingly, make decisions for them in a manner that we would generally find inappropriately paternalistic for the elderly, even when there has been some reduction of their mental faculties.[48] In addition, the elderly usually seek to live independently, whereas young children cannot.[49] These differences have great significance for the role that elderly citizens, their families, and the state should play with respect to the dependency that attends old age.[50]

The way in which dependency needs for the elderly are met is becoming an increasingly important issue as the American population ages. In 1900, 3.1 million Americans were over the age of 65. In 2004, this number had increased to 36.3 million. Even this number is expected to double in the next 25 years, as 78 million baby boomers become senior citizens.[51] The caretaking needs of this population of citizens are substantial. The aging process in many respects reverses the childhood pattern of increased independence; the elderly grow more reliant on others for caretaking. Senior citizens are much more likely to suffer severe, chronic illnesses than the general population, and this likelihood increases as they age.[52] Additionally, the chronic conditions experienced by seniors are far more likely to cause substantial limitations in daily living, including in driving, walking, dressing, or eating.[53] This means that many elderly adults need substantial amounts of caretaking, including aid in activities such as dressing, bathing, and getting around, both inside and outside of their homes.[54]

Caretaking Needs

When it comes to how the state should seek to organize caretaking for senior citizens, at first glance, it may make sense to assign this responsibility to their grown children. Principles of reciprocity would support this assignment: These parents took care of their children's dependency needs when they were young; children now should do the same for their parents. On further consideration, however, there are better reasons why the state should not place legal responsibility for caretaking on adult children.

It may very well be that, if we were constructing a society from scratch, we would set it up in a way that made it possible for adult children to assume the bulk of parents' caretaking responsibilities.[55] For better or worse, however, this is not the society in which we live. Most senior citizens have long lived apart from their children and prefer to live independently. Ninety percent of adults 60 and older say they want to stay in their home or community rather than uproot themselves late in life.[56] Few children now live within a short distance from their parents; many, in fact, have moved across states or across the country. Further, the women who have historically performed the bulk of caretaking tasks for older family members now largely work in the paid workplace, which limits their time for caretaking.[57] It also keeps them from performing caretaking tasks that must be performed during business hours, such as taking an aging parent to doctors' appointments. Many of these grown children also now have children of their own, further increasing their time and stress burdens. And unlike the strong social norm that parents should care for minor children, the norm that once supported caretaking for aging parents has waned to some extent.[58]

Given these circumstances, although the state should support and encourage caretaking of the elderly by family members, it should not legally assign such responsibility to family members. Instead, the state should seek to construct networks of care for aging citizens that are not dependent on delivery through grown children. The goal of these networks should be to ensure access to care in a manner that preserve seniors' autonomy to the extent possible. Dependency, in this view, is not like a light switch that is turned either off or on. Rather, dependency needs can range from lesser to greater, and can be meshed with senior citizens' interest in autonomy. To do so, where possible, care should be provided in a manner that supports senior citizens living independently within their communities. There are a number of caretaking models currently being tried that seek to provide exactly this kind of assistance for elderly residents with moderate and intermediate levels of dependency;[59] the state should support the most promising of these models. Exploring alternatives to allow elderly people to live independently and with dignity while meeting their caretaking needs should be a core part of the state's mission.

The state should also seek to make available a broad range of options for senior citizens as their need for caretaking increases. In this regard, the limits of a model in which seniors remain in suburban single-family homes that are built for privacy rather than community and caretaking must be acknowledged. The state must develop alternatives to this model for the frail elderly, in order to allow them to receive higher levels of caretaking in a more amicable setting. One successful example of such a model is the New Canaan Inn, which was created by citizens of New Canaan, Connecticut in 1981. At the inn, senior citizens live in their own apartments, yet still get the benefit of having a shared community with a common living room and dining room where meals are provided.[60] Residents not only receive the caretaking they need through the inn's network of services, they can also remain more integrated in the town's community since the inn is a short walk to downtown.

With that said, the supportive state should still seek to encourage and support caretaking by adult children and other family members. In many cases, children will be the people best positioned to know their parents' needs and desires. Moreover, the bonds of love that most children feel for their parents, as well as the moral obligation to them, are strong motivators to act in their parents' best interests. There are a number of measures the state can adopt to facilitate such caretaking. It can strengthen family leave provisions such as the Family and Medical Leave Act,[61] by converting its now unpaid leave to leave with pay, and extending its coverage beyond medical care. Supporting caretaking for senior citizens also gives the state good reason to support work schedules with flexible hours and to mandate that part-time workers receive comparable benefits based on hours to full-time workers, so that family members who work have the ability to care for their loved ones. The state should also seek to reduce the obstacles that our existing models of housing can pose to family caretaking by, for example, subsidizing loans to families who renovate their homes to include space for aging family members, and granting zoning variances to those who wish to add a separate mother-in-law's apartment for a caretaker or aging parent to live in. Finally, for those families who take in elderly family members, the state should seek to ensure that supplementary caretaking is available to them, including well-trained home-care assistance, respite services, and high-quality day programs for senior citizens.[62]

Financial Dependency

Intertwined with other dependency needs of elderly citizens are serious issues of financial dependency. In 2010, 3.5 million elderly persons in the United States lived in poverty.[63] This represents a rate of 9 percent of senior citizens. Although this is a significant figure, it is still a considerably lower rate than in the past. In 1960, for example, the official poverty rate of the elderly was 35 percent, more than twice that of nonelderly adults.[64] Even that figure represents a steep decline from poverty rates earlier in the century.[65] Social Security, which is received by more than 90 percent of U.S. retirees,[66] is a key reason for this drop in poverty rates. Indeed, a study by Gary Engelhardt of Syracuse University and Jonathan Gruber of M.I.T. investigating the drop in elderly poverty from 1967 through 2000 concluded that the entire decrease in poverty rates during these years was the product of Social Security benefits.[67] Although the fiscal instability of the Social Security program may have been exaggerated in recent political debates, the political controversy over this program is real and ongoing.[68] The theoretical issue that underlies this controversy—to what extent the state should play a role in dealing with the financial needs of elderly citizens—therefore merits separate discussion.

Perhaps the most obvious alternative in a liberal polity that treats citizens as responsible for choosing their own life course is to place the financial burden squarely on the shoulders of the senior citizens themselves. The justification for taking this route is that the elderly, in contrast to young children, have had the opportunity to plan for this stage of their lives and should have saved accordingly. Although there is no question that some responsibility for planning and saving should be imposed on senior citizens, there are still serious difficulties with treating this responsibility as solely an individual issue. First, many factors about this last stage of life are difficult to predict on an individual level—how long citizens will live, how long they will be able to work, whether they will experience serious or lengthy medical conditions, and so forth.[69] This uncertainty makes it hard for individuals to know how much to save. Further, even with the best-laid plans, economic circumstances can change for many reasons not within citizens' control, including workers being laid off or prematurely retired, company pensions being defunded, stock-market crashes that deplete retirement savings, or lingering financial responsibilities for children. In addition, many crises can deplete savings with little notice. The medical costs of an unexpected illness of the individual or a family member can—and often does—bankrupt even a prudent planner.[70] Should senior citizens no longer be able to live on their own, the national average annual cost for a semiprivate room (double occupancy) in a Medicare-certified nursing home is $73,000 ($200.00/day), a figure that would quickly consume the savings of most senior citizens.[71] Finally, developments in medicine, particularly of expensive medical treatments, can impose costs on citizens that would have been difficult to predict in earlier years.[72]

At the least, then, any expectation that citizens will be able to save individually for their own retirement will be violated on a relatively frequent basis, often for reasons beyond the individual's control. In a world in which individual savings for retirement were the expectation, what should happen to these citizens? One possibility is that grown children should be required by law to support needy parents.[73] As with the issue of caretaking, however, there are strong reasons to avoid holding grown children financially responsible for such support. Although wealthy children might be able to shoulder these responsibilities, for poor and middle-class families they would impose a heavy, and for many, an insuperable burden, especially if those families are struggling to raise their own children at the same time.[74] Furthermore, the same factors that make it difficult for senior citizens to save adequately for their retirement—difficulties in predicting their financial position, lifespan, health status, and so forth—would make it difficult for their children to do the same for them. On top of that, grown children have their own uncertainties to contend with—unexpected layoffs, for instance, or unexpected illnesses. As Ian Shapiro counsels, while imposing financial responsibilities for aging parents on their grown children would have made more sense in the past, "[i]n the contemporary world, when people work, save, and insure as individuals throughout their adult lives, it makes little sense to try to reintroduce them to the household economy as life's ending approaches."[75]

For those seniors who lack sufficient savings through no fault of their own, in the absence of other financial support, there is little question that the state should provide them with at least a subsistence level of support. In a liberal polity committed to human dignity, whether or not citizens' basic needs are satisfied should not be dependent on the vagaries of the labor market or a thousand other factors beyond individual control. Even in cases in which senior citizens arrived at their sorry financial situation through what might be deemed imprudence, although it is a closer issue, there is still a strong argument to be made that these senior citizens should be provided some basic level of income support as well. Just as we should still try to rescue the drowning swimmer who negligently swam in waters beyond his or her capability, the moral injunction to protect the vulnerable requires providing at least some basic provision to those who have been financially imprudent in earlier years, as does our commitment to human dignity.

Given the risk to the state of having to subsidize senior citizens who have not managed to save for their own financial needs when they were younger, the wiser course for the state is to establish a system that combines an expectation of individual responsibility with guaranteed income supports by the state, along the general lines of our current Social Security system. In such a system, able adults should be required to contribute to a retirement fund in their working years, from which they will receive basic support in later years. Pooling worker contributions avoids the problems of individual uncertainty about what will happen at the end of life. Furthermore, the mandate of compulsory savings also avoids the moral hazard that some citizens will not save sufficiently during their productive lives in the belief that the state will later support them if they lack adequate savings.[76] Any infringement on individual autonomy that mandating contributions to the fund imposes is justified by the fact that, in the absence of state-mandated contributions, the state would have some obligation to subsidize citizens who do not accumulate sufficient savings.

This combination of individual and state responsibility puts the liberal democratic state in its proper role of recognizing and responding to the mix of autonomy and dependency that comprises the human condition. Mandating that citizens contribute to a common fund recognizes that adults in their productive years should be saving for their later years. At the same time, it also recognizes that dependency at the end of life is a common fact, even if there are many issues about that dependency that cannot be predicted. The state therefore constructs institutions that respond realistically and humanely to this fact, making clear that dealing with dependency is properly a joint responsibility of both the state and its citizens.

Although the outlines of the current Social Security program comport with the theory of the supportive state, the current minimum level of support it provides does not. The Social Security benefits formula is, as it should be, progressive, so that lower earners' eventual benefits represent a larger portion of their average lifetime earnings than do higher earners' benefits. It is not progressive enough, however. Currently, some retirees who have worked low-wage jobs for long periods of time receive benefits insufficient even to place them above the poverty line.[77] Those who have worked diligently and contributed prudently are entitled to a decent living standard as they age. This requires adoption of some form of adequate minimum benefit that Social Security now lacks.

CONCLUSION

The state has an important responsibility to ensure that societal institutions are structured in a manner that supports meeting citizens' dependency needs. When it comes to dealing with the caretaking needs that result from dependency, this responsibility of the state requires that fundamental changes be made in the labor market to ensure that family members have adequate opportunity for caretaking. The state need not go so far as to set up society in a manner that maximizes opportunities for family caretaking, but it must arrange institutions in such a way that they at least allow family members to meet the basic needs of dependents with reasonable diligence. In addition, when it comes to older citizens, the state must ensure the availability of caretaking networks outside of families to meet needs for care that occur in the later years of life. The state's responsibility to ensure that senior citizens' issues of financial dependency are humanely met also requires it to ensure institutions that share responsibility between these seniors and the state. In the next chapter, I consider the extent to which the state's duty changes when it deals with relationships among generally able adults.

CHAPTER 4

The Supportive State and ("Horizontal") Relationships Among Adults

For centuries, the state's putting its seal of approval on heterosexual marriage, and only heterosexual marriage, as the normative family structure was taken as a matter of course. In the last 15 years, however, public agreement on this issue has collapsed. In its place, controversy has been brewing over the role the state should play with respect to intimate relationships between adults, or "horizontal" relationships. This debate was catalyzed by recent state-court decisions striking down same-sex marriage bans,[1] as well as the political reaction to these decisions.[2] But it has been spurred on, as well, by the increasingly varied ways in which Americans organize their family lives.[3]

The emerging conversation has been complex. Some argue in favor of retaining traditional, heterosexual marriage.[4] Many others argue for change. Of these, some contend that marriage rights should be extended to same-sex couples.[5] Others contend that the rights and privileges presently confined to married couples should be extended not only to same-sex couples, but to cohabiting couples,[6] as well as a variety of other relationships.[7] Still others, including some gay rights advocates, believe that the state has no legitimate business privileging adult relationships at all, and that it should remove itself completely from sanctioning marriage and other intimate relationships.[8]

In this chapter, I consider how the supportive state should treat horizontal relationships. This issue is a complicated one because these relationships implicate a range of important liberal democratic goods in complex and contradictory ways. Because of this, any workable approach must seek nuanced ways to ameliorate the tension among these goods and, where necessary, to make trade-offs among them. It must also balance the state's high normative aspirations against its commitment to protecting its most vulnerable citizens.

In the first part of the chapter, I explore the interplay of goods at stake in horizontal relationships and the difficult issues they raise concerning the state's role. I do this by considering arguments on both ends of the spectrum of the current marriage debate: on the one hand, commentators who argue that the state should continue to privilege only heterosexual marital relationships; and, on the other hand, those who argue that the state should abolish privileging any horizontal relationships. Both sides reach such widely divergent results because they focus on a narrow range of the spectrum of important goods at stake in these relationships. In the next part of the chapter, I construct an approach that balances the important goods in this area through four principles that, together, should guide the supportive state in crafting its policies regarding relationships among adults. At base, these principles seek to balance the traditional liberal goods of individual autonomy and equality with the recognition of both children's and adults' dependency needs. At the same time, they strike a balance between promoting family forms that support important goods and protecting vulnerable citizens outside these family forms. Under them, the state supports a broad range of relationships that further caretaking, but this support is limited in particular ways.

Finally, at the end of the chapter, I consider two difficult issues that the state must confront with respect to regulating horizontal relationships. When it comes to the issue of whether civil marriage should be retained as an institution, the supportive state is agnostic: It values the institution of marriage for the energy that it, because of its cultural associations, channels into caretaking relationships; yet it is concerned that the singular cultural cache associated with marriage devalues the many other valuable forms of caretaking relationships. I then explore the complicated question of whether and how the state should seek to encourage two-parent families over single-parent families. Although the supportive state has legitimate reasons to adopt measures that encourage and seek to stabilize multiple-parent families, it must do so in a manner that does not jeopardize the welfare of children in single-parent families. Doing so requires far more nuanced policies than many of those now on the table to promote two-parent families.

EXISTING CONCEPTIONS OF THE STATE'S RESPONSIBILITY FOR HORIZONTAL RELATIONSHIPS

How should the state treat relationships among adults? The spectrum of views on this issue runs the gamut from those who say that the state should privilege only heterosexual marital relationships to those who argue that the state should end all privileges for horizontal relationships. Looking at the arguments on either end of the spectrum gives us a grasp of the complicated issues at stake here.

The Case for Traditional Marriage

Defenders of traditional marriage sometimes argue that the state should privilege heterosexual marriage because of reasons that are unrelated to the societal goods associated with it. On the whole, these arguments are flawed. For example, in his book, *It Takes a Family,* former Senator Rick Santorum argues that the state should support traditional families, and only traditional families, because this form of family is "fundamentally *natural.*"[9] Even leaving aside the unambiguous evidence of same-sex sexual relationships and partnerships in animals that undercut the blithe equation of "natural" with "heterosexual,"[10] the fact of the matter is that marriage is a social institution that is subject to societal control. If all that was at stake was what is "natural," there need be no discussion about the role of the state.

David Blankenhorn, a pro-marriage activist, and the president of the Institute for American Values, does little better when he argues that the state should continue to privilege only heterosexual marriage because marriage is fundamentally about assuring children a biological father and mother. As Blankenhorn acknowledges, marriage is a social institution that has been in place across societies from as far back as we can trace civilization.[11] In that time, it has varied from culture to culture and across time depending on the needs, desires, and cultural understandings of those involved with it. For example, in some times and places, the property aspects associated with it have been more prominent. In others, marriage's utility for larger kinship structures has been emphasized. To say that a complicated institution in which billions have participated from different cultures over thousands of years "is" about any single thing is nonsensical. Certainly for much time the understanding of marriage as both an affective relationship between the partners, the purpose emphasized by many advocates of same-sex marriage, and as the institution in which to bear children, the purpose emphasized by Blankenhorn, were bound up more tightly than they are today. Now that these two strands have been to some extent unraveled, there is no definitive way to determine which of them is more fundamental. What we do know is that in our society, as Blankenhorn notes, citizens conceive *each* of these understandings of marriage individually to be important.[12]

The issue of how the state should deal with relationships among adults, then, should not turn on what form of relationships are "natural," or what marriage somehow intrinsically "is," but, rather, on how privileging particular relationships either furthers or stymies important goods. Both Santorum and Blankenhorn provide more substantial justifications for the state to privilege the heterosexual marital family when they argue that it creates the best environment for children.[13] Leaving aside for the moment the accuracy of their contention, it is certainly true that children's welfare is a good that should be weighed heavily by a liberal democracy. But is there a reason to privilege *only* heterosexual marriage, if other forms of relationships also further other important goods? Why not, for example, also recognize same-sex marriage because it helps meet the caretaking needs of the adult partners? Blankenhorn's answer is that marriage properly links sex with reproduction in order to ensure that every child receives their birthright of having a biological mother and father responsible for them.[14] He argues that to the extent that the state allows same-sex marriage, children's interests will be threatened because the notion of marriage as giving them a birthright to two biological parents will be weakened.[15] This, in turn, will lead to fewer children being raised by both their biological father and mother, to the detriment of children's welfare. There are a number of problems with this argument.

First, again setting aside the truth of the claim that children who are raised in heterosexual marital families are generally better off than other children, the notion of limiting access to marriage to further the welfare of children appears far more unpalatable once we substitute some other possible restriction in place of same-sex marriage. For example, it is unlikely that any of us would be comfortable with the state refusing to allow poor people to marry on the ground that research demonstrates that their children have less favorable outcomes than those of well-to-do parents. Neither would we likely prohibit adults with low I.Q.s from marrying, although I.Q. is in part inheritable and low I.Q.s can diminish children's life prospects. Part of the reason we would not bar marriage in these cases is that we think of the institution as at least in some part a matter of human dignity and autonomy, in addition to thinking of it as an institution in which to raise sound children. In this context, the reason it may appear less offensive to exclude same-sex couples than these other couples from the institution of marriage seems more a matter of historical prejudice and an easy acceptance of the exclusion of gays and lesbians from matters of human dignity than concern for the welfare of children.

Another reason we do not bar people from marrying whose circumstances we may not deem optimal for rearing children is our awareness of both the benefits of and the limits of the power of formal institutions such as marriage. Prohibiting people from marrying would not keep all, or perhaps even most, of them from having children. This makes it possible that restricting marriage will worsen the well-being of the children who would be born anyway by excluding their parents from an institution that would stabilize their relationship to the children's benefit. Given the proliferation of gay and lesbian couples who have decided to have children outside the institution of marriage when access to this institution was not permitted to them, this certainly seems a realistic possibility if same-sex marriage continues to be denied to them.[16]

By the same token, Blankenhorn's argument depends on the extent to which the state's excluding same-sex couples from marriage will reinforce his desired perception that children have a right to grow up in a marital family with their biological parents. With the frequency of divorce and remarriage today, the increasing use of assisted reproductive technologies that rely on eggs and sperm from third persons, and surrogacy arrangements that expand the possible number of biological parents beyond two,[17] it is, at the very least, a questionable proposition whether that particular genie can be put back in the bottle. Against this possibility must be weighed the very certain benefits to caretaking for same-sex adults and the benefits to children reared in these families that are lost by restricting marriage to opposite-sex couples.[18]

Finally, Blankenhorn's argument that children need both a father and mother assumes a stark and essentialist gender divide that is incompatible with the goal of sex equality. Blankenhorn tells us that "Marriage's affective dimensions are inextricably linked to its purpose of bridging the primary divide in our species," which he asserts is the divide between men and women.[19] While Blankenhorn is exceedingly vague on what exactly this sex divide consists of, his view that women and men are so completely different, and that children need exposure to their very different traits and characteristics, echoes the now outmoded view that men and women, by nature, are starkly and essentially disparate creatures suited for very different roles in society.[20] This view of gender complementarity has long been rejected by those who study gender differences. It has also been recognized as outdated by the Supreme Court, which has repeatedly pointed out that reliance on categorical gender classifications "carr[ies] the inherent risk of reinforcing stereotypes about the 'proper place' of women and their need for special protection."[21]

But I have until now put aside the accuracy of Blankenhorn and Santorum's claims that children do best when they are raised from birth by two married, biological parents of the opposite sexes. Although these marriage proponents are correct that empirical studies suggest this form of family is a better environment for children to grow up in than other contenders, the other contenders in these studies *do not* include committed same-sex relationships in which the partners plan for and then raise a child from birth. Instead, these empirical studies compare how children fare in married, heterosexual families with biological children only against single-parent families, cohabiting heterosexual families, and families with a biological parent who later marries a step-parent.[22] There are clearly significant differences between these families and the same-sex families whom the authors seek to exclude from state support.

Is it the case that the heterosexual marital family is appreciably better for raising children than a same-sex marital family? Because same-sex marriage is so new, we do not yet have good comparative longitudinal data on these two forms of marital households. Yet the data we have already strongly suggest that children raised in two-parent same-sex families do comparably well on measures of well-being to children raised in heterosexual families.[23] In Gregory Herek's words, despite considerable variation in the quality of their samples, research design, measurement methods, and data-analysis techniques, the findings have been remarkably consistent: "[E]mpirical research to date has consistently failed to find linkages between children's wellbeing and the sexual orientation of their parents."[24] As Charlotte Patterson summarizes this research:

> [T]he clarity of findings in this area has been acknowledged by a number of major professional organizations. For instance, the governing body of the American Psychological Association (APA) voted unanimously in favor of a statement that said, "Research has shown that the adjustment, development, and psychological well-being of children is unrelated to parental sexual orientation and that children of lesbian and gay parents are as likely as those of heterosexual parents to flourish" (APA, 2004). The American Bar Association, the American Medical Association, the American Academy of Pediatrics, the American Psychiatric Association, and other mainstream professional groups have issued similar statements.[25]

Moreover, evidence also suggests that children born into both heterosexual and homosexual families who use sperm banks for the purposes of conception, and who, therefore, have only one parent who is biologically related to the child do similarly well.[26] Thus, although all the evidence won't be in for years, there is little support for the notion that children who are the product of same-sex marriages would fare any better or worse than their counterparts raised in opposite-sex marriages. Certainly, the presence of two same-sex parents has far less effect on children's well-being than such factors as the quality of the parents' relationship with the child, the level of stress in the parents' relationship, and the income level of the family.

So where does this leave us? In terms of identifying the critical issues at stake in the state's treatment of horizontal relationships, Santorum and Blankenhorn correctly identify children's welfare as an important good that should be taken into account, even if that good is not so clearly tied to heterosexual marriage as they would have it. In many other respects, however, their accounts are notable as much for the goods they leave out as those they

consider. Santorum and Blankenhorn pay little attention to key tenets of liberalism that are tied to the good of autonomy. These include a respect for
individuals' choosing their own life course, a belief that citizens' freedom will
generally redound to the health of the polity, a profound vigilance against
standardization by the state, and the concern that the majority will use state
power to impose its own beliefs on the minority without good public reasons
to do so.[27] While there might be goods on the other side of the scale that would
outweigh these tenets, and the welfare of children could certainly be one of
them, we have no good evidence of this when it comes to excluding same-sex
relationships and a lot of evidence to the contrary.

In addition, Santorum and Blankenhorn also give short shrift to the good
of equality. I have already mentioned how Blankenhorn's advocacy of gender complementarity conflicts with a commitment to sex equality. Privileging
only marital heterosexual relationships presents a further danger in that it
reinforces a form of association historically marked by gender inequality. As
Martha Fineman bluntly puts it, public policy that encourages heterosexual
marriage for the sake of children thereby constitutes the state's willingness
to sacrifice women's interests for children's.[28] Furthermore, privileging heterosexual marriage cuts against the goal of societal equality for gays and
lesbians. As with its commitment to autonomy, liberalism's commitment to
equality—particularly with respect to characteristics as deeply rooted as sexual orientation and gender—is strong. This goal might conceivably need to be
compromised because of liberalism's commitment to other important goods,
but is no evidence here of such a conflict.

Further, in arguing that the state should funnel an array of relationship
benefits to heterosexual marriage and only heterosexual marriage, Santorum
and Blankenhorn's proposals undercut socioeconomic equality in that they
would ensure that a vast range of benefits continue to be directed to those
who have, on some number of measures, already been fortunate. Not all in
society have an equal chance of getting and staying married. Coming from
a stable, well-to-do family significantly increases one's chances of doing so.
What's more, those citizens left out of the institution of marriage will likely
be those who most need state benefits, including financial benefits. Because of
economies of scale, adults in live-in relationships generally have an easier time
financially than those who live alone.[29] Funneling privileges to those who have
both the wherewithal and the happenstance to be in a committed relationship
therefore steers societal resources toward those who have traditionally been
the haves, rather than the have-nots. As Judith Stacey argues, "The more eggs
and raiments our society chooses to place in the family baskets of the married,
the hungrier and shabbier will be the lives of the vast numbers of adults and

dependents who, whether by fate, misfortune, or volition, will remain outside the gates...."[30]

On a related issue, arguments for privileging certain relationships—in Blankenhorn and Santorum's case, heterosexual marriage and only heterosexual marriage—raise issues about the balance that the state should strike between, on the one hand, incentivizing particular ways of life that are deemed to have beneficial consequences and, therefore, rewarding those who adopt these ways of life, and, on the other hand, directing resources toward those who are most in need, who will often be those least able to adopt those behaviors rewarded by the state. Blankenhorn and Santorum focus on rewarding ways of life they deem salutary for the public good. In contrast, much of the focus of the political left when it comes to state welfare policy has been to ensure that the state protects citizens when misfortune happens—when they lose their jobs, or have a health crisis, or their family falls apart. It is this concern that makes the left push for a viable social safety net. In truth, while both sets of considerations must be taken into account, neither can be allowed to overbalance the other.

The Case Against Marriage

Those at the other side of the spectrum who advocate that the state eliminate civil marriage, not surprisingly, attend largely to a range of important goods that marriage advocates ignore. Queer theorist Michael Warner's powerful argument against gay rights advocates who seek same-sex marriage is a case in point. Warner contends that the gay community's current push for same-sex marriage runs the risk of requiring the wholesale "repudiation of queer culture's best insights on intimate relations, sex, and the politics of stigma."[31] The ethical heart of these lessons is centered on human dignity. These lessons emerge somewhat paradoxically from queer culture's experience with sex and its indignities:

> [T]he ground rule is that one doesn't pretend to be *above* the indignity of sex.... A relation to others, in these contexts, begins in an acknowledgement of all that is most abject and least reputable in oneself. Shame is bedrock. Queers can be abusive, insulting, and vile toward one another, but because abjection is understood to be the shared condition, they also know how to communicate through such camaraderie a moving and unexpected form of generosity.... The rule is: Get over yourself. Put a wig on before you judge. And the corollary is that you stand to learn most from the people you think are beneath you. At its

best, this ethic cuts against every form of hierarchy you could bring into the room....[32]

Warner adds that this ethic "is actually truer to the core of the modern notion of dignity than the usual use of the word is.... Dignity in [this] sense is not pomp and distinction, it is inherent in the human."[33] He argues that marriage is the means through which the state has historically sought to privilege and promote a particular, monogamous model of heterosexual sexuality, and to stigmatize all other ways of life as morally tainted. Warner therefore sees the expansion of marriage to same-sex couples as more of the same—the blatant imposition of the majority's view of what is morally proper on the minority, and the denial of equal regard for the human dignity of all.[34]

Warner's vision of state disestablishment of marriage skillfully weaves together many of the values a liberal democracy respects. Not only does he powerfully mobilize the call for human dignity, and recognize that it encompasses a promise of equality for all, he also makes a powerful case for the individual autonomy that liberals hold dear: It is up to citizens rather than the state to determine what course in life is right for them, and neither should the state delegitimize some relationships and activities (such as sex outside of marriage) based solely on the private preferences of the majority. Somewhat less obvious but still a contributor to Warner's account is the good of community: As Warner presents it, the recognition that all are partners in shame leads to a recognition of fellowship, a willingness to learn from one another, generosity, and a spirited sense of community.

Yet Warner's emphasis on human dignity cuts both ways. As I have argued, once the dependency of the human condition is taken into account, supporting human dignity requires not just protecting individual autonomy, but also supporting caretaking. As our society is organized, some large portion of the caretaking that citizens need will come, if it comes at all, from those with whom we share close relationships. Long-term caretaking relationships contribute particular, important benefits to the polity because they satisfy dependency needs in a way that casual sex between two (or more) persons—whether these people are straight, gay, bisexual, or queer—does not. There are therefore reasons for the state to privilege particular relationships that do not turn on the illegitimate, private preferences of some citizens. Although liberal suspicions about the danger of an overweening state are legitimate, the importance of support for caretaking should not preclude the state acting to foster these relationships.

At the heart of the difficulties with the disestablishment approach is the fragility of its ethical base to accomplish the caretaking that must occur in any good society. The question is not whether Warner's vision is normatively attractive—it is in many respects. The question is whether state disestablishment of adult relationships could reasonably be expected to give rise to the responsibility and commitment that human dependency and the consequent need for caretaking entail. Warner dismisses the claim that his vision, as effectuated in queer culture, will lead to relativism, self-indulgence, or libertinism, arguing that queer culture polices itself, and the recognition of the common bond between queers creates a generosity and sense of ties among them that overcome these tendencies.[35] Although this may be the case within queer subculture, this sense of generosity and community seem far less likely to happen spontaneously in the more heterogeneous culture outside of queer life. Disestablishment advocates, then, are overly optimistic that the state's promotion of respect for all forms of life will lead to the committed ties that human dependency requires. Given their importance, a liberal democracy can and should be able to encourage the norms of commitment and responsibility that foster caretaking.

Some marriage disestablishment proponents base their argument, not on the claim that the state should not be picking and choosing between different goods, as Warner does, but instead on the claim that privileging adult relationships is the wrong means to support particular goods. For example, feminist Martha Fineman supports disestablishment based on the same good that the promarriage advocates rely on: children's welfare. Fineman argues that, contrary to marriage advocates, state support for the marital family ultimately redounds to children's detriment. In today's society, she points out, children grow up in a wide variety of family forms. A state that truly seeks to support the welfare of children, Fineman contends, would support child rearing in all the contexts in which it occurs, not just for children whose parents are married.[36] As a result, Fineman argues, the state has no legitimate stake in furthering relationships between capable adults, and therefore should abandon civil marriage as an institution. In the new regime she proposes, legal relationships between adults would be governed by private contracts negotiated between them.[37] This would leave marriage as a purely religious institution for those couples who choose to enter it, with no civil consequences.

In taking this position, however, Fineman does not properly credit the legitimate normative aspirations of the state. While the state should certainly focus attention on ensuring that all existing children are supported in their relationships with their parents, it may also aim higher and seek to promote those family forms that better foster children's welfare so that future children are born into sounder circumstances. On this point, Santorum and Blankenhorn are right. They are wrong, however, in arguing that same-sex relationships have no place in this mix, and in disregarding the costs to vulnerable citizens that can be imposed by policies meant to achieve such aims.

Moreover, Fineman, in arguing that the state should eliminate marriage as a civil status, ignores a legitimate reason that the state should be interested in horizontal relationships. The fact of the matter is that it is not just children who need caretaking: adults do, as well. This gives the state an important reason to support relationships between adults.

In sum, there are a complicated array of goods at stake in the state's regulation of intimate relationships among adults. An adequate theory of horizontal relationships needs to recognize this in developing principles to regulate these relationships. Considering all of these goods and principles together yields a more complicated—but ultimately a better—picture of what the state's role should be with respect to adults' relationships.

THE SUPPORTIVE STATE'S FRAMEWORK FOR RELATIONSHIPS BETWEEN ADULTS

What stance would the state take on relationships between adults if it considered the broad range of important goods and principles implicated in intimate adult relationships? These include not only autonomy and human dignity, but also furthering caretaking and human development for children and adults, equal opportunity for all citizens, and sex equality. Such an approach should take into account this array of important principles and interests, give each due weight, and, as far as possible, ameliorate the tension among them.

There are actually two separate but related issues that must be considered with respect to the state's approach to relationships. The first issue is whether the state should *recognize* relationships between adults for the purpose of assigning rights and responsibilities *between these adults*. The second is whether the state should *privilege* relationships between adults, in the sense that those who participate in these relationships should receive either *benefits from or rights against the state or third parties*. I argue that both of these issues should be answered in the affirmative, although the issue of whether the state should recognize relationships is an easier one to answer than whether it should privilege them.

State Recognition of Adult-Adult Relationships

When it comes to whether the state should recognize relationships between adults for the purpose of assigning rights and responsibilities between them, the answer is clearly "yes." Although proponents of disestablishment such as Fineman have argued that relationships between adults would be better dealt with through private contracts negotiated by the partners, the interdependent nature of intimate relationships between adults, particularly when they are long-term, can create large economic inequities and imbalances of power in the absence of regulation. In the face of these inequities, a state's failure to impose at least default rules on such couples, as Mary Shanley recognizes, would abandon the state's interest in securing justice and equality in these relationships.[38]

Those who advocate a regime of contract to regulate intimate relationships overlook serious difficulties that arise with respect to the fairness of such contracts. When persons contract about affective relationships they generally do not deal at arms length with one another. They may sometimes not zealously guard their own interests, out of concern for the other person or because of a mistaken (but extremely prevalent) belief that their own relationship will last for life. As a result, they may agree to an unfair contract. Furthermore, the courses of lives and relationships are often so difficult to predict that contracts entered into *ex ante* may not fairly and justly resolve what occurs *ex post*. In addition, in a regime of contract, those in a weaker bargaining position—traditionally women—may negotiate less favorable terms for themselves that will lead to inequality both in the course of the relationship and also if and when it ends. For these reasons, the state's establishment of a fair default position—for example, requiring that earnings by either partner during the relationship be owned jointly by the partners—to which couples may opt to contract out of is a better alternative than encouraging all partners to bargain individually.

Moreover, in a regime that provided for no civil status for horizontal relationships, and in which such relationships were governed exclusively by contract, even those who negotiate unfavorable contracts could be lucky compared to those who negotiated no contracts at all. Some will have no contract because they could not afford a lawyer. Others will not because the motivation to express one's love publicly, which many would say is their motivation to enter marriage,[39] would not similarly impel them to enter into a contract to protect themselves against their partner. If and when these relationships end, the partners would have neither the default protections currently in place based on their status as spouses, nor contractual claims against one another. Again this would operate to the detriment of primary caretakers, since they would have no claim to income earned by their partners during the relationship.[40] A regime in which the state recognizes relationships among adults for the purpose of apportioning rights and obligations fairly among them therefore better furthers the ends of fairness and justice than a regime of contract.

Of course, the state could assign rights and obligations based on the functional characteristics of the relationship even without providing couples with a route to formalize their relationships. For example, the American Law Institute's *Principles of the Law of Family Dissolution* imposes particular responsibilities on unmarried cohabitants whose relationships meet certain functional criteria.[41] In a regime in which civil marriage and other formalized commitments between adults were eliminated, a similar scheme could be applied to all couples. Under such an approach, the couple's functional characteristics—how long they lived together, whether they had children together, and so forth—could be used to determine the rights and responsibilities that each has with respect to the other.

Eliminating a civil route for formalizing relationships would still be a mistake for two reasons, however. First, this formalization helps to identify the intent of its members and their own understandings with respect to the intended primacy and permanency of the relationship. In entering into a marriage, participants indicate their assent to a specific formal status that comes with a set of enforceable legal rights and responsibilities.[42] And surely such understandings should be relevant in determining the default rules that apply to that particular relationship. For example, a commitment to a permanent relationship should be pertinent to the state's determination of whether and how long income should be redistributed between parties who have separated.[43]

Second, and still more important, the state's making available routes through which citizens can formally commit to the permanency and depth of their relationships serves the state's interest in increasing the stability of familial caretaking relationships. As Elizabeth Scott thoughtfully explains about civil marriage:

> The formality of marital status, together with the requirement of legal action for both entry into marriage and divorce, clarifies the meaning of the commitment that the couple are making and underscores its seriousness.... The package of substantive legal obligations that goes with the formal status of marriage serves independently to promote stability in the relationship.[44]

Providing routes for couples, as well as those in other forms of intimate relationships, to formalize their commitments thereby increases the likelihood these citizens will stay together to provide one another the care that each needs, establish a stable relationship in the event of children, and try hard to weather the difficult times with their partners.[45]

State Privileging of (Some) Adult-Adult Relationships

The supportive state should *recognize* relationships between adults for the purpose of assigning default rights and responsibilities among their participants,
but should it also seek to *privilege* such relationships? In my view, the answer
should be "yes" because of the goods that these relationships further. These
privileges, however, must be limited in particular ways since they conflict with
other important liberal goods and values, including principles of autonomy
and equality. The following four principles for the supportive state's treatment
of adult relationships together seek to accommodate the range of important
goods at stake.

1. Freedom to Enter into Consensual Relationships

Liberalism's great respect for individual autonomy requires that the state give
individuals the freedom to engage or not engage in consensual relationships
with others as they choose. The right to determine one's own personal relationships free from interference by the state is central to the value of individual
self-determination and the human dignity on which liberalism is grounded.[46]
Under this principle, for example, a citizen whose vision of the good life is
to have sexual relationships with as many other citizens as possible should
be able to fulfill that vision without interference by the state (barring issues
such as public health concerns), regardless of the majority's own private views.
Although this goal in life may seem silly to many of us, and sinful to others,
barring some legitimate public reason, the state has no grounds to proscribe
this conduct. This principle would prohibit state criminal statutes still on the
books in several states that outlaw fornication and cohabitation outside of
marriage.[47]

2. Support of (a Broad Range of) Long-Term Caretaking Relationships

Although the liberal state must tolerate all consensual relationships, it need
not give all such relationships a level playing field. It is true, as Michael Warner
argues, that the liberal democratic state should not favor some relationships
over others based on citizens' private notions of morality.[48] It can and should,
however, seek to support relationships that further important public goods in
which the liberal state has a legitimate interest. Given the dependency inherent in the human condition, it is not only autonomy that is necessary to support human dignity but also caretaking and human development. Supporting

long-term relationships is an important way to further these goods. Without minimizing the violence and other harm that sometimes occurs in relationships between adults, or ignoring the sex inequality that has marked heterosexual relationships, the crux of the matter is that dependency is an inevitable fact of life for adults as well as for children, and a liberal state must contend with that fact. Because of its interest in the health, well-being, and dignity of its citizens, the liberal state has a vital interest in the success of relationships that foster caretaking, and should provide these relationships with the institutional support that will help them flourish.

Given that a primary reason for the state to privilege adult intimate relationships is caretaking, the state has an interest in supporting a considerably broader range of relationships than the heterosexual couples who can now choose to marry. For example, the state has an interest in supporting relationships of nonmonogamous couples or, at the opposite end of the spectrum, those whose relationships are not sexual. By the same token, the state also has an interest in supporting caretaking in family groupings that involve more than two adults.[49] Thus, the state has valid reasons to support all the following horizontal relationships involving caretaking: two elderly sisters who live together and take care of one another, a nonmonogamous homosexual couple, a commune of five adults who live together with their children, and a heterosexual married couple.

3. Limits on the Privileges Available to Long-Term Caretaking Relationships

Promoting the health and stability of horizontal relationships is only one goal that a flourishing liberal democracy should pursue, and only one of many principles that should influence the state's decision-making. State distribution of privileges in favor of these relationships therefore has to be weighed against alternative principles of distribution, including need. As I have argued, claims of need should not monopolize the field when it comes to state action: a flourishing society must be able to act on aspirations for a better future, as well. For this reason, the state may provide certain benefits to encourage long-term relationships, even though those benefits may not reach those currently most in need. With that said, claims of need must still be given considerable moral weight, and properly limit the privileges accorded these relationships, even if they do not bar them entirely.

In addition, the recognition of the limits on the state's ability to ensure the existence and stability of relationships must also be factored into the state's family policy. Liberalism's profound recognition of the limited institutional competence of the state to accomplish particular ends—what might be called liberal humility—should be an important element of the state's approach to relationships among adults. Liberal humility requires recognizing that the state has only a moderate ability to encourage citizens to develop and maintain healthy caretaking relationships. Although the state can establish certain institutional preconditions and incentives that support relationships, ultimately whether healthy relationships will develop and be sustained has a great deal to do with characteristics of the individuals involved and dumb luck, which are beyond the state's ability to affect. Ignoring these limits on the state's competence can cause the state to over-invest resources when it only has a modest power to affect results. And its attaching too many incentives to such relationships can cause citizens to enter into and remain in them in name only or, worse, to remain in abusive relationships that the state has no good interest in supporting.

Further, the fact that healthy relationships depend on so many factors unrelated to individual desert is also reason to limit the benefits the state provides to relationships. Even if eligible citizens seek to marry, for many, entering and remaining in this institution will depend on circumstances that they can do nothing about. For example, one partner may simply decide that he or she no longer loves the other partner and leave, with no fault on the part of the other partner. The state's investing its resources only in marriage means that this wider group of citizens will, many through no fault of their own, be ineligible for these benefits. These considerations should cause the state to limit the privileges that support relationships in two specific ways. First, state support of caretaking relationships between adults cannot undercut the state's responsibility to ensure that all its citizens have the means and opportunity to pursue dignified lives. This means, at a minimum, that a just society should seek to deliver basic social goods, such as health care, to everyone in society, regardless of family membership. Insofar as the state distributes these goods based on a particular relationship status, it neglects its most basic responsibilities.

Second, the state should limit privileges for relationships to those tied to the specific public goods in which the state has a legitimate interest—for example, caretaking or sex equality. Singling out families for more generalized favorable treatment—while it might still further the goal of encouraging and supporting families—stands in tension with principles of fairness and equality among all citizens, both those within and those not in such families, particularly insofar as it redistributes economic resources to those who are, on average, better off. Under this principle, the state may allow caretaking leaves from work, hospital visitation privileges for the families of sick citizens, and special immigration privileges for the partners of citizens, but may not allow general tax breaks for those in caretaking relationships that are unrelated to the extra expenses incurred in caretaking. Thus the state would have little justification for funnelling general economic support to those in adult-adult relationships, given that these adults, on average, do better financially due to the economies of scale of living together. In contrast, economic redistribution to those in caretaker-dependent relationships could be better justified by the consideration of the cost to caretakers of caring for dependents, including the interruption from working continuously in the paid work force.[50]

One important way in which the state can legitimately foster relationships among adults that conform to this principle is, as I suggested earlier, by providing a civil route through which adults can formalize their commitment to others. These formal commitments increase the likelihood that a relationship will last. They also serve as an expressive vehicle for the state to announce its support for stable caretaking relationships without redistributing tangible privileges in favor of such relationships and, hence, away from those who might need them more. The state's endorsement of such formal commitments is still not, of course, without cost to those who do not enter them. To the extent that the state endorses such commitments, those who do not enter into them may feel a lack of societal respect or even societal disapprobation. However, given the importance of caretaking relationships, the stability that such formalization contributes to these relationships outweighs the costs of this potential stigmatization in my view.

4. Guarding against Injury to Other Important Goods

Finally, the supportive state must take account of the risks that supporting families can pose to other important liberal goods. Three such risks merit particular attention. First, state support for caretaking relationships poses the threat of increasing gender inequality, insofar as the relationships supported are heterosexual. Second, privileging familial relationships may also increase inequalities of wealth and opportunity, since closer families may be more likely to distribute resources within their family. Third, the state's encouraging family relationships could make it more likely that family members will be so engaged with their own families that they will disengage from community life.

A. SEX INEQUALITY Any proposal that the state should promote intimate caretaking relationships must contend with the fact that heterosexual relationships, and especially the institution of heterosexual marriage, have been deeply intertwined with women's unequal status in society.[51] Leaving current political realities aside, the state might, of course, deal with this troubling association by privileging only those long-term caretaking relationships that are not heterosexual, such as homosexual relationships or platonic relationships. Alternatively, and far more palatable politically, the state could privilege heterosexual relationships along with other relationships, at the same time that it seeks to eliminate the inequality within these relationships.

One of the most important ways to pursue this latter option is for the state to adopt policies that encourage parents to share caretaking of children, since a large measure of gender inequality is associated with women assuming disproportionate childrearing responsibilities.[52] To accomplish this goal, as I discussed in Chapter 3, the state should adopt a model of public support for caretaking that allows both parents to share equally in caretaking and in the paid workplace. For example, the state might require employers to adopt family leave and flex-time policies that can be taken by parents sharing child care between them.[53] Public schools, too, could play a role in this endeavor, teaching children that both fathers and mothers should have equal roles in nurturing their children, and helping them to understand the importance of these caretaking tasks. In Anita Shreve's words, "the old home-economics courses that used to teach girls how to cook and sew might give way to the new home economics: teaching girls *and boys* how to combine working and parenting."[54]

B. INEQUALITIES OF WEALTH AND OPPORTUNITY The state's support of family ties runs the risk that closer family bonds will lead to wealth being more tightly held within families and therefore to increased disparities of wealth and opportunities across families.[55] The state should do a few things to address this risk. First, it must ensure that all citizens have the financial means and education to achieve (at the very least) some basic threshold of opportunity, even when their families cannot provide this without aid. Second, it should set up incentives to encourage family members with significant wealth to redistribute it outside of families, such as through charitable tax exemptions. Finally, when citizens do make bequests within families, the state should seek to reduce, although not eliminate, disparities in wealth that continue between generations. As Michael Walzer argues, there are significant reasons to allow family members to express their love through bequests to family members, as well as significant reasons to tax these bequests to further equality and fund legitimate state expenditures.[56] Walzer concludes, rightly, in my view, that the state should moderate between these goals by giving some weight to each when determining the extent of taxation of such gifts.[57]

C. RETREAT FROM CIVIC LIFE For civic as well as economic reasons, the state should also seek to encourage families to serve as a source of support for their members, but not function as islands unto themselves. This is a more significant issue in our era than it was in the past. The social circles of adult Americans have narrowed dramatically in the past decades.[58] A number of factors likely contribute to our shrinking social lives: Primarily because of women's increased labor force participation,[59] American families have added more than 10 hours working outside the home per week. In families without children, husbands and wives combined to put in a 58-hour paid workweek in 1968 and a 68-hour workweek in 2000; in families with children the parents combined for a 53-hour paid workweek in 1968 and a 64-hour workweek in 2000.[60] This, as well as longer commutes,[61] place American families in a far greater time crunch than in the past. Recent time-analysis studies, however, suggest that parents still spend roughly the same number of hours each week caring for children as in the past.[62] Their commitment to child care leaves them less time for socializing with other adults and for community activities than they once had.[63] This time crunch is particularly evident among the highly-educated middle class, which is the group that most contributes to voluntary community associations.[64]

These developments pose a significant threat to the health of the polity. A liberal democracy requires both solid ties between citizens and flourishing civic associations in order to thrive. Without them, the trust and confidence in others that is necessary for society to function well flags.[65] Further, the weakening of bonds between citizens also poses risks for social equality—it is far easier to see someone as properly unequal if we can see them as the "other." Finally, weaker community ties threaten the important caretaking that can occur outside of families. Not all people can or will choose to live in families. Even when citizens do, family members will not always be around in times of need, or be able to meet all caretaking and human-development needs. As the networks of volunteers from the San Francisco gay community who took care of those stricken with AIDS in the 1980s demonstrated, caretaking outside of family bounds serves an important role in a healthy society. Yet this caretaking is dependent on the existence of vigorous networks of citizens. For all these reasons, the supportive state must seek to encourage the conditions that promote civic bonds among citizens.

To foster the strong ties that a healthy polity requires, the state should support caretaking relationships in a manner that still encourages strong bonds between citizens and communities. Some part of this goal can be accomplished through measures that are both family and community friendly, such as policies that help workers reduce long work hours and commuting times, including maximum hour laws, and public transportation and zoning policies that discourage urban sprawl and its attendant long commute times.[66] At the same time, the state should seek to encourage at least some deprivatization of the nuclear family form as it has taken shape in the United States. The pattern of child rearing in which parents have sole responsibility for child care inside a private home isolates children and caretaking parents from the larger community. In privileging caretaking relationships, the state should seek to construct institutional arrangements that incorporate parents and dependents into the life of the community and share caretaking responsibilities within the community. Tax subsidies for co-housing developments, in which some cooking and childcare are performed cooperatively, and supports for child-care cooperatives, are two measures by which the state can pursue these ends.

DIFFICULT ISSUES IN REGULATING INTIMATE ADULT RELATIONSHIPS

I have argued that the state should both recognize and encourage intimate relationships among adults that foster caretaking. Yet two difficult issues remain with respect to regulating these relationships. The first concerns the form or forms through which the state formalizes intimate relationships. Specifically, should the state make available a single formalized status such as "domestic partnership" for all adult relationships? Or should the state make available a number of different formalized statuses for different types of relationships? In the latter case, the state would presumably continue to formalize some relationships as marriages, while formalizing others in a variety of ways. The second concerns the measures that the state may legitimately use to encourage two-parent families over single-parent families.

Domestic Partnership for All or Marriage for Some?

The most difficult issue with respect to how the state should treat adults' long-term caretaking relationships is not, in my view, whether the state should accord some civil status to these relationships, or whether it should privilege caretaking relationships over other relationships. Instead, it is whether all such horizontal relationships should be formalized within a single legal category, such as "domestic partnership," or whether relationships should be categorized separately according to the general type of relationship at issue.

In the latter case, the state would retain a civil status for conjugal relationships such as marriage (which, out of fairness, as well as for the goods associated with them, would need to be expanded to same-sex couples), but also recognize other forms of adult-adult relationships such as domestic partnerships between friends who cohabitate.

Each of these alternatives has significant benefits and costs. Grouping all adult relationships into a single legal status has the advantage of guarding against the possibility that any particular subcategory of relationship, namely marriage, would be unfairly privileged in the political process as against other horizontal relationships. By the same token, clustering different types of horizontal relationships together into the same legal category would send a strong message that marriage occupies no paramount place in the legal hierarchy, announcing clearly that there are a number of ways that caretaking relationships can be forged and maintained in society, all of which should be respected.

This approach comes with two significant downsides, however. First, it would keep the state from tailoring the particular obligations and benefits assigned to that status to the type of caretaking relationship at issue. For example, when a child is born to one of the parties within a conjugal relationship, it makes sense to accord a presumption of parenthood to the other partner. There is less reason to accord such a presumption in a nonconjugal caretaking relationship, however. The same is true for inheritance rights: As a default matter, it makes sense to assign a presumption that conjugal partners intend their partner to inherit, since most individuals in such relationships leave their estates to their partners.[67] It may make less sense to apply this presumption to other types of long-term caretaking relationships.

Second, although moving away from the category of marriage has the benefit of eliminating marriage as *the* privileged category, it has the related disadvantage that much of the positive cultural resonance associated with marriage—the notion that the institution is a serious, long-term bond of commitment based on love between two people who come together and take one another permanently as family—will also be lost.[68] Eliminating marriage may therefore weaken the resolve of those in relationships to work through rough periods. It could also dissuade those who would otherwise have married from formalizing their relationships, since the new form of formalization the state adopts will not have the same cultural resonance that swearing one's love through marriage does.[69]

The alternative of retaining a conjugal status such as marriage but also developing other formalized categories of relationships that adults could choose to enter has the benefit of retaining the cultural and legal force associated with marriage. This alternative would also allow the state to tailor specific bundles of rights to the particular types of relationships at issue. For example, the state could adopt a formalized legal status for adults (not necessarily limited to two) who live together but are not involved in a sexual relationship, including adult siblings; for couples who do not live together but are in a long-term, committed caretaking relationship; and more. The downside of this approach, however, is that it runs the risk that marital relationships will continue to be perceived as superior to other relationships and disproportionately assigned privileges.

At the level of theory, there is no clear winner between these two alternatives—each has its own set of benefits and costs. At the level of political reality, though, popular ideology (not to mention the $50 billion a year wedding industry)[70] is so invested in the value of marriage that eliminating civil marriage is almost impossible. As a result, those who seek to topple marriage from its pedestal as the preferred family form and to develop equal regard for a broader category of relationships would likely do better to focus their attention on decentering marriage by proliferating other categories of status relationships among adults, rather than seeking to eliminate marriage as a civil status and replacing it with a civil partnership category.[71] This strategy of broadening the categories of relationships that receive legal protections and support and distributing a subset of the bundle of rights now received by marriage among these different relationships is not only the most pragmatic course to take given existing political realities, but a course that offers significant promise in furthering the goods that a liberal democracy needs to flourish.[72] Disaggregating the privileges awarded based on the range of goods at issue also helps deconstruct the monolithic notion of "The Family" and the orthodoxy surrounding it. This approach makes clear that there are many kinds of relationships that contribute important public goods, and that no one-size-fits-all family is the ideal.

Encouraging Two- (or More) Parent Families

There should be no question that a vigorous liberal democracy should be able to privilege some relationships over others for important public ends. And certainly creating a stable environment for children is such an important end. All other things being equal, close, stable family relationships are better for children than more distant or unstable relationships. Further, while many of the greater difficulties associated with single-parent families can be attributed to lack of adequate legal and social supports,[73] the trauma of a family breakup or divorce itself has significant consequences.[74] In addition, having the emotional and financial resources of two loving adults in the household available to the child, again, all other things being equal, is better than having the resources of just one.[75] This gives the state a legitimate interest in preferring two-parent (or more) families to single-parent families.

The issue of *how* the state may seek to encourage such multiple parent families is a difficult one, however. The state's duty to ensure that children have the caretaking and other resources necessary to meet their basic dependency needs and to promote a minimally-adequate level of human development exists whether or not the state believes that parents have made a wise choice about their family form. And it exists even if the state fears that ensuring that today's children have necessary resources will send the wrong signals about better and worse family forms and thereby hurt future children: The duty to support existing children adequately is paramount. Because of it, for example, the state may not withhold welfare benefits to low-income families based on their mothers' having additional children out of wedlock, if doing so would deprive the children in these families of necessary resources.

Above this required threshold of support, however, the state has good reasons to adopt measures that encourage and seek to stabilize multiple-parent families. In choosing among such measures, the state should still seek to harmonize the important liberal goods at stake. In other words, the state's goal should be to construct policies that avoid zero-sum situations in which furthering some goods operates to the detriment of others. Developing such policies will require careful attention to the ways in which relevant goods may conflict.

By this criterion, the state's seeking to further two-parent families by awarding them economic resources not awarded to single-parent families is a peculiarly bad tool to harmonize these goods, since doing so keeps resources from the families who need them most and therefore increases inequality. The state would do better to adopt measures that do not pose such stark trade-offs. For example, the state could encourage multiple-parent families by providing job-training programs and educational subsidies for youths who are at risk of becoming parents, since studies show that increasing the prospects for young adults' futures makes it significantly less likely that they will bear children while they are young and single.[76] Such programs do not directly pit the important interests of current children against those of future children, and also have the virtue of increasing equal opportunity.

Along the same lines, the state should treat proposals that seek to strengthen marriage by making divorce more difficult, such as proposals that seek to return to fault divorce laws, with a skeptical eye. Tightening up divorce laws by returning to fault divorce, despite furthering the state's interest in promoting marriage, would severely infringe on citizens' autonomy interests. The state would therefore do better to adopt proposals such as premarital counseling requirements that avoid this stark trade-off of goods.[77] By the same token, as Linda McClain argues, many marriage-promotion policies risk perpetuating sex inequality within marriage.[78] Given that women more often seek divorces than men, the state could usefully support such relationships by encouraging men to be better partners through assuming an equal share of housework and carework.[79] Such measures would infringe less on individuals' autonomy than stricter divorce laws and, at the same time, increase sex equality.

In determining the measures that the state should take to further such relationships, it is important to keep in mind the limits of the state's institutional competence to deal with the complexities of these relationships. The state can make it more difficult for individuals to get out of marriage; it cannot, however, keep affection and caretaking alive within such relationships. In those cases in which parents' relationships with one another are unsuccessful, rather than attempting to keep them in the marriage, the state's efforts would be better focused on ensuring that both parents have a continued, meaningful role in the child's life. As courts and commentators have increasingly recognized, the fact that two adults divorce one another does not mean that one of them must also divorce the child.[80] The state's goal in this situation should be, insofar as it is possible, to facilitate harmonious parenting relationships between both parents and the child. At the top of the list of policy changes that the supportive state should make to pursue this goal should be moving family courts away from litigation as the standard model to resolve divorce disputes, since it heightens animosity between the parties, and toward a model such as collaborative dispute resolution that facilitates cooperation between the parties.[81]

CONCLUSION

Determining the stance that the supportive state should take with respect to adult intimate relationships is so difficult because these relationships implicate a number of goods that are central to American ideals—and which, at best, jibe uneasily with one another. Each of these goods—human dignity, autonomy, equal opportunity, sex equality, children's welfare—is too important to the liberal democratic project to be sacrificed wholesale to any of the others. By the same token, none ranks so supreme that it should be deemed completely to trump the others. What is called for, then, rather than focusing on a single good or two and ignoring the others, is a family policy that stitches the relevant goods together into a more nuanced set of principles that allows each of these goods to be given its due.

This does not mean, of course, that a set of principles can be arrived at that allows each of these goods unmitigated scope, uncompromised by the others. As Isaiah Berlin succinctly counsels, the world is full of situations "in which we are faced with choices between ends equally ultimate, and claims equally absolute, the realization of some of which must inevitably involve the sacrifice of others."[82] It does mean, however, that there will be places in which this tension between goods can be ameliorated through thoughtful policies. It also means that, where these tensions cannot be mitigated, the supportive state must make hard choices between these goods consciously and carefully.

CHAPTER 5

The Supportive State, Family Privacy, and Children

As a general matter, the state should support families' capacity for caretaking and human development while giving families the autonomy to make decisions about how to conduct their own affairs. Focusing on how children fit into the mix, however, raises thorny issues when it comes to this policy of family privacy. One set of issues comes from the state's responsibility to protect children from harm. The fact of children's vulnerability, in concert with their presence within families, makes the relationship between parents and the state a complex one when it comes to protecting children's welfare. Most parents love their children and generally try to do what is best for them. Yet this is not true of all parents. And even some parents who love their children fail to safeguard their welfare adequately, or even abuse them. How should the state construct its relationship with families to best promote children's welfare and shield them from harm?

Hard questions also arise about how best to protect children's interests more broadly than in cases of child maltreatment. The state's support for a policy of family privacy, without more, generally reinforces parents' authority over their children. In making family decisions, different parents will exercise this authority in different ways. Some will defer to their children's opinions often. Others will do what they think is best for their children, but pay less attention to their opinions. Still others will pursue their own interests and views while paying little attention even to the interests of their children. This inequality of power between parents and children creates a particular cause for concern because, unlike adults, children generally cannot exit from families when they disagree with decisions that are made. To what extent should the state seek to protect children's interests by allowing them rights that alter this balance of power?

Finally, a last set of difficult issues about family privacy arises when it comes to parents' authority to direct children's upbringing. Parents have strong claims to be able to raise their children in the manner they see fit (barring abuse and neglect), and to be able to influence the persons they will become. But what should happen when parents seek to raise their children in a manner contrary to liberal democratic values? In some cases, parents do so without being purposeful, as when they model traditional gender roles to their children without stopping to think about them. In other cases, parents who reject liberal credos in their own lives deliberately seek to pass along illiberal or undemocratic views to their children. For example, some Southern Baptist parents may seek to pass on their church's belief that wives should graciously submit to their husbands. To take another example, some Christian conservatives may undermine their children developing the virtue of civil tolerance by teaching them that gay men and lesbians should not be entitled to civil rights because homosexuality is a sin. Furthermore, some fundamentalist parents may seek to keep their children cloistered from other ways of life to preclude their straying from their religion.[1] This seclusion can stifle children's opportunity to develop the autonomy necessary to choose their own course in life. What position should the state take in these situations?

In this chapter, I address all three of these sets of questions: How the state best constructs its relationship with families to protect children from harm; whether to give children rights within their families; and how the state should respond to parents who pass on illiberal beliefs. The mainstream answer to this spectrum of issues has been simply to affirm the doctrine of family privacy except in the case of specific and extreme circumstances such as abuse or neglect. In this approach, as the discussion of John Rawls in Chapter 1 revealed,[2] what happens within families is generally not the state's concern. The supportive state's position is not diametrically opposed to the mainstream position, but it is more nuanced. Like the mainstream view, it respects the value of family privacy. It does not, however, conceive of this privacy as an all-or-nothing issue. For one thing, it recognizes that family autonomy is never complete, and that the state inevitably affects the way that families function in the ordinary course of affairs. For another, although it gives considerable weight to families' own decisions about how to conduct their affairs, it recognizes that family privacy, like individual autonomy, is one of a range of goods that must be supported in a flourishing society. Family privacy therefore no longer serves as the trump card of state policy that it does in the mainstream view.

In its place, the supportive state aims to adopt policies that, to the extent possible, align the interest in family privacy with other important goods, including children's welfare, their interest in autonomy, and the development of their civic virtues. As I argue in the first part of the chapter, a child welfare system that supports families in the ordinary course of affairs can both decrease the number of crises that call for intrusive interventions by the state, as well as do a better job at improving children's welfare than the current child welfare system. Such a policy of state support to parents, I contend in the second part, also does a better job serving children's interests than does a platform of "children's rights." I point out, however, that there are some specific instances—the most significant of which is pregnant girls' right to choose abortion—in which children's interests call for granting them particular rights. When it comes to parents who seek to pass on illiberal ways of life, I assert in the last part of the chapter, the state cannot allow their desires, no matter how well meaning or deeply held, to curtail children's developing civic virtues or the necessary autonomy to direct the course of their own lives. With that said, in most cases, the state can pursue these developmental objectives in other institutions besides the family, thereby minimizing infringements on parents' autonomy.

FAMILY PRIVACY AND THE CHILD
WELFARE SYSTEM

What role should the state play to best safeguard children's welfare? In this section, I contrast two very different approaches to state involvement. The first is the approach currently used in the child welfare system in the United States. In it, the state's responsibility for children's welfare is treated as residual, in the sense that parents alone are expected to provide the conditions that children need to thrive; only after parents fail to protect children adequately does the state properly step in.[3] When this point is reached, because the parents are conceived as being at fault for having failed to safeguard children autonomously, coercive state intervention is deemed warranted. This intervention often takes the form of the state removing children from their home. Many of these children will later be reunified with their parents, others will remain in foster care, and still others will be adopted by new parents. Regardless of which of these alternatives transpires, almost all children in this system will be significantly damaged, both before and after the state becomes involved. Although there are certainly better and worse outcomes for children in this system, very few of these outcomes are good for the children involved.

The second approach, that of the supportive state, treats the issue of children's welfare very differently. In it, children's welfare is not a residual responsibility of the state that comes into play only after families fail, but rather a concurrent responsibility in the ordinary course of affairs. Instead of strong-arming families after a crisis has occurred, the state seeks to partner with parents so that families are less vulnerable to crises in the first place. In contrast to the existing system in which the government spends most child-welfare funds paying private companies and foster parents to care for children deemed inadequately parented,[4] the government would funnel its resources first and foremost into ensuring that existing families have the social supports to provide for children's well-being. The supportive state model, in contrast to the residual model, seeks to promote children's flourishing, rather than simply minimize the damage to them.

The Current Child Welfare System

Under the current system, state agencies responsible for children's welfare take no action unless and until they receive a report of mistreatment. Until that point, it is families, not the state, who are responsible for safeguarding children's welfare. Once a complaint of abuse or neglect is investigated and deemed substantiated, however, the parents are deemed to have failed. Coercive state intervention in the family is considered the appropriate response.

At this point, the Adoption and Safe Families Act of 1997 ("ASFA"),[5] the federal act which overhauled the United States' foster care system, seeks to assure that once the state does become involved, its relationship with families will be finite and, preferably, brief. The Act leaves in place the previous mandate that states should generally make efforts to keep the child in the home and, alternatively, to reunify the child if a period of foster care is necessary.[6] Yet in keeping with this approach's recalcitrance toward ongoing state support for families, current federal funding standards make it far more difficult for states to be compensated for providing assistance to preserve families than to be reimbursed for providing foster care or adoption for the child.[7] The numbers reflect these financial incentives: In 2002, the federal government spent at least nine dollars on foster care and three more dollars on adoption for every dollar spent to prevent foster care or speed reunification.[8] As a consequence, a relatively small proportion of families actually receive any assistance besides emergency services to help keep children out of foster care or to reunify children with their parents after removal.[9] Under the current approach, a staggering number of children—approximately 254,400 annually—enter the foster-care system.[10]

Once children are taken into care, ASFA limits the length of any efforts to reunify that the state may attempt by mandating that child welfare agencies seek termination of parental rights if a child has been in foster care for fifteen of the previous twenty-two months.[11] In keeping with this approach's dim view of families who cannot support children's welfare on their own, ASFA requires states to pursue efforts to find adoptive homes for children in foster care concurrently with efforts to reunite these children with their family, on the view that reunification efforts with such flawed parents are often unsuccessful.[12] The end state envisioned in this model is children living with families—whether their biological families or adoptive families—who can ensure children's health and welfare on their own.

There is substantial debate over whether many of these children are truly better served by taking them into foster care, rather than leaving them in their homes.[13] Recent data suggests that at least in cases on the margins for removal, children, particularly older ones, would be better off if they were left with their birth families.[14] Whether or not this is the case, most children who enter the child-welfare system will have already been significantly harmed by the state's failure to support their welfare until that point. Most of these children have been raised in poverty,[15] and have suffered its deleterious effects. By the time they enter care, the overwhelming majority will have some sort of physical or mental abnormality that requires medical attention, including greatly elevated rates of suicidal and homicidal ideation, as well as a high level of developmental delays.[16]

Taking these children into foster care causes them even further trauma. It is difficult to overestimate the emotional anguish experienced by these children as a result of being removed, even temporarily, from their parents, their siblings, and their home, regardless of whether they were maltreated there. As stated by an expert witness in *Nicholson v. Williams,* "The attachment between parent and child forms the basis of who we are as humans and the continuity of that attachment is essential to a child's natural development."[17] Most of these separations are for substantial periods of time: Once a child is placed in foster care, the median length of stay is 14 months, although a full 11 percent of children (43,083) stay five years or longer.[18]

A significant portion of the children taken into foster care will suffer even more than the inevitable trauma of separation from their families. The difficulty that states have had administering and monitoring the foster care system means that children who enter it are far from assured a benign experience. In this system, a significant number of children are shuffled from placement to placement.[19] They are, moreover, at far greater risk for physical abuse, sexual abuse, and neglect than in nonfoster families.[20] In fact, the problems with the foster-care system have been so pervasive that, as Barbara Woodhouse notes, at the time that ASFA was being considered in Congress, 21 states had been forced to enter into consent decrees as a result of badly managed child-welfare systems.[21] The recurrent newspaper stories of foster care mismanagement and abuse that have emerged from state after state graphically illustrate how flawed this system is in actual operation. It should be no surprise then that many of the children who enter foster care—probably most—will be scarred for life. Adults between the ages of 20 and 33 who were in foster care as children suffer posttraumatic stress disorder (PTSD) at twice the rates of combat veterans. More than half (54.4%) of them have at least one mental-health problem, such as depression, social phobia, panic syndrome, or anxiety.[22]

Roughly half of the children taken into care will eventually be returned to their biological families.[23] However, it is not at all clear that the model of episodic state involvement that marks the current child-welfare system—in which the state only sometimes provides assistance for reunification, and, when it does, offers only limited, crisis-oriented services for relatively short periods of time—deals effectively with the deep-seated problems that generally prompt state intervention in the first place. One well-regarded older study found that 33 percent of caretakers with children in foster care suffered from severe mental or emotional problems; 60 percent had a family member with alcohol abuse problems; 53 percent had a severe health problem; and 76 percent of families had at least one child with a serious health problem.[24] The complexity of these parents' problems, in combination with the ineffectiveness of the short-term services occasionally offered to them, means that a large proportion of children will be returned to families that still have the same problems that first prompted the children's removal. Because of this, many of the children who enter the child-welfare system will cycle through it repeatedly.[25]

The other half of children who are not returned to their parents also have a tough road ahead of them. Many of these children will have their relationship with their biological parents legally terminated. In 2008 alone, this occurred for roughly 64,084 children in foster care.[26] Current law makes such termination far easier than in the past, on the assumptions that many families who need state support are irrevocably broken, that the state can do nothing to mitigate their problems, and that the children of such families would be better off elsewhere.[27] Yet because of the shortage of families willing to adopt from this pool of children, many of them will languish in foster care for years.[28] For example, in 2010, about 53,000 children were adopted from foster care. This left 107,000 children in the system waiting to be adopted.[29] Older children, African-American children, and children with disabilities have a particularly poor chance of being adopted.[30] As a result, many children will linger in foster care until they "age out" of the system, an upbringing that is devastating based on almost any measure of wellbeing.[31] Even for those children who do find adoptive families, the permanent separation from their birth families takes a wrenching emotional toll.[32]

This model also imposes heavy emotional costs on the tens of thousands of parents who lose their children every year, sometimes permanently, because they cannot meet the responsibility assigned to them. This toll falls disproportionately on the poor, who make up the vast majority of the parents involved in the foster care system.[33] African American parents similarly have their children removed at a far greater rate than their counterparts.[34] Many of these parents cannot afford the conditions and services—decent housing, medical care, mental health care, adequate child care while they work—that the current system requires parents to provide their children.[35] That poor children are removed from their parents at such disproportionate rates, and that so many of these children are African American, poses a strong challenge to the foundational belief that basic rights, including the right to rear one's own children, should not depend on a person's wealth or race.

Finally, the dominant model imposes heavy costs on the state, both financial and otherwise. At first glance this model seems relatively cost-effective because it assumes that parents alone can and should bear financial responsibility for children. However, at closer inspection, this turns out not to be the case. A study by the Urban Institute calculated that states spent upward of 22 billion dollars on child welfare funding in 2002 from federal, state, and local sources, most of it for foster care,[36] and that is only what they paid directly. The vast indirect financial costs resulting from the damage to children under the prevailing system resulting from juvenile delinquency, loss of productivity, and adult criminality are far higher—by one estimate 103.8 billion dollars annually.[37] Even more important are the vast non-financial costs to the polity from having hundreds of thousands of its most vulnerable citizens, each of whom should be developing their capabilities to become flourishing adults and productive members of society, instead become physically, mentally, and emotionally damaged, many of them for life, by the current system.

In sum, the current foster care system is premised on a conception of the relationship between families and the state that serves no one's interests well, most particularly children's. In it, state support for children's welfare is largely limited to the coercive removal of children from their families only after their families have "failed." The consequence is a system that is costly to the polity, excruciating for parents, and, most importantly, devastating to children.

The Supportive State and Children's Welfare

In contrast to the current child welfare system, the supportive state's approach is premised on the view that children's welfare is a concurrent rather than residual responsibility of the state, and that this responsibility is best met through supporting families in the normal course of events. In assuming a role as an active partner in securing children's welfare, the state seeks to head off many problems before they become crises that require coercive intervention. In addition to the more-limited goal of preventing child maltreatment to at-risk children, this approach pursues the broader goal of supporting the development of flourishing children.

A necessary centerpiece of the supportive state's child welfare program is a set of policies designed to alleviate child poverty. As I mentioned earlier, the harms that poverty visits on children have significant effects on children's physical and mental health.[38] It also curtails their educational and employment prospects.[39] In addition, poverty prevents parents from establishing the conditions that their children need to stay safe,[40] and the stress associated with it elevates child maltreatment rates.[41]

Another central element of the supportive state's child welfare program would involve ensuring the availability of developmentally-enriching early education and childcare programs. Such programs not only keep children safe and well-supervised during a significant part of the day, clear evidence also links early education programs to a broad variety of other benefits for children. These include higher levels of education and employment for those who participate in them as children.[42] They also include more immediate benefits to children enrolled in some types of programs in the form of significantly

reduced levels of child maltreatment.[43] For older children, after-school programs that ensure children are cared for safely and constructively until their
parents return home from work are a basic, much-needed way for the state to
support children's well-being.[44]

All children should be ensured access to such programs. Yet the state has a
special responsibility to ensure access to low-income children, given welfare
regulations that require even primary caretakers with young children to participate in the paid workforce.[45]   In the absence of public provision of early
education programs, the state should subsidize these programs for low-income
families. France's model provides one example of how such a system could be
constructed. In contrast to the spotty subsidization and unregulated private
day care in the United States, in the French model, infants and toddlers from
three-months old have child care provided in day-care centers and day-care
homes, which are government licensed. For children from two-and-a-half to
five-years of age, subsidized preschools that are open until early evening are
provided. Cost is on a sliding-scale basis.[46]

The supportive state would also ensure sufficient access to low-income
housing so that parents have a decent home in which to raise their children.
Several studies show that a substantial percentage of children taken into foster
care, in some studies as high as 30 percent, could remain safely in their own
homes if their parents had access to decent housing.[47] The supportive state recognizes that it is more conducive to children's welfare to ensure decent housing with their own parents rather than with a stranger.

Likewise, policies that ensure access to mental health services and drug-
treatment programs would foster children's welfare and prevent the need for
coercive state intervention further down the road. A sizeable percentage of
children in the foster care system have parents with mental-health issues.[48]
Even more egregiously, between 35 and 85 percent of children entering foster
care need mental health treatment.[49] In fact, many of them enter the system
because their parents cannot afford the treatment they require.[50] Given that
the largest barrier to obtaining mental health services is the cost,[51] a supportive state would ensure the provision of affordable treatment to at-risk parents and children before they reach the point of crisis.[52] It would also ensure
that parents have access to publicly-funded substance- and alcohol-abuse
programs. Although studies implicate parental substance abuse in anywhere
between one-third and two-thirds of child maltreatment cases,[53] there is currently a severe shortage of treatment programs, particularly those suitable for
mothers with child-care responsibilities.[54] Once again, the supportive state
recognizes that providing these services to parents is more conducive to children's welfare than removing these children into foster care.

Finally, other spheres outside the family, including schools and neighborhoods, powerfully influence children's welfare. A supportive state would therefore ensure that these systems, too, are regulated in a manner that supports

children's well-being. The tight linkage between children's neighborhoods and their welfare means that the state should give priority to transforming blighted neighborhoods.[55] Such projects would not only reduce one of the risk factors for child maltreatment, they would increase the well-being of all of the community's citizens.

There can be little doubt that the implementation of this broad range of programs would require a significant financial investment on the part of the state. However, redirecting some of the more than $22 billion that federal, state, and local governments spend each year on the current child welfare system—most of it for foster care—would go far toward paying the bill for a system that truly supports children's welfare.[56] It would also avoid the much greater costs indirectly imposed on the polity after children who have been in the foster care system become adults. Even more importantly, the supportive state's system would help prevent the incalculable physical, mental, and emotional damage that now befalls hundreds of thousands of our most vulnerable citizens. In its place, it offers the possibility of supporting the development of sound children who will one day become vigorous and active citizens and productive members of society.

Would adopting the supportive state approach mean that the state would never have to coercively intervene in families, and be able to shut down foster care programs? Of course not. Even with all the institutional prerequisites in place, there will still be parents who either cannot or will not adequately protect their children's welfare. In these cases, the state should breach family privacy when it has reason to believe that parents are abusing or neglecting their children or are otherwise not raising them in a manner likely to produce at least minimally competent adult citizens. The "minimally competent" standard for intervention allows the state to step in on those occasions in which there is a significant risk of harm, but it helps prevent the state from overreaching in other cases. Setting a relatively high bar for coercive intervention helps protect against overzealous action by the state bureaucracy. The history of the child-welfare system in the United States is replete with instances in which state agents, many of them well meaning, have inappropriately removed children from their parents' care, particularly children from poor and minority families.[57]

In sum, the primary thrust of the state's efforts to improve children's welfare should come, not through coercively removing children from their homes, but through routinely supporting families and other institutions that profoundly affect the wellbeing of children. The broad scope of parental responsibilities and the intricate intertwining of parents' and children's lives make it unrealistic to expect that parents will always act in their children's best interests. However, the state can do far better than it currently does to establish conditions that facilitate parents' promoting their children's wellbeing and safety. It is in their homes, rather than removed from their families, that children have the best chance of growing into flourishing adults and sound citizens.

FAMILY PRIVACY AND CHILDREN'S INTERESTS

Even when abuse and neglect are not present, the issue of children's unequal power within families still remains. If the state gives families a wide berth for decision making, unless it takes some action to shore up children's rights within families, it will generally be their parents who make important decisions. I have already argued that inequality within families should be a cause for concern when it comes to adults, and should lead to the state taking measures to redress this inequality.[58] Should the state take similar measures when it comes to children?

The Family and Children's Rights

Children's rights advocates forcefully argue that a strong doctrine of family privacy leaves children subject to unconstrained subordination by their parents. They contend that family privacy therefore sacrifices children's welfare to parents' rights.[59] These advocates call for measures to redress the imbalance of power between children and their parents, for example, by giving children representation to argue their own interests in court in certain cases, and by lowering the standards for state intervention in families so that the state can safeguard children's rights.[60]

Although these advocates are certainly right that children's welfare must be given great weight, they are wrong with respect to the best means generally to further this goal. State support for families with a strong but not unlimited doctrine of parents' rights and family privacy better serves children's welfare than does a vigorous platform of state intervention and children's rights.[61] The fact of the matter is that parents are generally well motivated to act in children's interests. Bearing or rearing a child is certainly not a guarantee that parents will love their children and look out after their interests; in most instances, however, it works out that way. Indeed, in a culture like ours in which there is a strong expectation that individuals will put their own interests first, the extent to which most parents will sacrifice their own welfare for their children's should be nothing short of astounding. Parents will work for years in jobs that they despise in order to put food on the dinner table or pay for health care for their children. They will work second and sometimes third jobs to enable their children to get the best education that they can obtain. And they will sacrifice sleep, time for themselves, and social time with friends and spouses for years on end to ensure that they have adequate time for their children. Again, although this is not true for all parents all the time, it is true for most parents at most times.

There are other reasons, as well, to reject arguments that parental authority disserves children's interests. As Elizabeth and Robert Scott point out, for children to flourish, they require a strong bond with their parents.[62] To the extent that the state's reducing parents' rights to raise their children as they see fit weakens this bond, children's interests are disserved.

Furthermore, whether overruling parents' decisions will serve children's welfare must be assessed by considering whose judgment and efforts will replace parents'. Children generally lack the maturity and judgment to fill this role. As I suggested in Chapter 2, autonomy, properly conceived as reasoned self-government, is not a capacity that simply springs up fully formed in humans; instead, it matures over time.[63] Although their opinions should generally be heard, children are still often not the best judges of their own long-term interests. While parents are certainly not infallible, they are generally better placed to ensure that children's long-term interests are pursued than are children themselves.

Neither is the state generally better positioned to second-guess parents' decisions or more motivated to act on children's behalf. The state can ascertain whether children have what they need to achieve some minimal standard of development—for example, that they have adequate food, shelter, and supervision. Over and above this threshold, however, it becomes far more difficult for the state to say what is in children's best interests without implicating comprehensive views of the good life, a position that the liberal state, with its respect for pluralism, should seek to avoid.[64] Furthermore, most decisions about children above this basic threshold require knowledge about the individual child and are, therefore, better made by parents than the state. Finally, state actors, even when they are diligent, will generally be less motivated to act on children's behalf than will parents.

This is not to say that parents will always act in their child's best interests rather than their own. Nor would we expect them to do this. Parents are human and have needs and desires apart from their children. Sometimes these needs and desires will conflict with their children's, and parents should not always have to choose their children's interests over their own. (Get up 20 minutes early to prepare a healthy, from-scratch school lunch, or sleep those extra 20 minutes and once again pack the cheese sandwich?) Indeed, always looking after their children's interests rather than their own is probably not a parenting position that could be sustained in the long term. Rather than seeking to police parents' choices to promote children's welfare, the state, in the absence of abuse or neglect, would do better to try to ameliorate possible conflicts between parents' and children's interests in order to make it easier for parents to support caretaking and human development. For example, instituting reasonable regulations on the hours that most employees are required to work would reduce the time pressures on families and therefore make it easier for parents to spend more time with their children. Likewise, the state's ensuring that employees have adequate leave time after the birth or adoption of a child can keep new parents from being so exhausted that they spend their child-care time in front of a television rather than more actively engaged with their child.

The Family and Adolescents

I have been discussing childhood as if it were a state in which children are at all times helpless beings who are completely dependent on their parents and other caregivers. Obviously this is a distortion of reality. Childhood is not a static state of dependency until the point at which children cross some magical line into adulthood, when they suddenly acquire maturity, judgment, and a host of other faculties. Instead, children mature over time into adults— sometimes gradually, and sometimes in fits and starts—and they make progress on some measures at different rates than others. There is no single point in time at which children can be conceived to transform into adults for all purposes.

Rather than reflecting the process of children's gradual development, the law typically deals with adolescence by ignoring it. In our system, children are generally deemed completely incompetent in a particular policy context until a designated point in time, when they are suddenly declared competent.[65] In this framework, childhood and adulthood are conceived as binary positions, rather than as part of a continuous spectrum.[66] At age 17, adolescents are considered children who are not allowed to vote; at age 18, they have full voting rights. At 20, they are deemed children who are too young to buy alcohol; at 21, they are adults who may purchase alcohol in any state. Generally, the law's dealing with adolescence in this manner works adequately.[67] As Elizabeth Scott notes, this system fosters at least a somewhat gradual transition into full adulthood by designating adolescents to be adults at different ages in different policy contexts.[68] This gives adolescents experience in shouldering some responsibilities without having to shoulder them all at the same time.

There will, of course, always be some adolescents who reach maturity earlier than the age at which they are legally recognized to be mature. Yet, the administrative costs to assess maturity in every individual case make it reasonable to deny them the relevant right until they reach the designated age.[69] Furthermore, having a bright-line age of 18 at which adolescents are declared adults for the purpose of emancipation from their parents also works tolerably well. So long as this bright-line rule also permits judicial emancipation of older minors who are sufficiently mature and who have important reasons not to wait for emancipation, the statutory scheme is a reasonable one for dealing with children's passage to adulthood.

Decision making within families, though, ideally will not directly track this legal model. Although children's interests are not well served by giving them formal legal rights to assert themselves against parents, parents should still listen to their children's views and take them into account. Liberalism's respect for autonomy and its closely-connected respect for human dignity counsels that adolescents' views of who they are and what is in their interests be given some weight, even if their judgments are not yet completely mature.[70] For adolescents to one day assume the responsibilities of adult citizens, they need considerable practice at decision making before that time. Ideally, their parents will give them gradually increasing responsibility as they mature, so that they are competent decision makers by the time they strike out on their own.[71] With that said, granting children legal rights against their parents is a poor vehicle to serve these objectives. Thus, parents' determinations about the friends with whom their teens may spend time, what time their curfew is, what school to send their children to, and whether they may get a tattoo should generally be left unquestioned by the state.

There are particular situations, however, in which the supportive state should make exceptions to the general rule of broad parental authority. In situations involving access to birth control, and treatment for sexually transmitted diseases, drug or alcohol abuse, and mental-health issues, there are good reasons to allow minors to consent to treatment on their own. This is not because minors have especially mature judgment in these areas; instead, it is because of the pragmatic concern that requiring parental consent will mean that children will not get treatment or contraceptives that it is in their interest to receive.[72] Put another way, in these situations, the threat to children's long-term welfare tips the scales in favor of allowing them decision making power. For this reason, a number of states allow adolescents birth control without parental consent, not because they believe these teens are ready for sex, but rather because of a concern that they will engage in sex anyway and, if parental consent for contraceptives is required, they will do so without birth control.

Minors and Abortion

The thorniest issue that arises with respect to how much control parents should have over their teens' lives occurs when teenage girls seek access to abortion. This issue has been the subject of extensive and intense political and legal controversy, in which participants have often taken their larger ideological views about abortion and sought to apply them to pregnant girls. Thus, opponents of abortion have argued that parents should be able to veto their daughters' decisions to obtain an abortion; meanwhile, pro-choice advocates have argued that pregnant teens should be treated as adults and should therefore be given the unrestricted right to consent to abortions. In the discussion that follows, I take as a given that abortion is a constitutional right for adult women, and consider only the manner and extent to which this right should be adjusted for pregnant teens, if indeed it should be adjusted at all. In doing so, I base my discussion on the admittedly large assumption that any difference between minors' and women's access to abortion should be grounded on the special circumstances imposed by their youth.

Although the supportive state should let parents be the final judges regarding most decisions about their teenagers, several reasons strongly counsel against giving them veto power over their child's abortion decision. First, given that abortion is currently a constitutionally-protected right for women, any power parents have to curtail their minor daughters' access should be exercised to protect daughters from immature decision making, rather than to interpose parents' own moral standards.[73] Abortion, however, involves a highly-contested moral choice about which different people reach different conclusions. Because of this, there are reasons to fear that parents will make this decision based on their own morality, rather than based on a determination of what is right for their child or what their child would decide if she were more mature.

Further, the decision of whether to carry a pregnancy to term or to terminate it is intimately related to bodily integrity, which, in our culture, is inextricably linked with one's very subjectivity. The body is not just a container for the "real" person within; instead, it is the embodied subject—the "I."[74] Courts invoke this concept when they insist that one's body is uniquely one's own to make decisions about, subjecting even relatively bodily minimal invasions of one's body to the highest degree of scrutiny. Given the centrality of the abortion decision to this conception of subjectivity, we should give great pause before allowing the abortion decision to be made by someone other than the teenager whose body is involved.

The critical link between the abortion decision and individual autonomy is compounded by the enormous implications this decision will have for the future course of the teen's life. As Justice Powell pointed out in determining the scope of teens' right to choose abortion:

> [T]he potentially severe detriment facing a pregnant woman ... is not mitigated by her minority. Indeed, considering her probable education, employment skills, financial resources, and emotional maturity, unwanted motherhood may be exceptionally burdensome for a minor. In addition, the fact of having a child brings with it adult legal responsibility, for parenthood, like attainment of the age of majority, is one of the traditional criteria for the termination of the legal disabilities of minority ... [T]here are few situations in which denying a minor the right to make an important decision will have consequences so grave and indelible.[75]

Refusing to allow a teen to make this decision for herself therefore imposes profound consequences on her, which will likely have deep and abiding effects on the trajectory of her life, without her consent.

The teens' interest in making this decision is especially acute because the abortion decision is only available for a short window of time. Most other decisions that parents make for their children postpone the teens' desires only temporarily. This is the case, for example, with a teen whose parents refuse to permit her to enlist in the military or to marry before she is legally eligible to consent. In contrast, the abortion decision is definitively time-contingent. The possibility of obtaining an abortion expires in, at most, months, and sometimes weeks or days. And once the time period for this decision passes, it can never again be regained.

Taken together, these reasons strongly counsel against giving parents an absolute veto over their pregnant daughter's abortion decision. What, then, about instead requiring the teen to notify her parents about the abortion decision? Given the moral complexity of the decision—a decision that many adult women find extremely difficult to resolve—the requirement that pregnant teens consult with their parents, who know them best and have more mature judgment, has considerable appeal.[76] There are, however, problems with even a parental notification requirement.

Although in an ideal world all pregnant adolescents would discuss the abortion decision with their parents, we do not live in an ideal world. In the world we live in, some teens vehemently resist telling their parents. For some, this is because of the fear of disappointing them, or angering them, or of being thrown out of the house. For others, this is because telling their parents raises a reasonable fear of domestic violence.[77] A small but still significant number will not tell their parents because the pregnancy is the product of incest. Regardless of the merit of their reasons, a blanket parental notification requirement keeps teens who cannot bring themselves to tell their parents about their pregnancy from obtaining an abortion.[78] Even if the teen is being ridiculous and immature in refusing to notify parents who would be both helpful and understanding, it is far from clear that a ridiculous and immature teenage girl who does not want to have a baby will be well served by giving birth to one. If the ultimate goal of parental notification laws is to ensure that teens think through their decisions and have abortions when it is truly in their best interest to do so, but not to have abortions when it is not in their best interest, requiring parental involvement in all cases falls short of this goal. Under this system, some teens will be unwilling to have the conversation and will, therefore, wind up having children even when it would be in their best interests to have an abortion.

States that adopt parental notification requirements would seem, at first glance, to leave a sufficient "out" for teens by allowing them to bypass parental notice through exercising a (constitutionally mandated) right to petition in court to obtain an abortion.[79] In this bypass procedure, the court may approve the teen's obtaining the abortion in the absence of parental notification if the minor demonstrates that she is sufficiently mature to make the abortion decision herself. If the court finds she is not sufficiently mature, it can still approve her obtaining an abortion if it determines that the procedure is in her best interests.[80] The rationale supporting parental notification with such a judicial bypass option is sound: It encourages pregnant teens to discuss this important decision with their parents; but those who cannot or will not do so will have their best interests protected through the bypass procedure.

In practice, however, judicial bypass procedures do not have this effect. As Carol Sanger points out, empirical studies of these provisions show that they have largely been passed in order to thwart teenagers' access to abortions, and have been relatively successful at achieving this goal.[81] It turns out that a substantial number of minors who will not notify their parents of their desire to seek an abortion are also deterred from filing bypass petitions because of the uncertainty of the court's decision, the need to skip school without their parents' knowledge, the difficulty in getting transportation to the courthouse, and the need to disclose intimate details of their sexual activity and their home life in court. The net result is that teen abortions drop significantly after the implementation of parental notification laws, even with bypass procedures, because teens are deterred from exercising their bypass rights.[82] Further, even when teens do file bypass petitions, judges seldom conduct a reasoned assessment of the merits of the case. Instead, they generally either sign all petitions presented to them or deny them all, depending on their personal views of abortion. The vast majority approve them, probably on the view that teens too young to consent to an abortion on their own would be better served by an abortion because they are not sufficiently mature to have a child.[83]

The supportive state can and should do better than current parental notification laws. While teens should still be encouraged to notify their parents, for those who cannot or will not discuss this issue with them, the goal should be to set up a system that still supports teens thinking through their available options clearly, without deterring those who believe abortion is in their interests from engaging in this process. One possible model of this ilk would allow pregnant teens to substitute for parental consent proof of counseling by an authorized counselor with whom she has discussed pregnancy, abortion, adoption, and state support for children. Allowing consultation with a counselor encourages the teen to discuss this difficult decision with a mature adult, even if she will not discuss it with her parents. Yet it should not have the deterrence effect that judicial bypass requirements do.[84] This model therefore recognizes the teen's interest in autonomy without assuming her judgment is as developed as it one day will be. It also seeks to safeguard the teen's best interests at the same time that it recognizes the importance of the parental tie by fostering communication between the teen and her parents.

THE FAMILY, THE STATE, AND CHILDREN'S UPBRINGING

A final set of issues concerning children's place in families relates to the extent that parents should control children's upbringing. In a liberal democracy that places a high value on individual autonomy and family privacy, we should start with the baseline assumption that parents should generally be able to raise their children as they see fit. This starting point takes into account how central the rearing of children is to many citizens' life plans. It also recognizes that parents are generally the people who love their children most and will most vigorously pursue their interests. These considerations, however, are not the only important ones at stake in how children are reared. After all, children are not only members of their families, they are also members of the polity, in which they will one day assume the mantle of collective self-rule. Because of this, the state has a strong interest in ensuring that children acquire the civic virtues and skills needed to be competent citizens. In addition, even apart from protecting the polity's own interests, the state has the responsibility to safeguard children's interests. As part of this responsibility, the state has a duty to ensure that children develop their capacity for autonomy. Ensuring the development of children's civic virtues and autonomy, though, requires a delicate negotiation with the principle of family privacy.

Civic Virtues

Throughout most of this book, I have argued that strong families do not just simply happen. Instead they require both the presence of particular conditions and a good deal of effort. The same is true for a healthy polity. A vigorous liberal democracy requires that its citizens possess certain virtues in order to flourish. Until recently, when scholars of liberal democracy paid attention to the need for civic virtues at all, they tended to minimize the virtues that citizens needed. In this view, because we live in a representative democracy, in which few citizens' involvement in collective self-rule extends beyond voting every few years, citizens require only minimal civic skills.[85]

The events of the last decade have not been kind to this view. The many failures to institute democracy in the Middle East during this period demonstrate that the simple holding of democratic elections is not enough to develop or sustain a liberal democracy dedicated to equal freedom for all. Recent history in the United States has also shown that the presence of a range of liberal democratic institutions is not enough to assure a government committed to political equality, the rule of law, and to the protection of the rights of its citizens. Without a citizenry committed to liberal democratic principles, we have seen, these institutional structures are susceptible to manipulation and abuse.

Among other things, a flourishing liberal democracy requires that citizens develop a commitment to political equality among citizens and to the protection of basic individual rights. As Eamonn Callan convincingly argues, young citizens must also come to accept what he calls, after John Rawls, "the burdens of judgment." By this, he means that they must come to recognize that reasonable people can and will disagree about fundamental issues surrounding the good life and religion, and that disagreements about such "comprehensive philosophies" cannot be resolved by any mutually accessible standards. Accordingly, citizens in a polity committed to individual freedom and pluralism must come to endorse the view that the power of the state should not be used to foist such comprehensive views on others.[86] In addition, citizens need to develop some capacity and willingness for autonomous thought and action: Without some independence of mind and spirit, citizens may become too easily led by the government, and too quick to believe inadequate justifications and explanations. ("They hate us because of our freedom.")

Families, however, sometimes function in ways that discourage the development of these traits and dispositions in children. May a state seek to remedy these deficiencies? Parents who discourage these traits inadvertently may not object to the state seeking to develop the requisite virtues in their children. Those parents who themselves reject liberal democratic norms, however, may have strong objections to such lessons. The depth of their response is understandable: There can be no doubt that parents have a deep investment in the people that their children will become. As Stephen Gilles observes: "For the overwhelming majority, the loving relationships we share with our spouses, our children, our siblings, and the parents who educated us are at the heart of our individual conceptions of the good life."[87] Therefore, Gilles argues, parents rather than the state should generally have the last word on how their children are raised.

Certainly when it comes to parents who strongly hold illiberal beliefs, such as those espoused by some fundamentalist Christians, the state's seeking to foster particular liberal democratic dispositions and virtues in their children could therefore come as a harsh blow. For example, the state's seeking to ensure that children are exposed to the deep differences in belief that exist in our pluralist society, and that they come to recognize the burdens of judgment, could do significant damage to these parents' attempts to pass on to their children their belief that there is only one correct path in life.[88] For them, morals and commitments are ordained by God or the natural moral order. To the extent that the state seeks to ensure that children learn to respect the possibility that there are other ways of life out there that make similar claims, and are exposed to the idea that some moral precepts are susceptible to critical evaluation and their adoption subject to voluntary choice, this education has the potential to undermine central tenets of these parents' views.[89]

Yet even recognizing the weighty interests that parents have in raising their children, and the profound damage that could be done to some parents' life plans by their children developing liberal democratic virtues, the state's interest in developing these virtues must still trump. The difficult enterprise of maintaining a vigorous liberal democracy requires imposing some constraints on individual liberty when it conflicts with other important goods, including civic virtue. These constraints on parents' liberty are necessary to securing liberty itself.[90] Those who contend that parents' private interests in rearing their children should be weighed more heavily than the state's miss a critical point: Without the state's ensuring that liberal democratic virtues are widely dispersed in the population, the state cannot sustain a liberal democracy capable of protecting the individual freedoms these parents seek to assert. An illiberal populace is more likely to support infringements on personal freedom. Its state would also need to exercise stricter controls on citizens because they would be less likely to respect the basic principles of liberal democracy. Accordingly, if respect for parents' autonomy could preclude children from developing civic virtues, still more extensive infringements on citizens' autonomy would result.

Furthermore, it must be recognized that the risks to personal liberties from allowing parents to pass on illiberal views do not fall equally on all citizens; instead, they fall particularly on citizens who are members of disfavored groups. Citizens not well-versed in liberal democratic ideals are far more likely to tyrannize marginalized groups, and to deny them political equality simply on the basis of their own comprehensive views, divorced from public reason. The political events of the past few years surrounding same-sex marriage represent one flagrant example of some citizens' efforts to continue to marginalize gays and lesbians based on their own comprehensive belief systems. The largest price for not teaching civic virtues out of deference to parents therefore will not be paid by the parents, or even by the polity generally, but rather by the political minorities who bear the brunt of the majority's illiberal impulses. While dashing of some of the hopes of parents who earnestly hold illiberal views for the persons whom their children will become should not be taken lightly, the rights of political minorities to the fundamental promise of liberal democracy should not be sacrificed for them.

Accordingly, although parents should generally be allowed to raise children as they see fit, their autonomy is limited not only by prohibitions on abuse and neglect, but also by the requirement that children must be educated for civic virtue. Put another way, simply because parents hold views contrary to liberal democratic ideals, the state is not required simply to fold its tent and go home. As Stephen Macedo counsels, liberal democracy's respect for pluralism requires that the state allow citizens to espouse illiberal views and to practice these views in their own lives. It does not, however, require that the state give such views a level playing field when it comes to the next generation.[91] For the state to do so would recall Robert Frost's definition of a liberal as someone who cannot defend themselves in an argument.[92] Instead, the state may and should educate children for civic virtue precisely because of the freedom it values so dearly.

To what extent should the state's duty to educate children for civic virtues cause it to seek to influence the ways that families function? Feminist theorists have for some time argued that families' failure to model norms such as sex equality impede development of critical civic virtues in children. If families are "not environments in which justice is normally practiced, work equally shared, and people treated with equal dignity and respect," how will children be able to develop a sense of justice?[93] As Nancy Rosenblum points out, however, ensuring congruence between the norms that families model and liberal democratic virtues is necessary only if children cannot develop these virtues outside their families.[94] In Rosenblum's words, even if children do not see particular virtues modeled at home, the disposition for these virtues "can be shaped on the playground, at school, in secondary associations, and at work."[95] No doubt that Rosenblum is largely right: There are other ways to develop children's dispositions for many liberal democratic virtues that do not depend on the lessons that parents communicate at home. For example, it is only because the disposition for gender justice could be developed outside of families that second-wave feminism could emerge in the 1970s from the young women raised in the patriarchal 1950s. Many of these women gained their thirst for equality and justice not from the families in which they were raised, but from their experiences outside of them, including the antiwar movement and feminist consciousness-raising groups.[96]

Three tenets that should guide the supportive state when it comes to children's civic education follow from this discussion. First, to the extent possible, the state should seek to develop liberal democratic virtues in children through institutions other than the family. Doing so preserves the good of family privacy to the extent possible, even if it does not leave parental autonomy unbounded. The most important institution aside from families in which liberal democratic dispositions can be developed is clearly the public schools. However, the requisite traits can also be fostered by the state in other places, including community centers responsible for after-school care and activities, civic service programs, and even (through state regulation) private schools.

Second, the state should gently encourage families to function in ways congruent with liberal democratic norms. I have already discussed public policies by which the state can encourage families to move away from gendered family roles, including through use-it-or-lose-it family leave for fathers.[97] The state can also use other means to nudge families toward congruence with liberal democratic norms: For example, celebrating Martin Luther King, Jr.'s birthday as a federal holiday encourages parents to raise awareness about civil rights and the importance of equality.

Third, and finally: Where civic virtues cannot be developed in children without more significant interventions in family decision making, the state should seek to minimize the extent of the intrusions on parental autonomy. It may be the case, for example, that some children who are home schooled do not have adequate opportunity to develop liberal democratic dispositions. If this is so, the state should seek to redress this deficit by more minimal interventions, such as requiring these children to attend after-school programs. Only if these alternatives prove impracticable or unsuccessful should the state move to bigger interventions, such as banning home schooling entirely and requiring children to attend brick-and-mortar schools.

Autonomy

Not only does the state have the responsibility to ensure the development of civic virtue in children, it must also ensure that they develop autonomy. An integral part of liberalism's conception of the value of human life is the notion that one's life plans and commitments are, on some basic level, *owned* by the person who holds them. This does not mean that persons must have consciously chosen this plan or built every aspect of it from scratch. It does, however, mean that they could renegotiate the plan if they determined it no longer suited them.[98] As Eamonn Callan succinctly puts it, at a bare minimum, each child "must learn to ask the question of how we should live, and … how we answer it can be no servile echo of the answers others have given, even if our thoughts commonly turn out to be substantially the same as those that informed our parents' lives."[99] This prohibition on ethical servility means that parents cannot foreclose a child's ability to pursue other ways of life than the parents' own. The state has a duty to foster this threshold level of autonomy in children even over their parents' objections: Liberalism does not allow one person to serve simply as a pawn to satisfy another's life plan, even when the other person is a parent.

Of course, many parents who seek to prevent their children from developing autonomy are no mere hypocrites. They have themselves abjured the norm of autonomy in their own lives. Or, rather, as both Michael Sandel and Nomi Stolzenberg point out, they do not see themselves as *choosing to reject* the norm of autonomy, but rather see themselves as *having been chosen* for another course.[100] To these parents, the state's seeking to foster children's capacity for autonomy hijacks children from their proper course in life. To some parents, the state's actions risk setting children on the road to eternal damnation.

Despite the strength of these parents' beliefs, the liberal state cannot tolerate what Eamonn Callan refers to as "parental despotism."[101] Liberalism gives considerable weight to parents' life plans because it conceives these plans as embodiments of the free will these citizens possess and the commitments they have made. Respecting these plans is therefore essential to respecting their human dignity. The very reason for giving serious attention to parents' desires for their children's education requires denying their desires to keep their children ethically servile: Insofar as the parents' claims are based on liberalism's respect for individuals' choices about their path in life, it cannot be used to deny those parents' children the same opportunity to choose their own paths.[102]

The extent of the autonomy that the state should promote, however, is the subject of some disagreement. Several scholars argue that the state should do more than ensure children are not ethically servile: it should encourage children to distance themselves from their parents' ways of life.[103] Most prominently, Eamonn Callan suggests that the state should encourage children to see their life paths as open and subject to their own choice.[104] Callan calls this type of education "educating for the 'Great Sphere,'" after Bruce Ackerman's description of a liberal education focused on developing autonomy. In Callan's words:

> The essential demand is that schooling properly involves at some stage sympathetic and critical engagement with beliefs and ways of life at odds with the culture of the family or religious or ethnic group into which the child is born. Moreover, the relevant engagement must be such that the beliefs and values by which others live are entertained not merely as sources of meaning in *their* lives; they are instead addressed as potential elements within the conceptions of the good and the right one will create for oneself as an adult.[105]

The purpose of this education, according to Callan, is to help children "explore the globe in a way that permits them to glimpse the deeper meanings of the dramas passing on around them. At the end of the journey, however, the now mature citizen has every right to locate himself at the very point from which he began—[or] to strike out to discover an unoccupied portion of the sphere."[106] Taking a similar tack, Meira Levinson argues that a key function of the state in promoting children's autonomy is to "balance[] out a current maldistribution of power that unjustly favors parents" by encouraging children to think about different ways of life other than their own.[107]

The supportive state, however, over and above instilling the threshold level of autonomy necessary to prevent ethical servility, does not seek to dampen parents' ability to pass on their way of life to their children. There is a big difference between ensuring that children are not ethically servile and teaching them to become so detached from their parents' way of life that they consider it merely as one among a series of equally-weighted alternatives. The supportive state endorses the former position, but not the latter. Autonomy, as Thomas Spragens advises, is a good that should be optimized, not maximized.[108] We value it as an intrinsic element in a fully human life; yet a life spent pursuing as much autonomy as possible could lead citizens to see themselves as rootless, and to have no firm sense of an ethical perspective.[109] Liberalism demands that one's background and ties cannot completely dictate the person's future, at least without one's autonomous assent; it does not require, however, that they count for nothing. To suggest otherwise would justify Stephen Macedo's likening of liberal culture to Californian culture—in which people constantly try on new lifestyles and principles without buying wholeheartedly into any of them (besides that of personal freedom).[110]

The supportive state recognizes that seeking to instill such a heightened sense of autonomy would undercut the legitimate hopes of many parents that their children will grow up connected to their way of life.[111] Parents' vision of successful parenting will seldom involve introducing their children to a way of life completely foreign to their own; instead, parents generally hope to introduce their children to their religious traditions, their political principles, their ethnic heritage, even their sports teams. We want our children to be comfortable with our working-class roots; to understand the Polish-American culture of our family; or, as the children of Holocaust survivors, to internalize the motto "never again." We want these things not only because we see our children in some sense as extensions of ourselves, and their life plans as—at least in some way—an extension of our own, but also because so much that is significant to parents about parenting involves the relationship between parent and child. In Robert Reich's words, "[r]aising a child is never merely a service rendered unto another person but is the collective sharing of a life."[112] We therefore want our children to understand and identify with us.

For many, though not all parents, the point is not necessarily to have the child live the same life or adopt exactly the same principles; many of us hope our children achieve better lives than those we have lived—with more education, more wealth, more achievements, and so forth. But even as we want them to surpass us, we also want them to understand and accept their roots, to be comfortable returning to our households, and to appreciate the meaning of our rituals.[113] Children must be given the tools to withdraw from such ways of life when they cannot embody this identity from the inside out. They do not, however, need to be given a hand-engraved invitation to create their identity from scratch when they would be comfortable with forging a life out of material closer to home. To teach children that their parents' conception of the good is only one of a multitude that children should consider equally carefully for adoption does not do justice to parents' legitimate hopes for raising their children.[114]

Indeed, the view that parents should stamp their imprint on their children as lightly as possible rests on a misguided notion of what happens in childrearing.[115] To begin with, although children certainly do not come into the world simply as blank slates, neither do they come into the world with a completely developed personality simply waiting to unfold. Rather, the person a child will eventually become results from the complex relationship between the child and her environment, including her family. In the course of her rearing, some of the child's traits will inevitably be fostered and others dampened.

Furthermore, the very process of parenting involves a sharing of one's own life that cannot but influence the child's identity. Just as we love our children not because they are the best children in the world, but because they are ours, so children come to identify with their parents and family because of their relationship with them. David Archard demonstrates this by the example of a father who takes his child to see a sports team play:

> Such trips are one of the important activities father and son share. Inasmuch as the father visibly supports the team it is hard to see how the son would not come to share this passion... This is, it should be noted, not simply a case of a parent choosing for his son, of the son's life merely being an 'extension' of the father. It is a genuine case of sharing.....[116]

Insofar as parenting involves sharing one's life with a child, it necessarily involves communicating one's passions to one's children, whether these be sailing, community service, watching sports together, or gardening. Sharing these activities is important for a number of reasons, including allowing children to get to know their parents; teaching them the value of engaging in activities that fulfill one's passions; and for the more practical reason of allowing parents to retain some of their own pleasures while still fulfilling the responsibilities of parenting. Doing so, however, will inevitably influence the child's sense of self and of what activities are worth engaging in.

The point is that children develop special affinities—for their families, for their local sports team, for particular songs—not because these things are especially good in an objective sense, or because we would choose them if we stepped back and made this choice solely on a rational basis—but because it is *our* family or team or song. In Amy Gutmann's words,

> We need not claim moral superiority (or ownership) to say any of this. We need claim only that some ways of life are better than others *for us and our children* because these orientations impart meaning to and enrich the internal life of family and society. To focus exclusively on the value of freedom, or even on the value of moral freedom, neglects the value that parents and citizens may legitimately place on *particularly* prejudicing the choices of children by their familial and political heritages.[117]

So long as these attachments forged in children go hand in hand with their capacity to rethink them should they decide they are not a good fit, the state should not encourage young citizens to distance themselves from these attachments.

Parents' influence on their children's personalities is not only an inevitable fact, it is also, on the whole, a good thing.[118] Encouraging children to see their future as unconditionally open to all possibilities risks undercutting the liberal, democratic and other virtues that parents, schools, and society seek to instill in children. We do not, in educating our children, really want them to wind up any place at all on the moral globe; we instead want them to be good, responsible citizens and family members. Our being successful at instilling these values, of course, limits children's futures and decreases their freedom by making some paths less possible than they would otherwise be. Yet this is as it should be. As Shelley Burtt wisely counsels, "The question is not how little impact a parent can make on a child's view of the world (how neutral parenting can be) but how fully parents can discharge their obligation to guide children to a productive, satisfying adulthood."[119] Parents need not introduce the golden rule as one that a child could as easily reject as accept; they may and should instead impress its importance on children.[120]

In sum, while the state must ensure that children are not ethically servile to their parents, its duty to educate children for autonomy does not require more.[121] There are good reasons why parents should have a thumb on the scales when it comes to the lives their children will lead. The state should ensure that parents do not take away the scales from their children entirely, and should ensure that the scales are not so weighted in favor of parents' views that children have no capacity or realistic option of rethinking them. But except to ensure these things, the state should generally not seek to counterbalance parents' thumbs.

Taking this stance allows the supportive state to do justice both to children's membership in their family and the polity. Befitting children's membership in their family, parents may generally bring children up to adopt parents' own beliefs and creeds. Befitting children's membership in the polity, the state should seek to ensure their commitment to liberal democratic virtues and that they are not ethically servile. Where these two goals conflict, the supportive state should remedy gaps in children's education through institutions other than the family to the extent possible. Ensuring the presence of more than one domain in which children can develop their commitments helps ensure that failings in one domain can be compensated for in the other. In addition, the presence of two educators who are both conjunctively responsible for developing children's sense of themselves in the world reduces the possibility that either may so completely dominate children's perspectives that they fail to develop the critical perspective necessary to be good citizens or lead full lives.

CONCLUSION

The supportive state transforms family privacy from the last word in the conversation over state action to the introduction of this conversation. Supporting family privacy, in its view, requires state action to help ensure that strong families have strong capabilities, rather than simply requiring that the state leave families to themselves. Furthermore, family privacy is no longer the be-all end-all of state policy. It is instead an important good that the state should support alongside other important goods, including children's welfare, human development, and civic virtues. To the extent possible, the supportive state should seek policies that ameliorate the tension among these goods. Where head-to-head conflicts between family privacy and other liberal democratic goods still remain, however, there are some cases in which the high cost of maintaining family privacy means it must give way to other important goods. These tradeoffs are inevitable where there are a range of important goods that must be fostered, as is the case in any flourishing liberal democracy.[122]

NOTES

INTRODUCTION

1 I use the terms *liberal theory, liberal,* and *liberalism* throughout this book to refer to the Anglo-American line of political thought stretching from John Locke through John Stuart Mill and on to such recent thinkers as John Rawls that focuses on the importance of liberty, self-government, and the equal worth of citizens. This use of the term is therefore broader than the use of the term *liberal* in common parlance to refer to those who hold political beliefs at the opposite end of the political spectrum from conservatives. Under my use of the term, both Speaker of the House of Representatives Nancy Pelosi, who qualifies as a liberal under common usage, and Supreme Court Justice Antonin Scalia, who is generally considered a political conservative, are liberals.

2 See Martha Nussbaum, "The Future of Feminist Liberalism," in Eva Feder Kittay and Ellen K. Feder (Eds.), *The Subject of Care: Feminist Perspectives on Dependency* (Lantham, MD: Rowman & Littlefield, 2002), 186.

3 In 2005, 10.8 million people (4.7 %) over the age of 15 reported having one or more disabilities for which they required assistance with daily activities. (Matthew W. Brault, Current Population Reports, "Americans With Disabilities: 2005," 4 [2008], available at http://www.census.gov/prod/2008pubs/p70-117.pdf [accessed Aug. 5, 2009]).

According to a report based on 2002 census data that considered the duration of disabilities, "more people reported needing assistance for 1 to 5 years (40.7 %) than reported needing help for less than 1 year (23.3 %) or needing help for more than 5 years (34.1 %)" (Erika Steinmetz, Current Population Reports, "Americans With Disabilities: 2002," 7 [May, 2006], available at http://www.census.gov/prod/2006pubs/p70-107.pdf [accessed Aug. 5, 2009]).

4 The number of adults requiring assistance for one or more daily activities increases for each subsequent age group: 1.9 percent for those 25–44, 3.4 percent for those 45–54, 5.7 percent for those 55–64, 7.6 percent for those 65–69, 9.6 percent for those 70–74, 16.1 percent for those 75–79, 29.2 percent for those 80 and over (M. W. Brault, "Americans With Disabilities: 2005," 3, 4).

5 See ibid. As the demographers at the U.S. Census Bureau summed up disability levels in the elderly population: "20 percent of older Americans have chronic

disability, about 7 percent to 8 percent have severe cognitive impairments, and about 30 percent experience mobility difficulty. Census 2000 counted about 14 million civilian noninstitutionalized older people, representing 41.9 percent of the older population, who had some type of disability" (Wan He, Manisha Sengupta, Victoria A. Velkoff and Kimberly A. DeBarros, Current Population Reports: Special Studies, "65+ in the United States: 2005," 59 [2005], available at http://www.census.gov/prod/2006pubs/p23–209.pdf [accessed Aug. 5, 2009] [citations omitted]). Roughly 40 percent of adults aged 75 or older cannot perform one or more daily activities, such as meal preparation and eating, bathing, dressing, toileting, and walking or driving by themselves (National Academy on an Aging Society, "Caregiving: Helping the Elderly with Activity Limitations," 2 [2000], available at http://www.agingsociety.org/agingsociety/pdf/Caregiving.pdf [accessed March 8, 2010]). According to the Census Bureau, although the disability rates of the elderly population are declining, that population is on the threshold of a boom, as Baby Boomers begin to turn 65 beginning in 2011. By 2030, the population of senior citizens is expected to have doubled from its 2000 rate, growing from 35 million to 72 million, and representing 20 percent of the total U.S. population at the latter date. This will mean that there will be many more senior citizens with caretaking needs (Wan He, "65+ In the United States 2005," 60).

6 In addition to caring for children, a 2003 study by the National Alliance for Caregiving and the AARP estimated that there are 44.4 million American care givers (21 percent of the adult population) who provide unpaid care to an adult age 18 or older. These caregivers are present in an estimated 22.9 million (21 percent) U.S. households (National Alliance for Caregiving and the AARP, "Caregiving in the U.S.," 8 [2004], available at http://www.caregiving.org/data/04finalreport.pdf [accessed Aug. 5, 2009]). The great majority of caregivers (83 percent) are helping relatives (National Alliance for Caregiving and the AARP, "Caregiving in the U.S.," 7). By 2020, it is expected that 40 percent of the workforce will care for an elderly relative (Martha Lynn Craver, "Growing Demand for Elder Care Benefits," *Kiplinger Business Forecasts* [May 29, 2002]). See also Sarah Rimer, "Blacks Carry Load of Care for Their Elderly," *New York Times* (March 15, 1998), section 1, 1 ("[N]early one in four American families is taking care of an elderly relative or friend, doing everything from changing diapers to shopping for groceries."); *Congressional Record 139,* 1969 (1993) (statement of Rep. Lynn Schenk ("[W]omen can expect to spend seventeen years of their lives caring for their children and eighteen years caring for an elderly relative.").

7 See Martha Fineman, *The Autonomy Myth: A Theory of Dependency* (New York: New Press, 2005).

8 Frances E. Olsen, "The Myth of State Intervention in the Family," *University of Michigan Journal of Law Reform, 18,* 835, 836 (1985).

9 Heidi Shierholz & Elise Gould, "A Lost Decade: Poverty and Income Trends Continue to Paint a Bleak Picture for Working Families," (2011), available at http://www.epi.org/publication/lost-decade-poverty-income-trends-continue/ (accessed May 25, 2012) (relying on 2010 Census bureau data). The United States' pre-aid poverty rate of 26.6 percent for children is similar to France's (27.7 percent), Ireland's (24.9 percent), New Zealand's (27.9 percent), and the United Kingdom's (25.4 percent). After government aid, however, these countries have much lower actual poverty rates than our own. Compared to our

21.9 percent actual poverty rate, France's is 7.5 percent; Ireland's is 15.7 percent; New Zealand's is 16.3 percent; and the United Kingdom's is 15.4 percent.
To take one example of the differences in effectiveness of transfer programs, the
poverty rate in France dropped to roughly 27 percent of its original rate (from
27.7 percent to 7.5 percent) after government taxes and transfers; in comparison, the U.S. poverty rate dropped only to 82 percent of its original level (from
26.6 percent to 21.9 percent) (Sylvia Allegretto, Economic Policy Institute, "U.S.
Government Does Relatively Little To Lessen Child Poverty Rates," available at
http://www.epi.org/content.cfm/webfeatures_snapshots_20060719 [accessed
Aug. 10, 2009]).

10 U.S. Department of Labor, "Women in the Labor Force: A Databook," 17–18 (2009),
available at http://www.bls.gov/cps/wlf-databook-2009.pdf (accessed February 28,
2010).

11 Ibid.

12 Janet C. Gornick and Marcia K. Meyers, *Families That Work: Policies for Reconciling
Parenthood and Employment* (New York: Russell Sage Foundation, 2003), 30.

13 See Chapters 1, 3.

14 See Michael Hout and Caroline Hanley, "The Overworked American Family:
Trends and Nontrends in Working Hours 1968–2001," (2002), available at
http://ucdata.berkeley.edu/rsfcensus/papers/Working_Hours_HoutHanley.pdf
(accessed Sept. 30, 2009) ; Jerry A. Jacobs and Kathleen Gerson, "Overworked
Individuals or Overworked Families?" *Work and Occupations, 28,* 40 (2001).

15 See Chapter 1, notes 94–101, and accompanying text.

16 See Chapter 1, notes 106–08, and accompanying text.

17 See Chapter 1, note 109, and accompanying text.

18 UNICEF, Innocenti Research Centre, "Child Poverty in Perspective: An
Overview of Child Well-Being in Rich Countries: A Comprehensive Assessment
of The Lives and Well-Being of Children and Adolescents in The Economically
Advanced Nations," 26 (2007), available at http://www.unicef.org/media/files/
ChildPovertyReport.pdf (accessed June 20, 2009), 26. This measure of parent-child
interaction put the United States behind Australia, Austria, Belgium, Canada, the
Czech Republic, Denmark, France, Germany, Greece, Hungary, Iceland, Ireland,
Italy, Japan, Netherlands, Norway, Poland, Portugal, Spain, Sweden, Switzerland,
and the United Kingdom. Only Finland and New Zealand had lower rankings. The
OECD is an organization of thirty countries, most of which are regarded as high-
income economies. The United States is a member.

19 This composite measure put the United States behind Austria, Belgium,
Canada, the Czech Republic, Denmark, Finland, France, Germany, Greece,
Hungary, Ireland, Italy, the Netherlands, Norway, Poland, Portugal, Spain,
Sweden, and Switzerland. Only the United Kingdom was given a lower ranking
(Ibid., 2).

20 Women not only provide the great majority of care work for their children, but
also for aging relatives. They make up 61 percent of caregivers for adults. (National
Alliance for Caregiving and the AARP, "Caregiving in the U.S.," 9).

21 See Ann Crittenden, *The Price of Motherhood* (New York: Metropolitan Books,
2001), 88; Gornick and Meyers, *Families That Work,* 46.

22 Gornick and Meyers, *Families That Work,* 47 (citing Jane Waldfogel, "Understanding the 'Family Gap' in Pay for Women with Children," *Journal of Economic Perspectives, 12*[1] 137 [1998]).

23 Sarah Avellar and Pamela J. Smock, "Has the Price of Motherhood Declined Over Time?: A Cross-Cohort Comparison of the Motherhood Wage Penalty," *Journal of Marriage & Family,* 65, 597, 604 (2003).

24 Crittenden, *The Price of Motherhood,* 88; Gornick and Meyers, *Families That Work,* 47.

25 Jerry A. Jacobs and Kathleen Gerson, "Overworked Individuals or Overworked Families?," 40; Michael Hout and Caroline Hanley, "The Overworked American Family: Trends and Nontrends in Working Hours, 1968–2001," 11–12.

26 A study by sociologists at Duke University and the University of Arizona comparing data from 1985 and 2004 found that the mean number of people with whom Americans can discuss matters important to them dropped by nearly one-third, from 2.94 people in 1985 to 2.08 in 2004 (Miller McPherson, Lynn Smith-Lovin, and Matthew E. Brashears, "Social Isolation in America: Changes in Core Discussion Networks Over Two Decades," *American Sociological Review, 71,* 353 [2006]). In the same time period, the percentage of people who talk to at least one person outside of their family about important matters decreased from about 80 percent to about 57 percent, while the number of people who depend totally on their spouse has increased from about 5 percent to about 9 percent (Ibid., 359). The study concluded that citizens have turned away from close ties formed in neighborhood or community contexts and toward relationships with close kin, especially spouses (Ibid., 358, 371).

27 See generally Robert Putnam, *Making Democracy Work: Civic Traditions in Modern Italy* (Princeton, NJ: Princeton University Press, 1994); *Bowling Alone: The Collapse and Revival of American Community* (New York: Simon & Schuster, 2000).

28 For example, researchers Stanley Feldman and John Zaller discovered that those who opposed welfare programs had little difficulty expressing philosophical grounds for their opposition; they relied on the liberty and autonomy venerated in the liberal tradition. In contrast, those who supported welfare programs generally could not provide philosophical justifications for their beliefs (Stanley Feldman and John Zaller, "The Political Culture of Ambivalence: Ideological Responses to the Welfare State," *American Journal of Political Science, 36,* 268, 292–299 [1992]).

29 Four of these states, Massachusetts, California, Connecticut, and Iowa, instituted same-sex marriage as a result of state supreme court decisions striking down same-sex marriage bans under the state constitution. See *Goodridge v. Department of Public Health,* 798 N.E.2d 941 (Mass. 2003); *In re Marriage Cases,* 183 P.3d 384 (Cal. 2008); *Kerrigan v. Commissioner of Public Health,* 957 A.2d 407 (Conn. 2008); *Varnum v. Brien,* 763 N.W.2d 862 (Iowa 2009). Two others, Vermont and New Hampshire, instituted same-sex marriage through legislative initiatives. However, California's brief foray into same-sex marriage was ended by voters in those states amending the state constitution. Meanwhile, in Maine, the legislature passed a law instituting same-sex marriage, but that law was rejected in a voter referendum

before it was put into effect. (Maria Godoy, "State by State: The Legal Battle Over Gay Marriage," NPR.com, available at http://www.npr.org/news/specials/gaymarriage/map/ [accessed Feb. 15, 2010]).

30 As of 2010, 29 states had adopted state constitutional amendments that bar same-sex marriage; many of these states also had legislation barring same-sex marriage. In addition to those 29 states, 12 states had adopted legislation similar to the federal Defense of Marriage Act of 1996 ("DOMA") (1 U.S.C. § 7 [2010], 28 U.S.C. § 1738C [2010]). These state statutes, often called mini-DOMAs, bar the state from recognizing a same-sex marriage celebrated in another state (See Human Rights Campaign, "Statewide Marriage Prohibitions," [2010], available at http://www.hrc.org/documents/marriage_prohibitions_2009.pdf [accessed Feb. 28, 2010]). This figure includes Hawaii, whose state constitution does not ban same-sex marriage, but authorizes the state legislature to do so (See ibid.).

31 The Federal Defense of Marriage Act of 1996, or "DOMA," declares that no state must give effect to a same-sex marriage celebrated in another state, and that the term *marriage* for purposes of federal law is confined to the union of a man and woman (Pub. L. No. 104–199 [1996], 110 Stat. 2419 [1996], codified at 1 U.S.C. § 7 [2010], 28 U.S.C. § 1738C [2010]).

32 See Terrence Dougherty, National Gay and Lesbian Task Force Policy Institute, "Economic Benefits of Marriage under Federal and Massachusetts Law" (2004), available at http://www.thetaskforce.org/downloads/reports/reports/EconomicBenefitsMA.pdf (accessed June 20, 2009).

33 In 2008, the divorce rate was 3.5 per 1,000 population, nearly half the marriage rate of 7.1 per 1,000 population (National Vital Statistics Reports, "Births, Marriages, Divorces and Deaths: Provisional Data for 2008" 57 [19] [2009], available at http://www.cdc.gov/nchs/fastats/divorce.htm [accessed Feb. 28 2010]).

34 The 2000 U.S. Census counted 601,209 same-sex partner households. That is a 314 percent increase from the 1990 Census, although changes in the manner of coding these responses likely led to significant undercounting in the earlier census. It is possible that actual numbers are higher than even the 2000 Census reveals due to underreporting of these relationships (David M. Smith and Gary J. Gates, The Urban Institute, "Gay and Lesbian Families in the United States: Same-Sex Unmarried Partner Households," [2001], available at http://www.urban.org/publications/1000491.html [accessed June 20, 2009]).

35 In 1960, 9 percent of children lived in single-parent homes (Wendy Sigle-Rushton and Sara McLanahan, The Center for Research on Child Well-Being, "Father Absence and Child Well-Being: A Critical Review," 3–4 [2002], available at http://www.rwjf.org/files/research/Father%20Absence%20-%20Fragile%20Families.pdf [accessed Jan. 24, 2010]). In 2007, that figure rose to 25.8 percent of children (U.S. Census Bureau, "America's Families and Living Arrangements: 2007, Children by Presence and Type of Parent(s), Race, and Hispanic Origin," Table C-9 [2007], available at http://www.census.gov/population/www/socdemo/hh-fam/cps2007.html [accessed June 20, 2009]).

The rise in single-parent families is largely attributable to an increase in the number of families in which the parents were never married (George Akerlof,

Janet Yellen, and Michael Katz, "An Analysis of Out-of-Wedlock Childbearing in the United States," *Quarterly Journal of Economics, 111,* 277, 285 [1996]). Although the increase in rates of nonmarital births had begun to stabilize in the mid-1990s after a two-decade rise, since 2002 it has again begun to rise steeply. More than 1.6 million babies were born to unmarried mothers in 2006, the highest number ever recorded in the United States. The 2006 total (1,641,946 births) was nearly 8 percent greater than in 2005 (1,527,034) and a 20 percent increase from 2002 (1,365,966). This makes the percentage of all births to unmarried women in 2006 38.5 percent, up from 36.9 percent in 2005 and 34 percent in 2002 (Joyce A. Martin, Brady E. Hamilton, Paul D. Sutton, Stephanie J. Ventura, Fay Menacker, Sharon Kirmeyer, and T.J. Mathews, "Births: Final Data for 2006," *National Vital Statistics Reports,* 57[7], 2, 11 [2009]) (report for the U.S. Dept. of Health and Human Services, prepared by the Centers for Disease Control and Prevention, the National Center for Health Statistics, and the National Vital Statistics System).

36 In 2007, the American Community Survey reported 6.42 million cohabiting couples, compared to just 439,000 cohabitating couples in 1960 ("American Community Survey, 2007 1-Year Estimates,"[2007], available at http://factfinder.census.gov/servlet/ADPTable?_bm=y&-geo_id=01000US&-ds_name=ACS_2007_1YR_G00_&-_lang=en&-_caller=geoselect&-format= [accessed June 20, 2009]; U.S. Census Bureau, "1960 Census of Population, Persons by Family Characteristics" [1999], available at http://www.census.gov/population/socdemo/ms-la/tabad-2.txt [accessed June 20, 2009]).

37 Reynolds Farley and John Haaga (Eds.), *The American People: Census 2000* (New York: Russell Sage Foundation Publications, 2005), 88.

38 Ibid.

39 Among the best work this conversation has produced are Martha Fineman's *The Autonomy Myth;* Linda McClain's *The Place of Families* (Cambridge: Harvard University Press, 2006); Ian Shapiro's *Democratic Justice* (New Haven: Yale University Press, 2001); and Michael Warner's *The Trouble with Normal* (Cambridge: Harvard University Press, 1999).

40 See note 1.

41 John Rawls, *A Theory of Justice* (Cambridge: Harvard University Press, 1971).

42 These liberal revisionists include both *civic liberals,* who seek to incorporate a more community-oriented ethic into liberalism, and liberal feminists, who generally focus on issues of caretaking. The first group includes many theorists sympathetic to communitarian critiques of liberalism, which argued that liberalism was too focused on individual rights, most particularly freedom, rather than other, more community-oriented goods. In contrast to communitarians, whose project was largely critical of liberalism, civic liberals sought to respond by arguing that liberalism could adapt to these critiques. Among the best of these works are Stephen Macedo, *Diversity and Distrust* (Cambridge: Harvard University Press, 2000); Thomas Spragens, *Civic Liberalism: Reflections on Our Democratic Ideals* (Lanham, MD: Rowman and Littlefield Publishers, 1999); and Eamonn Callan, *Creating Citizens* (New York: Oxford University Press, 1997).

Taking a somewhat parallel path, liberal feminists have argued for reformulations of liberalism that combine its concerns of justice, freedom, and equality with support for the value of care. Among the best of these are Martha Nussbaum, *Sex and Social Justice* (New York: Oxford University Press, 1999); Linda McClain, *The Place of Families;* Joan Tronto, *Moral Boundaries: A Political Argument for an Ethic of Care* (New York: Routledge, 1993); and Eva Feder Kittay, *Loves Labor: Essays on Women, Equality, and Dependency* (New York: Routledge, 1999).

43 As Isaiah Berlin eloquently recognized, "[t]he world that we encounter in ordinary experience is one in which we are faced with choices between ends equally ultimate, and claims equally absolute, the realization of some of which must inevitably involve the sacrifice of others" (Isaiah Berlin, "Two Concepts of Liberty," in *Four Essays on Liberty*, 118, 168 [1969]). The trade-offs involved among goods are in part the reason that liberal society places such emphasis on the individual's right to his or her own free choice. Yet some societal goods cannot adequately be pursued on an individual level. In such cases, again in Berlin's words: "[t]he extent of a man's, or a people's, liberty to choose to live as they desire must be weighed against the claims of many other values, of which equality, or justice, or happiness, or security, or public order are perhaps the most obvious examples" (Ibid., 168, 170).

44 See the feminist theorists cited in note 42.

45 See Eamonn Callan, *Creating Citizens,* 10; Amy Gutmann, *Democratic Education* (Princeton, NJ: Princeton University Press, 1993), 139.

46 See, for example, Fineman, *The Autonomy Myth,* which I discuss in Chapter 3.

47 See, for example, Michael Warner, *The Trouble with Normal,* which I discuss in Chapter 4.

48 See, for example, Rick Santorum, *It Takes a Family* (Wilmington, DE: Intercollegiate Studies Institute, 2005), which I discuss in Chapter 4.

49 See, for example, David Blankenhorn, *The Future of Marriage* (New York: Encounter Books, 2007), which I discuss in Chapter 4.

50 *Meyer v. Nebraska,* 262 U.S. 390, 402 (1923).

51 Shapiro, *Democratic Justice,* 87.

52 See, for example, Peter Steinberger, *The Idea of the State* (Cambridge, UK: Cambridge University Press, 2005), 12, who argues "that an ongoing and recurrent failure on the part of political theorists to be clear about what they mean when they use the word 'state' has led to an entire range of important theoretical confusions."

53 Spragens, *Civic Liberalism,* xiii.

CHAPTER 1

1 John Rawls, *A Theory of Justice* (Cambridge, MA: The Belknap Press of Harvard University Press, 1971).

2 Alan Ryan observed that *A Theory of Justice* "has sparked off more argument among philosophers, and has been more widely cited by sociologists, economists, judges, and politicians than any work of philosophy in the past hundred years" (Alan Ryan, "John Rawls," in Quentin Skinner [Ed.], *The Return of Grand Theory in the Human Sciences* [New York: Cambridge University Press, 1985], 101). His

influence on contemporary legal thinking, as described by one commentator, has been "profound" (Lawrence B. Solum, "Situating Political Liberalism," *Chicago-Kent Law Review, 69,* 549–550 [1994]) (describing "the staggering number of law review articles citing *A Theory of Justice*"). See also Thomas Nagel, "The Rigorous Compassion of John Rawls: Justice, Justice, Shalt Thou Pursue," *New Republic,* Oct. 25, 1999, 36–37.

3 Rawls, *A Theory of Justice,* 3. Social justice is so fundamental, Rawls counseled, because "[e]ach person possesses an inviolability founded on justice that even the welfare of society as a whole cannot override" (Ibid).

4 The original position is meant "to show how the idea of society as a fair system of social cooperation can be unfolded so as to find principles specifying the basic rights and liberties and the forms of equality most appropriate to those cooperating, once they are regarded as citizens, as free and equal persons" (John Rawls, *Political Liberalism* [New York: Columbia University Press, 1993], 27).

5 Rawls, *A Theory of Justice,* 303.

6 Ibid., 7.

7 Ibid., 7, 462–463.

8 See Susan Moller Okin, *Justice, Gender, and the Family* (New York: Basic Books, 1989), 97. For example, Rawls suggests that persons in the original position might be thought of as heads of families, and states that he will generally follow this interpretation (Rawls, *A Theory of Justice,* 128). He makes explicit that his goal in doing so, however, is simply to ensure that the decisional rules chosen in the original position would be fair to future generations. From this motivational assumption, Rawls derives his "just savings" principle (Ibid., 128–129, 284–293).

9 Rawls, *A Theory of Justice,* 74. Later in the book, Rawls extended this argument to character: "The assertion that a man deserves the superior character that enables him to make the effort to cultivate his abilities is equally problematic; for his character depends in large part upon fortunate family and social circumstances for which he can claim no credit" (Ibid., 104).

10 Ibid. Rawls again broached the subject later in the book, when he pointed out that families create unequal opportunities for individuals (Ibid., 511–512). See also Martha Nussbaum, "Rawls and Feminism," in Samuel Freeman, (Ed.), *The Cambridge Companion to Rawls* (Cambridge University Press, 2009), 500.

11 Okin, *Justice, Gender, and the Family,* 97.

12 Ibid.

13 Rawls recognizes that, in limiting his conception to the good of virtue, he is excluding other possible goods: "This standard, however, is not to be confused with the principles defining the other virtues, for the basic structure, and social arrangements generally, may be efficient or inefficient, liberal or illiberal, and many other things, as well as just or unjust. A complete conception defining principles for all the virtues of the basic structure, together with their respective weights when they conflict, is more than a conception of justice. It is a social ideal" (Rawls, *A Theory of Justice,* 9).

14 Ibid., 4, 7, 9.

15 Ibid., 302.

16 See notes 9–10, and accompanying text. See also James Fishkin, *Justice, Equal Opportunity, and the Family* (New Haven: Yale University Press, 1983), 63–65.

17 Rawls, *A Theory of Justice,* 462–463. Similarly, when Rawls later in the book considered the problem that families will lead to unequal opportunities for individuals, he asked, "Is the family to be abolished then? Taken by itself and given a certain primacy, the idea of equal opportunity inclines in this direction" (Ibid., 511).

18 Ibid., 6 (arguing that "even though justice has a certain priority, being the most important virtue of institutions, it is still true that, other things equal, one conception of justice is preferable to another when its broader consequences are more desirable").

19 Ibid., 545. As Rawls's defenders have argued, Rawls's description of persons in the original position was intended as a moral construct that models benevolence, rather than, as some of his critics have argued, an ontological construct meant to represent reality. See, for example, Linda C. McClain, "'Atomistic Man' Revisited: Liberalism, Connection, and Feminist Jurisprudence," *Southern California Law Review,* 65, 1171 (1992). Linda McClain's position that Rawls, in fact, recognized the social nature of human beings and articulated a notion of social union and interdependency is right on target, and she points out that Rawls himself cautioned against reading the original position in the way these critics suggest (Ibid., 1206–1211). Rawls stated, "[t]here is no inconsistency, then, in supposing that once the veil of ignorance is removed, the parties find that they have ties of sentiment and affection, and want to advance the interests of others and to see their ends attained" (Rawls, *A Theory of Justice,* 129). With that said, Rawls's theory is vulnerable to the charge that he neglects dependency by not attending to it elsewhere in his theory.

20 The basic critique that Rawls neglects dependency and the consequences of that neglect for "equality and social justice" is made powerfully by Eva Feder Kittay, in *Love's Labor* (New York: Routledge, 1999). Much of my argument in this section builds on Kittay's critique.

21 See Rawls, *A Theory of Justice,* 4, 60–62. Kittay notes that Rawls's failure to grasp the inevitability of dependency is evident in his response to the charge that he should have discussed the situations of dependent persons with severe mental and physical handicaps (Kittay, *Love's Labor,* 77). According to Rawls, such difficult cases are better left to the later legislative stage (John Rawls, *Justice as Fairness: A Restatement* [Cambridge, MA: The Belknap Press of Harvard University Press, 2001], 171–176). Yet it is only seeing humans as generally able and independent that could lead Rawls to see such dependent persons as special cases rather than one end of a continuum that represents the human condition, and which should be dealt with as a basic matter of social organization. As Kittay states, "[d]ependency must be faced from the beginning of any project in egalitarian theory that hopes to include *all* persons within its scope" (Kittay, *Love's Labor,* 77) (emphasis in original). See also Martha Nussbaum, "The Future of Feminist Liberalism," in Eva Feder Kittay and Ellen K. Feder (Eds.), *The Subject of Care: Feminist Perspectives on Dependency* (Lanham, MD: Rowman and Little Publishers, 2002), 51.

22 Kittay, *Love's Labor,* 77. See also Okin, *Justice, Gender, and the Family,* 103–104.

23 See National Alliance for Caregiving and AARP, "Caregiving in the U.S., Executive Summary 2009," 4 (2009), available at http://www.caregiving.org/data/CaregivingUSAllAgesExecSum.pdf (accessed Feb. 28, 2010) (stating that 66 percent of caregivers are female). See also *Congressional Record, 139,* 1969 (1993) (statement of Rep. Lynn Schenk) ("Women can expect to spend 17 years of their lives caring for their children and 18 years caring for an elderly relative.").

24 See Sarah Rimer, "Blacks Carry Load of Care for their Elderly," *New York Times* (Mar. 15, 1998), 1; National Alliance for Caregiving and AARP, "Caregiving in the U.S.," available at http://www.caregiving.org/pubs/data.htm, follow link to Caregiving in the U.S.: Findings from the National Caregiver Survey (2004), 15–16, for a breakdown of differences in caregiving among different ethnic groups (accessed Feb. 28, 2010).

25 See Paula England and Nancy Folbre, "Care, Inequality, Policy," in Francesca M. Cancian et al. (Eds.), *Child Care and Inequality: Rethinking Carework for Children and Youth* (New York: Routledge, 2002), 133.

26 As of 2007, 88 percent of direct care workers were female, 52 percent were members of a minority race or ethnicity, and 21 percent were foreign born. (PHI: National Clearinghouse on the Direct Care Workforce, "Facts 3: Who Are Direct Care Workers?," 1 [2007], available at http://www.directcareclearinghouse.org/download/NCDCW%20Fact%20Sheet-1.pdf [accessed Feb. 28, 2010]).

27 Rawls, *A Theory of Justice,* 19.

28 John Rawls, "The Idea of Public Reason Revisited," *University of Chicago Law Review, 64,* 765 (1997).

29 Ibid., 787 n. 58.

30 Ibid., 788.

31 Ibid.

32 Ibid., 789–790.

33 Ibid., 789.

34 Ibid.

35 Ibid., 792.

36 Ibid., 779. See also ibid., 789–790 ("Since wives are equally citizens with their husbands, they have all the same basic rights, liberties, and opportunities as their husbands; and this, together with the correct application of the other principles of justice, suffices to secure their equality and independence.").

37 Ibid.

38 Sharon Lloyd is one of the few scholars to note this (Lloyd, "Situating a Feminist Criticism," 1329–1330).

39 Rawls, "The Idea of Public Reason Revisited," 790.

40 Ibid.

41 See Martha Minow, "All in the Family and in All Families: Membership, Loving, and Owning," in Martha Nussbaum and David Estlund (Eds.), *Sex, Preference, and Family* (New York: Oxford University Press, 1997), 249.

42 See Frances Olsen, *The Myth of Family Intervention.* I discuss this issue in more detail in Chapter 2.

43 Rawls, "The Idea of Public Reason Revisited," 790.

44 Janet C. Gornick and Marcia K. Meyers, *Families That Work: Policies for Reconciling Parenthood and Employment* (New York: Russell Sage Foundation, 2003), 30.

45 Introduction, note 12, and accompanying text.

46 This includes 62 percent of mothers with children under 6, and 77 percent of mothers with children between the ages of 6 and 17 (Bureau of Labor Statistics, "Rise in Mother's Labor Force Includes those with Infants," [2005], available at http://www.bls.gov/opub/mlr/1986/02/rpt2full.pdf [accessed June 20, 2009]).

47 National Alliance for Caregiving, "The MetLife Study of Sons at Work: Balancing Employment and Eldercare," available at http://www.caregiving.org/data/sonsatwork.pdf (accessed June 20, 2009).

48 The 2007 Work, Family, and Equity Index found that paid maternity leave is guaranteed in 169 countries, with over half these countries providing 14 or more weeks of paid leave. In contrast, the United States is one of only four countries that do not guarantee paid leave for mothers in any segment of the workforce in connection with childbearing. Almost a third of the countries studied also ensure that fathers receive paid parental or paternity leave, which the United States does not require. Further, at least 107 countries require breaks for breastfeeding with almost all of those countries providing one hour or more per day; in at least 73 countries, these breaks are paid. Until the health care reform bill passed Congress as this book was in publication, the United States provided no protection for employees who are breastfeeding, even though it is proven to reduce infant mortality (Jody Heymann, Alison Earle, Jeffrey Hayes, "Project on Global Working Families, The Work, Family, and Equity Index: How Does the United States Measure Up? [2007]," available at http://www.mcgill.ca/files/ihsp/WFEI2007.pdf [accessed June 20, 2009]). Section 4207 of the Patient Protection and Affordable Care Act, however, now requires that employers provide breastfeeding employees with "reasonable break time" and a private, non-bathroom place to express breast milk during the workday, up until the child's first birthday.

49 42 U.S.C. 2000e-2000e17 (2009).

50 42 U.S.C. 2000e (2009).

51 29 U.S.C. 2601-2654 (2009).

52 *Chi v. Age Group, Ltd.,* 1996 Westlaw 627580 (S.D.N.Y. Oct. 29, 1996).

53 Courts analyze Title VII challenges under two different frameworks of analysis: disparate treatment doctrine, which prohibits practices motivated by discriminatory intent, and disparate impact doctrine, which prohibits employment practices that are neutral on their face but have a discriminatory effect in practice (*International Bhd. of Teamsters v. United States*, 431 U.S. 324, 335 36 n.15 [1977]). Because courts have limited disparate treatment analysis to situations in which women are treated differently from men with respect to job requirements for which they are similarly situated, that doctrine is generally inapplicable to policies that are applied equally to both sexes but that disadvantage working mothers because of heavier parenting responsibilities (See, for example, *EEOC v. Sears, Roebuck & Co.,* 628 F. Supp. 1264 [N.D. Ill. 1986], *affirmed,* 839 F.2d 302 [7th Cir. 1988]; *Record v. Mill Neck Manor Lutheran Sch. for the Deaf,* 611 F. Supp. 905 [E.D.N.Y. 1985]; *Barnes v. Hewlett-Packard Co.,* 846 F. Supp. 442 [D. Md. 1994]). Disparate impact doctrine, in prohibiting employment practices that have a discriminatory effect on women, could in

theory challenge job requirements that disadvantage working parents based on the disadvantage they cause to women. Yet in practice, courts have repeatedly refused challenges to such job requirements (See, for example, *Ilhardt v. Sara Lee Corp.*, 118 F.3d 1151, 1156 [7th Cir. 1997] [holding that disparate impact analysis was inappropriately applied to the plaintiff's claim that termination of part-time workers in the course of reduction in force disadvantaged working mothers; plaintiff failed to show that the reduction in force was a "particular employment practice within the meaning of Title VII" rather than "an isolated incident"]; *Barrash v. Bowen*, 846 F.2d 927, 932 [4th Cir. 1988] [holding that although policy denying women parental leave to breastfeed children "would have an adverse impact upon young mothers wishing to nurse their babies for six months, ... that is not the kind of disparate impact that would invalidate the rule, for it shows no less favorable treatment of women than of men"]; see also *Wallace v. Pyro Mining Co.*, 789 F. Supp. 867 [W.D. Ky. 1990] [similar]; *Maganuco v. Leyden Community High Sch. Dist. 212*, 939 F.2d 440, 444 [7th Cir. 1991] [holding disparate impact doctrine inapplicable to maternity leave policy because plaintiff failed to present sufficient statistical support]; *Armstrong v. Flowers Hosp.*, 812 F. Supp. 1183, 1191 92 [M.D. Ala. 1993] [holding that hospital policy requiring pregnant and nonpregnant nurses to treat AIDS patients does not violate disparate impact doctrine despite higher risks to pregnant women of treating AIDS patients]; *E.E.O.C. v. Sears, Roebuck & Co., 628 F. Supp. 1264, 1285* [N.D. Ill. 1986], *affirmed*, 839 F.2d 302 [7th Cir. 1988] [holding disparate impact doctrine inapplicable because plaintiffs failed to identify specific, facially neutral policies that disadvantaged women]; *Chi v. Age Group*, 1996 Westlaw 627 580 [S.D.N.Y. Oct 29, 1996] [rejecting claim that requiring employees to stay late has disparate impact on women "because Age Group's requirement that the person in charge of production be able and willing to work late is legitimately related to the position"]).

54   *Guglietta v. Meredith Corporation*, 301 F. Supp.2d 209, 215 (D. Ct. 2004).

55   See Introduction, notes 21–24, and accompanying text.

56   Pregnancy Discrimination Act of 1978, 42 U.S.C. § 2000e(k) (2006).

57   As the Supreme Court stated, "the State cannot single out pregnancy for disadvantageous treatment, but it is not compelled to afford preferential treatment" (*Wimberly v. Labor and Industrial Relations Commission*, 479 U.S. 511, 518 [1987]). See also *Stout v. Baxter Healthcare Corp.*, 282 F.3d 856 (5th Cir. 2002) ("The [PDA] does not protect a pregnant employee from being discharged for being absent from work even if her absence is due to pregnancy or to complications of pregnancy, unless the absences of nonpregnant employees are overlooked.").

58   *International Union, UAW v. Johnson Controls*, 499 U.S. 187 (1991).

59   Title VII of the Civil Rights Act of 1964, 42 U.S.C. § 2000e-2(e)(1) (2006).

60   See *Johnson Controls*, 499 U.S. at 205.

61   Ibid., 206–207.

62   Ibid., 203–204.

63   Ibid., 207.

64   The importance of the issues excluded by the antidiscrimination framework is driven home by the inane scope of the debate between the majority and the minority opinions in *Johnson Controls*. Neither side disputed that the statute did not

recognize harm to employees in their roles as persons who might wish to bear children, to future children, or to the communities of which these injured children might one day be a part. Instead, the debate centered only on whether the statute recognized financial harm to the employer from tort suits brought on behalf of children injured by fetal hazards (*Johnson Controls,* 499 U.S. at 208–211) (White, J., concurring in part and concurring in the judgment). Severe economic harm to an employer caused by a tort suit, the Court tells us, may be cognizable under Title VII. Severe harm to fetuses, however conceptualized legally, that would later serve as the basis for such tort suits cannot be.

65 And, indeed, it has been hailed as a victory for women by a number of commentators (see, for example, Amy S. Cleghorn, "Justice Harry A. Blackmun: A Retrospective Consideration of the Justice's Role in the Emancipation of Women," *Seton Hall Law Review, 25,* 1176 [1995]; Sheryl Rosensky Miller, "From the Inception to the Aftermath of *International Union, UAW v. Johnson Controls:* Achieving its Potential to Advance Women's Employment Rights," *Catholic University Law Review, 43,* 227 [1993]; Renee I. Solomon, "Future Fear: Prenatal Duties Imposed by Private Parties," *American Journal of Law & Medicine, 17,* 411 [1991]).

66 *Wallace v. Pyro Mining Co.,* 789 F. Supp. 867, 869 (W.D. Ky. 1990). See also *Derungs v. Wal-Mart Stores,* 374 F.3d, 428, 439 (6th Cir. Ohio 2004) (determining that the PDA requires pregnancy-related conditions to be treated as an illness only when incapacitating).

67 See H.R. Rep. No. 95–948, 5 (1978), reprinted in 1978 U.S.C.C.A.N. 4749.

68 *Troupe v. May Department Stores,* 20 F.3d 734 (7th Cir. 1994).

69 Ibid., 737.

70 Ibid., 738 (internal citations omitted).

71 *Johnson Controls,* 499 U.S. at 207. See also *United States EEOC v. Catholic Healthcare West,* 530 F.Supp.2d 1096, 1106 (C.D. Cal. 2008) (holding that a hospital could not prohibit pregnant employees from working in a fluoroscopy lab due to concerns about fetal safety; women must "make decisions about their own bodies and their own destinies"); *Peralta v. Chromium Plating & Polishing Corp.,* 2000 U.S. Dist. LEXIS 17416 (E.D.N.Y. 2000) (holding that an employer could not prohibit a pregnant employee from working due to concerns about her miscarrying her unborn child; the choice to work while pregnant belongs to each individual woman).

72 939 F.2d 440, 443–45 (7th Cir. 1991).

73 Ibid., 444.

74 Likewise, in *Piantanida v. Wyman Ctr.,* 116 F.3d 340, 342 (8th Cir. 1997), the Eighth Circuit concluded that an individual's caring for a child was not a "medical condition" bringing it within the protection of the PDA. The court instead characterized the decision to parent as the assumption of a "social role chosen by all new parents who make the decision to raise a child." The court then upheld the demotion of an employee on maternity leave on the grounds that the employer's discrimination against her based on her status as a new parent was gender-neutral and therefore did not violate Title VII.

75 See Joan Tronto, *Moral Boundaries: A Political Argument for an Ethic of Care* (New York: Routledge, 1993), 122 ("Care has little status in our society, except when it is honored in its emotional and private forms."). Katharine Silbaugh makes the

related point that housework's association with the domestic realm and that realm's perceived affectionate atmosphere causes housework to be perceived as not "really work" and, therefore, not accorded the benefits and protections accorded to wage labor (Katharine Silbaugh, "Turning Labor into Love: Housework and the Law," *Northwestern University Law Review, 91*, 1 [1996]).

76 See, for example, Peggie R. Smith, "Elder Care, Gender, and Work: The Work Family Issue of the 21st Century," *Berkeley Journal of Employment and Labor Law, 25*, 351 (2004); Martha Fineman, "Contract and Care," *Chicago-Kent Law Review, 76*, 1403 (2001); Jill Elaine Hasday, "Contest and Consent: A Legal History of Marital Rape," *California Law Review, 88*, 1373 (2000); Carole Pateman, *The Sexual Contract* (Stanford, CA: Stanford University Press, 1988); Lucinda M. Finley, "Transcending Equality Theory: A Way Out of the Maternity and the Workplace Debate," *Columbia Law Review, 86*, (1986); Frances Olsen, "The Myth of State Intervention in the Family," *Michigan Journal of Law Reform, 18*, 835 (1985); Frances Olsen, "Family and Market: A Study of Ideology and Legal Reform," *Harvard Law Review, 96*, 1497 (1983).

77 See Nancy Fraser and Linda Gordon, "A Genealogy of 'Dependency': Tracing a Keyword of the U.S. Welfare State," in *Justice Interruptus: Critical Reflections on the "Postsocialist" Condition* (New York: Routledge, 1997), 176; Olsen, "Family and Market," 1501.

78 Family and Medical Leave Act of 1993, 29 U.S.C. § 2601 (2010).

79 Ibid. 29 U.S.C. § 2612, §2614(a) (2010).

80 See, for example, *Schultz v. Advocate Health,* 2002 U.S. Dist. LEXIS 9517 (N.D. Ill. 2002) (awarding damages to a maintenance employee of a hospital for his termination due to taking leave to care for his elderly parents, who were experiencing medical issues); *Knussman v. Maryland,* 272 F.3d 625 (4th Cir. 2001) (entering judgment in favor of a Maryland state trooper on FMLA claim for denial of leave to care for newborn child). See also Diane E. Lewis, "When Dad Needs Time Off: *Knussman* Win Uncovers Double Standard that Often Lurks Within Leave Policies," *Boston Globe,* Feb. 7, 1999, G4.

81 Family and Medical Leave Act of 1993, 29 U.S.C. § 2611(2) (2010).

82 U.S. Department of Labor, "Family and Medical Leave Act Regulations: A Report on the Department of Labor's Request for Information," 128 (2007), available at http://www.dol.gov/whd/FMLA2007Report/2007FinalReport.pdf (accessed June 20, 2009).

83 See 29 U.S.C. 2614(a)(1) (2010).

84 U.S. Department of Labor, David Cantor et al., "Balancing the Needs of Families and Employers: Family and Medical Leave Surveys," viii, x (2001), available at http://www.dol.gov/whd/fmla/foreword.pdf (accessed June 20, 2009).

85 California was the first to do so by providing up to six weeks of paid leave in its new Unemployment Insurance Code. (California Unemployment Insurance Code 3301 (A)(1) [West 2010]). Two other states have followed California's lead: Washington and New Jersey. (See N.J. Stat. Ann. 43:21–26 [West 2009]; Wash. Rev. Code 49.86.030 [West 2009]).

86 29 C.F.R. 825.113 (1997) ("[L]eave to provide 'child care' would not ordinarily qualify as FMLA leave if the child is not a newborn [in the first year of life after birth]."

See also S. Rep. No. 103–3 (1993, 29) (Congress sought to exempt "minor illnesses which last only a few days and surgical procedures which typically do not require hospitalization and require only a brief recovery period").

87 *Kelley v. Crosfield Catalysts,* 962 F.Supp 1047, 1048(N.D. Ill. 1997), *reversed on other grounds,* 135 F.3d 1202 (7th Cir. 1998). See also *Seidle v. Provident Mutual. Life Insurance Co,* 871 F.Supp. 238, 246 (E.D. Pa. 1994) (holding that a child's ear infection is not a serious illness triggering mother's coverage by FMLA); *Perry v. Jaguar of Troy,* 353 F.3d 510 (6th Cir. 2003) (holding that caring for a child with attention deficit hyperactivity disorder does not qualify an employee for FMLA leave).

88 *Pang v. Beverly Hospital,* 94 Cal. Rptr. 2d 643, 647 (2000).

89 Ibid., 648.

90 Ibid., 650. See also Peggie Smith, "Elder Care, Gender, and Work: The Work-Family Issue of the 21st Century," *Berkeley Journal of Employment & Labor Law, 25,* 351, particularly 387–389 (2004).

91 The debates regarding welfare reform are a case in point. See, for example, "The 1998 Campaign," *New York Times,* Oct. 17, 1998, B4 (interview of then-New York governor George Pataki, in which he asserts that welfare reform "has changed people's lives and replaced a system that encouraged dependency with one that requires responsibility."); David Brooks, "More Than Money," *New York Times,* March 2, 2004, A23 ("[John] Edwards suggests that if we could take money from the rich and special interests, there'd be more for the underprivileged…Conservatives, on the other hand, believe that liberals have it backward.…If people live in an environment that fosters industriousness, sobriety, fidelity, punctuality and dependability, they will thrive."); David Brooks, "No U-Turns," *New York Times,* Mar. 29, 2007, A5 ("[I]n the 1970s…[p]eople were right to have…the "liberty vs. power" paradigm burned into their minds — the idea that big government means less personal liberty…[i]t's been replaced in the public consciousness with a "security leads to freedom" paradigm. People with a secure base are more free to take risks and explore the possibilities of their world."); John Vliet Spitzer, *New York Post,* June 6, 2007, 30 ("Multi-generational welfare dependency still exists, here and elsewhere - but it is no longer considered an entitlement. And that's as good a thing for the poor as it is for the taxpayers."); Mike Dorning, "Will Poverty Make a Political Comeback?" *Chicago Tribune,* June 3, 2007, C4 ("The nation's response to its 37 million poor, [John Edwards] decreed in a speech to the National Press Club last year, 'says everything about the character of America.'… [b]ut Republicans and conservatives often argue that far-reaching welfare programs breed dependency, hurting the poor in the long run, and that the best way to lift people out of poverty is to create an economy that provides jobs and opportunities."). It should be noted, however, that support for the middle-class and wealthy, including homeowner mortgage interest deductions, Social Security, farm subsidies for wealthy landowners, and support for particular industries are defined in the popular mind in a manner that does not raise the risk of dependency. See Nancy Fraser and Linda Gordon, "A Genealogy of 'Dependency': Tracing a Keyword of the U.S. Welfare State," 121.

92 Press Release, Bureau of Labor Statistics, U.S. Department of Labor, "Employment Characteristics of Families in 2008," 2 (May 27, 2009), available at http://www.bls. gov/news.release/famee.nr0.htm (accessed Feb. 28, 2010).

93 Part-time workers are often excluded from medical care and pension benefits, and are paid roughly 79 percent of what their full-time counterparts earn on an hourly basis, even when basic differences in human capital are controlled for (Gornick and Meyers, *Families That Work*, 62–63, 149–50).

94 See Lawrence Mishel, Jared Bernstein, Heidi Shierholz, *The State of Working America 2008/2009* (Ithaca, NY: Cornell University Press, 2009), 365.

95 Ibid.

96 Gornick and Meyers, *Families That Work*, 59.

97 Ibid., 60–61.

98 Ibid.

99 Ibid., 61. The comparison countries included Belgium, Canada, Denmark, Finland, France, Germany, Luxembourg, the Netherlands, Norway, Sweden, and the United Kingdom.

100 Ibid., 33 (citing Jerry A. Jacobs and Janet Gerson, "Hours of Paid Work in Dual-Earner Couples: The United States in Cross-National Perspective," *Sociological Focus, 35*(2), 169 [2001]).

101 Ibid.

102 Jeffrey Capizzano and Gina Adams, "The Hours That Children Under Five Spend in Child Care: Variation Across States," (Washington, D.C.: Urban Institute [2000]), available at http://www.urban.org/UploadedPDF/anf_b8.pdf (accessed Feb. 28, 2010).

103 Ibid. (citing Jennifer Ehrle, Gina Adams, and Kathryn Tout, "Who's Caring for Our Youngest Children? Child Care Patterns of Infants and Toddlers," [Washington, D.C.: Urban Institute (2001)], available at http://www.urban.org/url.cfm?ID=310029 [accessed Sept. 15, 2009]).

104 Ibid., (citing Capizzano, Tout, and Adams, *Child Care Patterns of School-Age Children with Employed Mothers*, 6 tbl. 1).

105 Ibid.

106 Eunice Kennedy Shriver National Institute of Child Health and Human Development, National Institute of Health, Department of Health and Human Services, "The NICHD Study of Early Child Care and Youth Development (SECCYD): Findings for Children up to Age 4 1/2 Years (2006)," available at http://www.nichd.nih.gov/publications/pubs/upload/seccyd_051206.pdf (accessed June 20, 2009). The NICHD study is the most comprehensive longitudinal study on this issue. It found that children who were cared for exclusively by their mothers did not develop differently from those who were also cared for by others. In contrast, children who experienced higher-quality care demonstrated slightly better cognitive and developmental skills for the first three years of their lives. The study suggests that children exposed to higher-quality day care (as compared with lower-quality day care) were more ready for school at age four and fared better in standardized literacy and number skills tests.

107 Suzanne Helburn et al., "Cost, Quality, and Child Outcomes in Child Care Centers: Public Report," (Denver: University of Colorado, 1995), 319, available at http://www.eric.ed.gov/ERICDocs/data/ericdocs2sql/content_storage_01/0000019b/80/14/22/e6.pdf [accessed Sept. 30, 2009]. A slightly later study reached a somewhat more optimistic conclusion about the percentage of child

care that is developmentally enriching (Edward F. Zigler, Katherine Marsland, and Heather Lord, National Institute of Child Health and Development [NICHD], Characteristics and Quality of Child Care for Toddlers and Preschoolers, *Applied Developmental Science, 4*[3] 116 [2000] [finding that positive caregiving experiences were characteristic for 28 percent of infants and 22 percent of toddlers in center-based care.]).

108 Gornick and Meyers, *Families That Work*, 53-54.

109 Ibid., 56 (citing Mary B. Larner, Lorraine Zippiroli, Richard E. Behrman, "When School Is Out," *Future of Children, 9*, 4 [1999]).

110 Ibid., 53 (citing Linda Giannarelli and James Barsimantov, "Child Care Expenses of America's Families," [Washington, D.C.: Urban Institute (2000)], available at http://www.urban.org/url.cfm?ID=310028 [accessed Sept. 15, 2009]) .

111 See Introduction, notes 21-24, and accompanying text. Ann Crittenden notes one study of female graduates of University of Michigan Law School, who averaged only 3.3 months out of the workplace, compared with almost no time off for their male counterparts, and who had spent an average of 10.1 months working part-time work, and averaged 10% fewer hours than male colleagues when they worked full-time. In Crittenden's words, "the penalties for these slight distinctions between the men's and women's work patterns were strikingly harsh. Fifteen years after graduation, the women's average earnings were not 10 percent lower, or even 20 percent lower, than the men's, but almost 40 percent lower" (Ann Crittenden, *The Price of Motherhood* [New York: Metropolitan Books, 2001] 96).

112 See note 93.

113 See Introduction, note 9, and accompanying text.

114 Sylvia Allegretto, Economic Policy Institute, "U.S. Government Does Relatively Little to Lessen Child Poverty Rates," available at http://www.epi.org/content.cfm/webfeatures_snapshots_20060719 (accessed Aug. 10, 2009).

115 Gornick and Meyers, *Families That Work*, 73-78.

116 Harriet Presser, *Working in a 24/7 Economy: Challenges for American Families* (New York: Russell Sage Foundation Publications, 2005).

117 These include coronary disease, sleep disturbances, gastrointestinal disorders, and chronic malaise; round-the-clock employment also raises the likelihood of workplace accidents (Gornick and Meyers, *Families That Work, 51-52* [citing International Labour Association, "Conditions of Work Digest: Working Time Around the World, International Labor Office" (1995); Harriet B. Presser, "Shift Work Among American Women and Child Care," *Journal of Marriage and the Family, 48* [3], 551 [1986]).

118 Jody Heymann, *The Widening Gap: Why America's Working Families Are in Jeopardy—and What Can Be Done About It* (New York: Basic Books, 2000).

119 Robert Putnam, *Bowling Alone: The Collapse and Revival of American Community* (New York: Simon & Schuster, 2001).

120 Recent work by Suzanne Bianchi and her colleagues of parents' weekly hours resulted in the unexpected finding that since 1965, when 60 percent of all children lived in families with a breadwinner father and a stay-at-home mother compared with 30 percent of all children today, the hours that married and single parents spend teaching, playing, and caring for children actually has risen. For married

mothers, the time spent on child-care activities increased to an average of 12.9 hours a week in 2000, from 10.6 hours in 1965. For married fathers, that time more than doubled, to 6.5 hours a week, from 2.6 hours. Single mothers, too, reported an increase in child-care hours—11.8 hours a week on child care, up from 7.5 hours in 1965 (Suzanne M. Bianchi, John P. Robinson, and Melissa A. Milkie, *Changing Rhythms of American Family Life* [New York: Russell Sage Foundation Publication, 2007], 1–2, 13, 16, 115–117, 137, 169–170, 175–178). See also Robert Pear, "Married and Single Parents Spending More Time with Children, Study Finds," *New York Times*, (Oct. 17, 2006), A12.

121 See Introduction, notes 26–27, and accompanying text.

CHAPTER 2

1 Arguing against the view that kings had a natural right of sovereignty over their subjects that had been passed down from Adam's paternal authority over his children, Locke contended that "the power of a magistrate over a subject may be distinguished from that of a father over his children, a master over his servant, [and] a husband over his wife" (John Locke, *Second Treatise of Government*, C.B. Macpherson, [Ed.] [Indianapolis: Hackett Publishing Company, 1980], 7 [emphasis omitted]).

2 The English Leveller, John Wildman, was an early harbinger of this individualism when he declared, at the time of the Putney Debates on October 29, 1647: "Every person in England hath as clear a right to elect his representative as the greatest person in England" (A.S.P. Woodhouse [Ed.], *Puritanism and Liberty: Being the Army Debates (1647–9) from The Clarke Manuscripts* [London: J.M. Denton and Sons Limited, 1992], 66).

3 Joyce Appleby, *Capitalism and a New Social Order: The Republican Vision of the 1790s* (New York: New York University Press, 1984), 20 (quoting William Lucy, *Observations, Censures, and Confutation of Notorious Errours in Mr. Hobbes His Leviathan* [London: 1663]). See also Robert Filmer, "Observations Concerning the Originall of Government," in Peter Laslett (Ed.), *Patriarcha and Other Political Works* (Oxford: B. Blackwell, 1949), 241 (criticizing Hobbes for "imagining a company of men at the very first to have been all created together without any dependency one of another, or as mushrooms...they all on a sudden were sprung out of the earth without any obligation one to another"); Susan Moller Okin, "Humanist Liberalism," in Nancy L. Rosenblum (Ed.), *Liberalism and the Moral Life* (Cambridge, MA: Harvard University Press, 1989), 39, 41 (stating that liberalism pays "remarkably little attention to how we *become* the adults who form the subject matter of political theories").

4 Thus, although the *Federalist Papers* are most often recognized for the authors' reliance on institutional checks to protect against tyranny and injustice, its authors emphasized that these checks were no substitute for virtue, which they considered an integral element of the new republic's success. In Madison's words:

   As there is a degree of depravity in making which requires a certain degree of circumspection and distrust: So there are other qualities in human nature, which justify a certain portion of esteem and confidence. Republican government pre-supposes the existence of these qualities in a higher degree than any other form. Were the pictures which have been drawn by the political jealousy of some among us, faithful likenesses of the human character, the inference would be, that there is not sufficient virtue among men for self-government; and that nothing less than the chains of despotism can restrain them from destroying and devouring one another.

(James Madison, "The Federalist No. 55," in Alexander Hamilton, James Madison, and John Jay, *The Federalist Papers* [New York: Bantam Classic, 1982], 342).

5 John Locke, *Second Treatise of Government,* 32 (emphasis omitted).

6 John Stuart Mill, "Considerations on Representative Government," in John Gray (Ed.), *On Liberty and Other Essays* (New York: Oxford University Press, 1991), 225.

7 Ibid.

8 John Stuart Mill, "On Liberty," in John Gray (Ed.), *On Liberty and Other Essays,* 91.

9 For the definitive discussion of Mill's views on women and feminism, see Susan Moller Okin, "John Stuart Mill: Liberal Feminist," in *Women In Western Liberal Thought* (Princeton, NJ: Princeton University Press, 1977), 197–232.

10 In Mill's words:

The family is a school of despotism, in which the virtues of despotism, but also its vices, are largely nourished. Citizenship, in free countries, is partly a school of society in equality; but citizenship fills only a small place in modern life, and does not come near the daily habits or inmost sentiment. The family, justly constituted, would be the real school of the virtues of freedom. It is sure to be a sufficient one of everything else.... What is needed is that it should be a school of sympathy in equality, of living together in love, without power on one side or obedience on the other.... The moral training of mankind will never be adapted to the conditions of the life for which all other human progress is a preparation, until they practice in the family the same moral rule which is adapted to the normal constitution of human society....

(John Stuart Mill, "The Subjection of Women," in John Gray [Ed.], *On Liberty and Other Essays,* 518–519).

11 Proving the assertion that liberalism's moral appeal comes at least significantly from its grounding in the value of human dignity is beyond the reach of this book. I note, however, that many of the most eloquent defenses of liberal systems of rights and liberties, including of the U.S. Constitution, ultimately ground them in the value of human dignity. For example, in interviews with Bill Moyers for the PBS series *In Search of the Constitution,* both Justice William Brennan and Professor Ronald Dworkin asserted that the bedrock value on which the Constitution, particularly the Bill of Rights, was built, was the value of human dignity. See "Introduction," in Michael J. Meyer and W.A. Parent, *The Constitution of Rights* (Ithaca: Cornell University Press, 1992), 3 (citing *In Search of the Constitution* "Mr. Justice Brennan" and "Ronald Dworkin: The Changing Store," Public Affairs Television, Inc., New York, 1987).

12 Thomas Paine, *The Rights of Man* (New York: Anchor, 1973), 320, 329–330.

13 See Martha Albertson Fineman, *The Autonomy Myth: A Theory of Dependency* (New York: New Press, 2004), 36; Eva Feder Kittay, *Love's Labor: Essays on Women, Equality and Dependency* (New York: Routledge, 1999), 27.

14 Joan Tronto was the first to make a sustained argument that political theory needed to include an ethic of care in her excellent book, *Moral Boundaries: A Political Argument for an Ethic of Care* (New York: Routledge, 1993).

15 See Fineman, *The Autonomy Myth*, 36.

16 As Thomas Spragens observes: "The goal was, and properly is, a political order in which all citizens are able to sail their own ships, as it were, and not to be either subservient crew members in the conduct of their own lives or adrift in boats with no rudders and luffing sails" (Thomas Spragens, *Civic Liberalism* [Lanham, MD: Rowman & Littlefield, 1999], 122).

17 See Kittay, *Love's Labor*, x–xi, 40–42; see also Introduction, note 8.

18 As Isaiah Berlin eloquently recognized, "[t]he world that we encounter in ordinary experience is one in which we are faced with choices between ends equally ultimate, and claims equally absolute, the realization of some of which must inevitably involve the sacrifice of others" (Isaiah Berlin, "Two Concepts of Liberty," in *Four Essays on Liberty*, [1969], 118, 168). The trade-offs involved among goods are in part the reason that liberal society places such emphasis on the individual's right to his or her own free choice. Yet some societal goods cannot adequately be pursued on an individual level. In such cases, again in Berlin's words: "[t]he extent of a man's, or a people's, liberty to choose to live as they desire must be weighed against the claims of many other values, of which equality, or justice, or happiness, or security, or public order are perhaps the most obvious examples" (Ibid. 168, 170).

19 Spragens, *Civic Liberalism*, xv.

20 See Nancy J. Hirschmann, "Rethinking Obligation for Feminism," in Nancy J. Hirschmann and Christine Di Stefano (Eds.), *Revisioning the Political: Feminist Reconstructions of Traditional Conceptions in Western Political Theory* (Boulder, CO: Westview Press, 1996), 157, 162; Nancy J. Hirschmann, "Freedom, Recognition, and Obligation: A Feminist Approach to Political Theory," *American Political Science Review, 83*, 1227, 1229 (1989); Virginia Held, "Mothering Versus Contract," in Jayne Mansbridge (Ed.), *Beyond Self Interest*, (Chicago: The University of Chicago Press, 1990), 287; Okin, "Humanist Liberalism," 41.

21 Okin, "Humanist Liberalism," 41.

22 See Stephen Macedo, *Diversity and Distrust: Civic Education in a Multicultural Democracy* (Cambridge: Harvard University Press, 2003); Spragens, *Civic Liberalism*; Michael Sandel, *Democracy's Discontent: America in Search of a Public Philosophy* (Cambridge: Harvard University Press, 1996). In Sandel's words, "despite its appeal, the liberal vision of freedom lacks the civic resources to sustain self-government. This defect ill-equips it to address the sense of disempowerment that afflicts our public life. The public philosophy by which we live cannot secure the liberty it promises, because it cannot inspire the sense of community and civic engagement that liberty requires" (Ibid., 6).

23 *Thornburgh v. American College of Obstetricians and Gynecologists*, 476 U.S. 747 (1986) (*overruled by Planned Parenthood of Southeastern Pennsylvania v. Casey*, 505 U.S. 833 [1992]).

24 Ibid., 772.

25 See Sandel, *Democracy's Discontent,* 102.

26 See Spragens, *Civic Liberalism,* 65.

27 See Tronto, *Moral Boundaries*; Kittay, *Love's Labor*; Okin, "Humanist Liberalism."

28 Martha Nussbaum, "The Future of Feminist Liberalism" in Eva Feder Kittay and Ellen K. Feder (Eds.), *The Subject of Care: Feminist Perspectives on Dependency* (Lanham, MD: Rowman & Littlefield Publishers, 2002), 186, 190.

29 Ronald Dworkin, *A Matter of Principle* (Cambridge: Harvard University Press, 1985), 191.

30 William Galston, *Liberal Purposes: Goods, Virtues, and Diversity in the Liberal State* (New York: Cambridge University Press, 1991), 80.

31 For communitarians, see Robert N. Bellah et al., *Habits of the Heart: Individualism and Commitment in American Life* (Berkeley: University of California Press, 1985); Alasdair MacIntyre, *After Virtue: A Study in Moral Theory* (Notre Dame: University of Notre Dame Press, 1981); Michael Sandel, *Liberalism & the Limits of Justice* (New York: Cambridge University Press, 1982); Sandel, *Democracy's Discontent;* Charles Taylor, "Liberal Politics and the Public Sphere," in Amitai Etzioni (Ed.), *New Communitarian Thinking* (Charlottesville, VA: University of Virginia Press 1995); Walzer, *Spheres of Justice: A Defense of Pluralism and Equality* (New York: Basic Books, 1990). For feminists, see Deborah Rhode, *Justice and Gender* (Cambridge: Harvard University Press, 1989); Carol Smart, *Feminism and the Power of Law* (London: Routledge, 1989); Iris M. Young, *Justice and the Politics of Difference* (Princeton: Princeton University Press, 1990); Martha Minow, *Making All the Difference, Inclusion, Exclusion, and American Law* (Ithaca: Cornell University Press, 1990); Hirschmann, "Rethinking Obligation for Feminism," 157.

32 John Rawls, *Political Liberalism* (New York: Columbia University Press, 1993), 218, 223.

33 See also Macedo, *Diversity and Distrust,* 169.

34 Both Martha Minow and Martha Nussbaum have taken the lead in pointing this out. See Martha Minow, "All in the Family and In All Families: Membership, Loving, and Owing," in David Estlund and Martha Nussbaum (Eds.), *Sex, Preference, and Family: Essays on Law and Nature* (New York: Oxford University Press, 1997), 250; Nussbaum, "The Future of Feminist Liberalism," 199; Martha Nussbaum, *Women and Human Development: The Capabilities Approach* (New York: Cambridge University Press, 1999), 261–64.

35 Rick Santorum, *It Takes a Family: Conservativism and the Common Good* (Wilmington, DE: Intercollegiate Studies Institute, 2005), 28–29.

36 Nussbaum, "The Future of Feminist Liberalism," 31. See also Sherry B. Ortner and Harriet Whitehead, *Sexual Meanings: The Cultural Construction of Gender and Sexuality* (New York: Cambridge University Press 1991); Jane Collier and Sylvia Yanagisako, *Gender and Kinship: Essays Toward a Unified Analysis* (Stanford, CA: Stanford University Press, 1990).

37 Nussbaum, "The Future of Feminist Liberalism," 199.

38 Hendrik Hartzog, *Man and Wife in America: A History* (Cambridge: Harvard University Press, 2000), 24.

39 Frances E. Olsen, "The Myth of State Intervention in the Family," *The University of Michigan Journal of Law Reform, 18,* 835, 836 (1985).

40 Ibid.

41 See William J. Carrington, Kristin McCue, and Brooks Pierce, "Using Establishment Size to Measure the Impact of Title VII and Affirmative Action," *Journal of Human Resources*, 35, 503 (2000).

42 See Paula Mergenhagen DeWitt, "Breaking Up Is Hard to Do," *American Demographics*, 14, 53 (1992).

43 Sunhwa Lee, Institute for Women's Policy Research, "Keeping Moms on the Job: The Impacts of Health Insurance and Child Care on Job Retention and Mobility among Low-Income Mothers," 34 (2007), available at http://www.iwpr.org/pdf/C360KeepingMoms.pdf (accessed June 20, 2009) (concluding that access to employer-provided health insurance significantly reduces the rate of leaving jobs: low-income mothers with employer-provided health insurance in their own name are nearly three times more likely to stay on the job compared to mothers with other types of health insurance, all other characteristics being equal). See also Jonathan Gruber and Brigitte Madrian, "Health Insurance, Labor Supply, and Job Mobility: A Critical Review of the Literature," National Bureau of Economic Research NBER Working Paper No. W8817, (2002), available at http://www.nber.org/papers/w8817.pdf (accessed June 20, 2009); Brigitte Madrian, National Bureau of Economic Research, "The U.S. Health Care System and Labor Markets," Working Paper 11980, 13 (2006), available at http://www.nber.org/papers/w11980 (accessed June 20, 2009).

44 Alice Kessler-Harris, *In Pursuit of Equity: Women, Men, and the Quest for Economic Citizenship in Twentieth-Century America* (New York: Oxford University Press, 2001).

45 See, e. g., Ronald B. Mincy, "Raising the Minimum Wage: Effects on Family Poverty," *Monthly Labor Review*, 113, 18 (1990) (discussing the higher than expected impact of raising the minimum wage on family poverty, and thus a family's ability to meet their children's needs).

46 MDRC, Lisa A. Gennetian et al., "Making Child Care Choices: How Welfare and Work Policies Influence Parents' Decisions," (2002), available at http://www.mdrc.org/publications/182/policybrief.html (accessed March 8, 2010) (finding that work requirements that are tied to child care subsidies affect the stability of care arrangements whenever there are changes in employment status or income).

47 Institute for Women's Policy Research, "Fact Sheet: Maternity Leave in the United States," 2 (2007), available at http://www.iwpr.org/pdf/parentalleaveA131.pdf (accessed March 8, 2010) (stating that "[w]omen workers who have some form of paid leave take on average 10.5 weeks off after childbirth, while women without any paid leave take 6.6 weeks").

48 Frederick Engels, "The Condition of the Working-Class in England," in *Karl Marx & Frederick Engels: Collected Works,* vol. IV (New York: International Publishers, 1975), 424–25. Some critics have contended that Engels' portrait of Manchester overstated the extent to which family ties eroded, because it understated the extent to which families actively resisted capitalism's corrosive effects. See Jane Humphries, "The Persistence of the Working Class Family: A Marxist Perspective," in Jean Bethke Elshtain (Ed.), *The Family in Political Thought,* (Amherst: University of Massachusetts Press, 1982), 197–222.

49 See Bendheim-Thoman Center for Research on Child Wellbeing, "Fragile Families Research Brief: Barriers to Marriage Among Fragile Families," available at http://www.fragilefamilies.princeton.edu/briefs/ResearchBrief16.pdf (accessed June 20, 2009).

50 See Deborah Weissman, "The Personal Is Political—and Economic," *Brigham Young University Law Review* 387 (2007). Weissman cites a number of studies documenting the link between domestic violence and economic and social circumstances. These include Rebecca Miles-Doan, "Violence Between Spouses and Intimates: Does Neighborhood Context Matter?" *Social Forces, 77,* 623 (1998) (observing the role that neighborhoods play in rates of intimate partner violence); Judy A. Van Wyk et al., "Detangling Individual-, Partner-, and Community-Level Correlates of Partner Violence," *Crime and Delinquency, 49,* 412, 415 (2003) (describing how social isolation increases the risk of domestic violence); Michael L. Benson et al., "Neighborhood Disadvantage, Individual Economic Distress, and Violence Against Women in Intimate Relationships," *Journal of Quantitative Criminology, 19,* 207, 210 (2003) (linking social isolation due to collapse of occupational networks to domestic violence); Jacquelyn Campbell et al., "Risk Factors for Femicide in Abusive Relationships: Results from a Multi-Site Case Control Study," *American Journal of Public Health, 93,* 1089, 1092 (2003) (measuring a fourfold risk increase as a result of an abuser's unemployment).

51 See Office of Justice Programs: Bureau of Justice Statistics, "Intimate Partner Violence" (2010), available at http://bjs.ojp.usdoj.gov/index.cfm?ty=tp&tid=971 (accessed March 8, 2010) (noting that in 2008 females age twelve or older experienced about 552,000 nonfatal violent victimizations by an intimate partner, while men experienced 101,000 nonfatal violent victimizations; in 2007, intimate partners also committed 14 percent of all homicides, with intimate partner homicide victims numbering 2,340—1,640 females and 700 males.)

52 See U.S. Department of Health & Human Service: Administration on Children, Youth and Families, "Child Maltreatment 2007," xii-xiii (2009), available at http://www.acf.hhs.gov/programs/cb/pubs/cm07/cm07.pdf (accessed March 12, 2010).

53 Santorum, *It Takes a Family,* 95.

54 Martha Fineman does an excellent job of both laying out and dispelling the myths of individual and family autonomy that circulate in popular discourse (Fineman, *The Autonomy Myth*).

55 Kittay, *Love's Labor,* 67–68. As Kittay quotes one caregiver: "Well, what goes round comes round" (Ibid., 68).

56 See Robert E. Goodin, *Protecting the Vulnerable: A Re-Analysis of Our Social Responsibilities* (Chicago: University of Chicago Press, 1985), 153.

57 For example, Mary Anne Case argues that "forced extractions from the collective in aid of [children's welfare] should kick in only after those with an individual responsibility, notably fathers, are forced to kick in their fair share, financially and otherwise" (Mary Anne Case, "How High the Apple Pie: A Few Troubling Questions About Where, Why, and How the Burden of Care for Children Should Be Shifted," Chicago-Kent Law Review, 76, 1753, 1785 ([2001]). The term "residual

responsibility" was coined by Duncan Lindsey (Duncan Lindsey, *The Welfare of Children* [New York: Oxford University Press, 1994]).

58 Goodin, *Protecting the Vulnerable*, 134.

59 Ibid., 136.

60 See pp. 71–73.

61 *Lawrence v. Texas*, 539 U.S. 558 (2003).

62 Michael Walzer, "Liberalism and the Art of Separation," *Political Theory*, 12, 315 (1984).

63 Frances E. Olsen, "The Family and the Market: A Study of Ideology and Legal Reform," *Harvard Law Review*, 96, 1497, 1510 (1983).

64 Catharine MacKinnon eloquently describes its flaws:

> [W]hile the private has been a refuge for some, it has been a hellhole for others, often at the same time. In gendered light, the law's privacy is a sphere of sanctified isolation, impunity, and unaccountability.... Everyone is implicitly equal in there. If the woman needs something—say, equality—to make these assumptions real, privacy law does nothing for her.

(Catharine MacKinnon, "Reflections on Sex Equality Under Law," *Yale Law Journal*, 100, 1281, 1311 [1991]). See also Carole Pateman, "Feminist Critiques of the Public-Private Dichotomy," in A. Phillips (Ed.), *Feminism and Equality* (New York: New York University Press, 1987); Olsen, "The Family and the Market," 1510.

65 MacKinnon, "Reflections on Sex Equality Under Law," 1311.

66 Reva Siegel, "The Rule of Love: Wife Beating as Prerogative and Privacy," *Yale Law Journal*, 25, 2117, 2170 (1996).

67 Catharine MacKinnon, *Toward a Feminist Theory of the State* (Cambridge, MA: Harvard University Press, 1991), 53.

68 *Eisenstadt v. Baird*, 405 U.S. 438, 453 (1972).

69 See Spragens, *Civic Liberalism*, 137–139. In Professor Spragens' words, "When liberal theorists and political leaders eulogized liberty, they had in mind not so much a concern with freeing individuals from social control generally but a concern with freeing these important social enterprises from the control of political authorities and social elites." See also Walzer, *Spheres of Justice*, 23.

70 See Spragens, *Civic Liberalism*, 140.

71 Alexis de Tocqueville, *Democracy in America*, Richard D. Heffner (Ed.) (New York: Penguin Group, 2001), 199.

72 Jean Jacques Rousseau, "The Social Contract," in *Discourse on Political Economy and the Social Contract*, Christopher Betts (Trans.) (New York: Oxford University Press, 1994), 87.

73 See Janet C. Gornick and Marcia K. Meyers, *Families That Work: Policies for Reconciling Parenthood and Employment* (New York: Russell Sage Foundation Publications, 2003), 27–28.

74 See generally Charles A. Reich, "Midnight Welfare Searches and the Social Security Act," *Yale Law Journal*, 72, 1347 (1962).

75 I address the complex issue of how the state should treat the difficult situation of minors who seek abortions in Chapter 5.

76 I address the issue of how the state should treat situations in which adult family members agree to some course of conduct, but that conduct has implications for sex equality, in Chapter 2.

77 For a perceptive discussion of how application of alimony and equitable distribution laws disadvantage mothers, see Ann Crittenden, "Who Really Owns the Family Wage?" in *The Price of Motherhood* (New York: Henry Holt, 2001).

78 See Elizabeth S. Scott, "Marriage, Cohabitation, and Collective Responsibility for Dependency," *University of Chicago Legal Forum*, 225 (2004). See also Joseph Veroff, Lynne Sutherland, Letha Chadiha, and Robert M. Ortega, "Predicting Marital Quality with Narrative Assessments of Marital Experience," *Journal of Marriage and Family*, 55(2), 326–337 (1993).

79 See Ira Ellman, Paul Kurtz, Elizabeth Scott, Lois Weithorn, and Brian Bix, *Family Law: Cases, Text, Problems*, 4th ed. (Charlottesville, VA: Lexis Law Publishing, 2004), 162.

80 In a study of 380 married couples, almost 75 percent of the husbands surveyed reported "taking all or most of the responsibility for big financial decisions" (Nancy Burns et al., "The Public Consequence of Private Inequality: Family Life and Citizen Participation," *American Political Science Review*, 91, 373, 376–78 [1997]).

81 *McGuire v. McGuire*, 59 N.W.2d 336 (Neb. 1953).

82 Ibid., 238.

83 Lee Teitelbaum, "The Family as a System: A Preliminary Sketch," *Utah Law Review* 537 (1996).

84 Three community property states currently require equal division of property between spouses: California (California Family Code § 2250 [West, 2009]); Louisiana (Louisiana Revised Statutes Annotated § 9:2801[4] [b] [West 2009]); and New Mexico (*Ruggles v. Ruggles*, 860 P.2d 182, 188 [N.M. 1993]).

85 The term is Lee Teitelbaum's (Teitelbaum, "The Family as a System," 559).

86 See my discussion of John Rawls, Chapter 1, pp. 29–30.

87 To cite just one piece of research, in a study assessing the opportunity cost to women of having children, Jane Waldfogel discovered that the difference between men's and women's pay in the 1970s was roughly the same across women, whether or not they had children. By 1991, however, 30-year-old American women without children earned 90 percent what men did; women with children earned only 70 percent compared to men (Jane Waldfogel, "Understanding the 'Family Gap' in Pay for Women with Children," *Journal of Economic Perspectives,12*, 137–156 [1998]).

88 Research demonstrates that the partner with more earning power generally controls financial decisions, even where couples pooled their resources. For example, "when a wife earned less than thirty percent of what her husband earned, she controlled the household's finances thirty-one percent of the time. When she earned over thirty percent of what her husband earned, however, she had financial control sixty-four percent of the time" (Jan Pahl, *Money and Marriage* [Basingstoke, UK: Macmillan, 1989]).

89 Nussbaum, *Women and Human Development*, 280.

90 See Linda McClain, *The Place of Families* (Cambridge: Harvard University Press, 2006), 4.

91 Three Nordic countries—Sweden, Norway and Denmark—have successfully adopted such use-it-or-lose-it policies (Gornick and Meyers, *Families that Work*, 134).

92 In the 1990s, the Swedish government engaged in such a campaign to convince employers and unions of the benefits of fathers taking parental leave; the number of paternity leaves rose appreciably as a result (Ibid., 137). For a recent discussion of the success of Sweden's campaign to increase the use of paternity leave, see Katrin Bennhold, "In Sweden, Men Can Have It All," *New York Times* (June 10, 2010), A6 ("From trendy central Stockholm to this village in the rugged forest south of the Arctic Circle, 85 percent of Swedish fathers take parental leave. Those who don't face questions from family, friends, and colleagues.").

CHAPTER 3

1 Case's comments were later published as "How High the Apple Pie? A Few Troubling Questions About Where, Why, and How the Burden of Care for Children Should Be Shifted," *Chicago-Kent Law Review 76*, 1753 (2001). The original conversation occurred, however, at Martha Fineman's November 20, 1999 "Uncomfortable Conversation on Children: Public Good or Individual Responsibility" symposium at Cornell Law School. As Case later described her position, "I was dragged reluctantly into that Conversation,…by people who had heard me express some of these thoughts in conversation; but even some of those people acknowledged that my role would be that of 'the turd in the punchbowl'" (Ibid., 1786, n.5 [citing remarks of Kathryn Abrams, presenting Case's position in a panel discussion beginning the symposium]).

2 Ibid., 1789.

3 Ibid., 1785.

4 Ibid., 1784.

5 See Chapter 2, pp. 55–57.

6 Case, "How High the Apple Pie?," 1767 ("The difficulty I have experienced goes beyond privileging certain kinds of family over others, and more broadly extends to a privileging of family matters over an employee's other life concerns."); Ibid., 1768–1769 ("If there must be legislation on parental status discrimination, I agree with Elinor Burkett about its scope. [According to] Burkett, 'Last time I checked, discrimination law generally cut both ways. We don't bar discrimination against women; we bar discrimination on the basis of gender, and so on. So why single out parents? Why not bar discrimination on the basis of family status? Why not make it illegal to presuppose that a nonparent is free to work the night shift or presuppose that nonparents are more able to work on Christmas than parents?'"); Ibid., 1769 ("I note that much that is complained of is not as a technical matter discrimination against parents, but rather a failure to discriminate in their favor. Consider the oft-cited case of the mother fired for her inability to do required overtime because of childcare responsibilities. There is no evidence that a worker with a different reason for being unavailable would have kept her job. What is being sought on behalf of such parents really is something more like 'special rights.' … ").

7 See Chapter 1, pp. 38–42.

8 Ibid., 1781–1782; Katherine Franke, "Theorizing Yes: An Essay on Feminism, Law, and Desire," *Columbia Law Review, 101,* 181, 192–195 (2001).

9 See Crittenden, *The Price of Motherhood,* 107.

10 Ibid., 87–131.

11 These claims bear a strong similarity to those made by opponents of welfare, who contend that increasing subsidies for children will encourage welfare mothers to bear more children. As an empirical matter, there is not much support for this proposition either. Researchers have found, at most, only a small positive correlation between welfare and childbearing, and only for particular groups of women without high-school degrees. See, for example, Philip Robins and Paul Fronstin, "Welfare Benefits and Birth Decisions of Never-Married Women," *Population Research and Policy Review, 15,* 21 (1996). The existence of even this correlation, however, is hotly contested because of the difficulty of separating out confounding factors. See, for example, Robert Fairlie and Rebecca London, "The Effect of Incremental Benefit Levels on Births to AFDC Recipients," *Journal of Policy & Analysis Management, 16* (4), 575 (1997).

12 Martha Albertson Fineman, *The Autonomy Myth: A Theory of Dependency* (New York: The New Press, 2005).

13 Ibid., 48.

14 Ibid., xviii.

15 Ibid., xvii.

16 Ibid.

17 Courts will find a contract "implied-in-law" even where there is no specific contractual agreement where one party has been unjustly enriched by the actions of another. For the doctrine to apply, however, the first party must have been reasonable to perform such services with an expectation of payment in the absence of an agreement. This might be the case, for example, where a surgeon performs emergency services on an unconscious patient. The case of parents' decision to rear children is not likely susceptible to the same argument. See generally John Edward Murray, *Murray on Contracts* (4th ed.) (New York: Lexis Publishing, 2001), §51(B).

18 See, for example, Robert Putnam, *Making Democracy Work: Civic Traditions in Modern Italy* (Princeton, N.J.: Princeton University Press, 1994); *Bowling Alone: The Collapse and Revival of American Community* (New York: Simon & Schuster, 2000).

19 See, for example, Case, "How High the Apple Pie?," 1773.

20 See Chapter 2, notes 11–12, and accompanying text.

21 See Linda McClain, "The Place of Families: The Domain of Civic Virtue in a Good Society: Families, Schools, and Sex Equality," *Fordham Law Review, 69,* 1617, 1682–1695 (2001).

22 John Stuart Mill, *On Liberty and Other Essays,* John Gray (Ed.) (New York: Oxford University Press, 1998), 91.

23 The term is Thomas Spragens's (Thomas A. Spragens Jr., *Civic Liberalism: Reflections on Our Democratic Ideals* [Lanham, MD: Rowman & Littlefield Publishers, 1999], 59, 64).

24 Rick Santorum, *It Takes A Family: Conservatism and the Common Good* (Wilmington, DE: Intercollegiate Studies Institute, 2006).

25 Ibid., 46.
26 Ibid., 69.
27 This lack of attention to how poor mothers who are required to return to work would care for their children occurred on a larger scale when Congress implemented welfare reform in 1996. See Lucie White, "Despair, Impasse, Improvisation," in Joel Hander and Lucie White (Eds.), *Hard Labor: Women and Work in the Post-Welfare Era* (New York: M.E. Sharpe, 1999).
28 Santorum, *It Takes a Family*, 94 (emphasis in original).
29 Ibid., 95.
30 See Introduction, pp. 5–6.
31 Mill, *On Liberty*, 91.
32 See Nancy Fraser, "After the Family Wage, A Postindustrial Thought Experiment," in *Justice Interruptus: Critical Reflections on the Postsocialist Condition,* (New York: Routledge, 1997), 41–43.
33 This terminology is Nancy Fraser's (Ibid., 43).
34 Personal Responsibility and Work Opportunity Reconciliation Act of 1996 (PRWORA), Pub. L. 104-193, 110 Stat. 2105, enacted August 22, 1996.
35 Under the family-wage model, to the extent that welfare payments were made to caregivers, they were seen as an aberration and an indication that the family had failed. Under the direct-subsidy model, direct support for caretaking would be deemed appropriate in the normal course of families' lives.
36 See Ann Crittenden, *The Price of Motherhood: Why the Most Important Job in the World Is Still the Least Valued* (New York: Macmillan, 2001); Susan Moller Okin, *Justice, Gender, and the Family* (Jackson, TN: Perseus Publishing, 1991); Linda McClain, "The Liberal Future of Relational Feminism: Robin West's 'Caring for Justice,'" *Law & Social Inquiry, 24,* 477 (1999).
37 See Katharine K. Baker, "Taking Care of Our Daughters," *Cardozo Law Review, 18,* 1495, 1521–1522 (1997); Maxine Eichner, "Getting Women Work That Isn't Women's Work: Challenging Gender Biases in the Workplace Under Title VII," *Yale Law Journal, 97,* 1397, 1401–1402 (1988).
38 Even ambitious proposals to subsidize family leave by contemporary standards do not generally seek to compensate caregivers for their opportunity losses in the market. Anne Alstott's book, *No Exit: What Parents Owe Their Children and What Society Owes Parents* (New York: Oxford University Press, 2004), is at least a partial exception. Alstott argues for a "caretaker resource account" to compensate parents for opportunities they lose as a consequence of caretaking. Alstott proposes that the caretakers of children under age 13 be given annual grants of $5,000, which they may use for child care, education, or retirement savings. Even she, however, suggests a level of compensation for caregivers' opportunity costs that is well below most caregivers' actual opportunity cost for caregiving. See Crittenden, *The Price of Motherhood*, 80, for a discussion of those costs.
39 See Crittenden, *The Price of Motherhood*, 40.
40 It is this strand that both Mary Anne Case and Katherine Franke tap into when they talk about the pressures of repronormativity, and which gives their critique such traction (Case, "How High the Apple Pie?"; Franke, "Theorizing Yes," 192–195). See

also Sharon Hays, *The Cultural Contradictions of Motherhood* (New Haven, CT: Yale University Press, 1996).

41 See, for example, Mary Eberstadt, *Home-Alone America: The Hidden Toll of Day Care, Behavioral Drugs, and Other Parent Substitutes* (Honeoye Falls, NY: Sentinel HC, 2004) (arguing against day care and working motherhood); Laura Schlessinger, *Parenthood By Proxy: Don't Have Them If You Won't Raise Them* (New York: HarperCollins, 2000) (similar); Robert Shaw, *The Epidemic: The Rot of American Culture, Absentee and Permissive Parenting, and the Resultant Plague of Joyless, Selfish Children* (New York: Harper, 2003) (title speaks for itself); Suzanne Venker, *Seven Myths of Working Mothers: Why Children and (Most) Careers Just Don't Mix* (Dallas: Spence Publishing Company, 2008) (to become healthy and productive, children require a full-time mother at home).

42 See Peter Stearns, *Anxious Parents: A History of Modern Childrearing in America* (New York: New York University Press, 2003), 1, 3 ("contemporary children [are] seen as more fragile, readily overburdened, requiring careful handling or even outright favoritism lest their shaky self-esteem be crushed"); Madeline Levine, *The Price of Privilege: How Parental Pressure and Material Advantage Are Creating a Generation of Disconnected and Unhappy Kids* (New York: Harper Paperbacks, 2008) (discussing the "anxious, overprotective, oversolicitous, intrusive parenting that has become commonplace in affluent communities").

43 Gornick and Meyers compare twelve countries including Belgium, Canada, Denmark, Finland, France, Germany, Luxembourg, Netherlands, Norway, Sweden, the United Kingdom, and the United States (Gornick and Meyers, *Families That Work,* 22).

44 Ibid., 5.

45 See especially ibid.

46 While Americans tend to scoff at this notion as impossible, these types of policies are common in Europe. As Gornick and Meyers write, "All across Europe, as of approximately 2000, normal full-time weekly hours are set at levels below the forty hours that is the legal norm in the United States—thirty-five hours in France and between thirty-seven and thirty-nine hours everywhere else. The incidence of very long hours (for example, beyond fifty hours a week) is limited in Europe by the European Union-wide policy of setting maximum weekly hours at forty-eight hours a week [including overtime]" (Ibid., 161).

47 Although American pundits and the American press frequently suggest that these generous social programs have devastated the economies of European nations, scholarly assessments suggest minimal support for this argument. For example, MIT Economics Professor Oliver J. Blanchard dismissed the idea that there is "any obvious relationship between the degree of social protection and the unemployment rate today" (Oliver Blanchard, National Bureau of Economics Research Reporter Research Summary [summer 2004], "Explaining European Unemployment," available at http://www.nber.org/reporter/summer04/blanchard.html [accessed June 20, 2009]). Princeton economist Paul Krugman concluded that in "a head-to-head comparison between the economies of the United States and Europe—France, in particular—shows that the big difference is

in priorities, not performance. We're talking about two highly productive societies that have made a different tradeoff between work and family time. And there's a lot to be said for the French choice." Krugman stated that French unemployment tends to run roughly four percentage points higher than in the U.S., but the bigger difference is that the French have made a tradeoff of less pay for more time with their families (Paul Krugman, "French Family Values," *New York Times* [July 29, 2005], A23).

48 Robert Goodin and Diane Gibson, "The Decasualization of Eldercare," in Eva Feder Kittay and Ellen Feder (Eds.), *The Subject of Care: Feminist Perspectives on Dependency* (Lanham, MD: Rowman & Littlefield Publishers, 2003), 246.

49 Ibid.

50 My thinking on the issue of how the state should deal with caring for the elderly was influenced by Ian Shapiro's excellent discussion of the issue in *Democratic Justice* (New Haven: Yale University Press, 2001), 196–229.

51 U.S. Department of Health and Human Services, "Administration on Aging, Profile of Older Americans," (2000), available at http://assets.aarp.org/rgcenter/general/profile_2000.pdf (accessed June 20, 2009); U.S. Census Bureau, "Facts for Features: Older Americans Month Celebrated in May," (2005), available at http://www.census.gov/Press-Release/www/releases/archives/facts_for_features_special_editions/004210.html (accessed June 20, 2009). This puts the expected increase in the 65-and-over population between 2000 and 2050 at 147 percent. By comparison, the population as a whole will have increased by only 49 percent over the same period (Ibid).

52 See Agency for Healthcare Research and Quality, "Preventing Disability in the Elderly with Chronic Disease Research In Action, Issue 3," 1 (2002), available at http://www.ahrq.gov/research/elderdis.htm (accessed October 25, 2008); Grace Christ and Sadhna Diwan, "Chronic Illness and Aging," 7 (2009), available at http://depts.washington.edu/geroctr/mac/ResourceReviews/HealthFiles/CI-Sec1-Demographics.pdf (accessed Mar. 2, 2010).

53 "Preventing Disability in the Elderly with Chronic Disease," 1–2.

54 U.S. Census Bureau, "We the People: Aging in the United States," 11 (2004), available at http://www.census.gov/prod/2004pubs/censr-19.pdf (accessed Mar. 12, 2010).

55 This type of care was the rule rather than the exception in post-war England. By one account, more than half of people 65 or older in Bethnal Green, a neighborhood in East London, lived with their children; another 38 percent had at least one child available within a five-minute walk; and 78 percent of older persons saw their children at least daily, while 97 percent saw them weekly. Peter Townsend, *The Family Life of Older People* (London: Routledge and Kegan Paul, 1957), 44, 49 (cited in Goodin and Gibson, "The Decasualization of Eldercare," 254–255).

56 See AARP, "Press Release, 9 in 10 Adults Age 60+ Prefer to Stay in Their Home and Community Rather Than Move," (2006), available at http://www.aarp.org/aarp/presscenter/pressrelease/articles/9_in_10_adults_age_60_prefer_to_stay_in_their_home.html (accessed Mar. 12, 2010) .

57 Emily K. Abel, *Who Cares for the Elderly? Public Policy and the Experiences of Adult Daughters* (Philadelphia: Temple University Press, 1991), 4, 128.

58 See, for example, Winnie Hu, "Ties That Bind, Ties That Break," *The New York Times* (August 2, 1998), 141, available at http://query.nytimes.com/gst/fullpage. html?res=9506EED81F38F931A3575BC0A96E958260 (accessed June 20, 2009) (describing movement of norms of Asian immigrants to the United States away from personally caring for parents).

59 See, for example, Shari Roan, "Not Leaving Home. Older Americans Want to Live Out Their Days in Familiar Comfort. Increasingly, They Can," *Los Angeles Times,* March 3, 2008, F1 (discussing the LIFE [Living Independently in a Friendly Environment] project, begun in 2005 to provide services that help people remain in place as they age); Frederick Kunkle, "Seniors Reach Beyond Family Ties. Fort Hunt Group Aims to Provide Services That Will Let Elderly Residents Age in Their Homes," *Washington Post,* (Dec. 2, 2007), PW9 (discussing Mount Vernon at Home, a nonprofit offering services to the elderly to help them remain in their own homes as they age); Jane Gross, "A Grass-Roots Effort to Grow Old at Home," *New York Times* (Aug. 14, 2007), A1 (discussing elderly neighbors combining resources to form a nonprofit providing services to help them remain in their own homes as they age); Martha T. Moore, "Programs Offer Seniors Option to Age at Home. More Assistance Projects Show Growing Older Doesn't Have to Mean Going Away," *USA Today* (Jan. 17, 2007), 3A (discussing Project Independence, a program funded by the state of New York providing services to help elderly remain in their own home, suggesting federal funds would create more of an impact); Jane Ellen Spiegel, "Food Program Pairs Children and Elderly," *New York Times* (Oct. 14, 2007), WE7 (discussing day-care centers in which seniors help children).

60 The inn is described in more detail in Delores Hayden's *Redesigning the American Dream: Gender, Housing, and Family Life* (New York: W.W. Norton & Co., 2002), 216–217. See also New Canaan Inn's Website, available at http://www.waveny.org/ nci_content.html (accessed June 20, 2009).

61 The Family and Medical Leave Act of 1993, Pub. L. 103–3, 29 U.S.C. §§ 2601–2654 (2008).

62 Goodin and Gibson, "The Decasualization of Eldercare."

63 U.S. Census Bureau, "Income, Poverty, and Health Insurance Coverage in the United States: 2010," 17 (2011), available at http://www.census.gov/prod/2011pubs/ p60-239.pdf (accessed May 25, 2012.

64 See Gary Engelhardt and Jonathan Gruber, "Social Security and the Evolution of Elderly Poverty," in Alan Auerbach, David Card, and John Quigley (Eds.), *Public Policy and the Distribution of Income* (New York: Russell Sage Press, 2006), 259–287.

65 Eugene Smolensky, Sheldon Danziger, and Peter Gottschalk, "The Declining Significance of Age in the United States: Trends in the Well-Being of Children and the Elderly Since 1939," in John L. Palmer, Timothy Smeeding, and Barbara Boyle Torrey (Eds.), *The Vulnerable* (Washington, DC: Urban Institute Press, 1988).

66 U.S. Social Security Administration, "The Future of Social Security, SSA Publication No. 05–10055, ICN 462560," (2008), available at http://www.ssa.gov/pubs/10055. html (accessed June 20, 2009).

67 See Engelhardt and Gruber, "Social Security and the Evolution of Elderly Poverty." The findings in Engelhardt's and Gruber's paper are further developed in a paper by David Card from the Department of Economics at the University of California,

Berkeley. See David Card, "Comment on Gary V. Engelhardt and Jonathan Gruber 'Social Security and the Evolution of Elderly Poverty'," (2004), available at http://urbanpolicy.berkeley.edu/pdf/Ch6CommCardonGruberEngelhardt.pdf (accessed June 20, 2009).

68 See David Rosenbaum, "At Heart of Social Security Debate, a Misunderstanding," *New York Times* (March 8, 2008), A19.

69 See Shapiro, *Democratic Justice*, 197.

70 According to the work of Melissa Jacoby and Elizabeth Warren, of those who filed for bankruptcy, 46 percent self-identify a medical reason (birth, death, illness, or injury) among their reasons for filing bankruptcy (Melissa Jacoby and Elizabeth Warren, "Beyond Hospital Misbehavior: An Alternative Account of Medical-Related Financial Distress," *Northwestern University Law Review*, 100, 535, 548 [2006]).

71 Genworth Financial, "Executive Summary: Genworth 2012 Cost of Care Survey: Nursing Homes, Assisted Living Facilities and Home Care Provides," (April, 2012), available at http://reversepartner.genworth.com/content/etc/medialib/genworth_v2/pdf/ltc_cost_of_care.Par.40001.File.dat/2012%20Cost%20of%20Care%20Survey%20Full%20Report.pdf (accessed May 25, 2012).

72 Shapiro, *Democratic Justice*, 197.

73 Currently 28 states still have filial responsibility statutes that impose responsibilities on adult children to provide for their indigent parents. Most states, however, no longer vigorously enforce these statutes (Allison E. Ross, "Taking Care of Our Caretakers: Using Filial Responsibility Laws to Support the Elderly Beyond the Government's Assistance," *Elder Law Journal*, 16, 167 [2008]).

74 Shapiro, *Democratic Justice*, 203.

75 Ibid., 203, 218–219.

76 Ibid.

77 See U.S. Social Security Administration, Office of Policy, "Income of the Aged Chartbook," (2004), available at http://www.ssa.gov/policy/docs/chartbooks/income_aged/2004/iac04.html (accessed June 20, 2009) (noting that the oldest age group (80 or older) has the highest poverty rate).

CHAPTER 4

1 See *Baehr v. Lewin*, 852 P.2d 44 (Haw. 1993); *Goodridge v. Department of Public Health*, 798 N.E.2d 941 (Mass. 2003); *In re Marriage Cases*, 183 P.3d 384 (Cal. 2008); *Kerrigan v. Commissioner of Public Health*, 957 A.2d 407 (Conn. 2008); *Varnum v. Brien*, 763 N.W.2d 862 (Iowa 2009). After the Hawaii Supreme Court's decision in *Baehr* declared its state's same-sex marriage ban to be suspect under the Hawaii Constitution, Hawaii voters amended the state constitution before the Hawaii Supreme Court finally ruled on the constitutionality of the same-sex restriction.

2 This backlash began with the reaction to the Hawaii Supreme Court's decision in *Baehr v. Lewin*. Following *Baehr*, Congress passed the Defense of Marriage Act (DOMA) of 1996, which declares that no state must give effect to a same-sex marriage celebrated in another state, and that the term *marriage* for purposes of

federal law is confined to the union of a man and woman. Pub. L. No. 104–199 (1996), 110 Stat. 2419 (1996) (codified at 1 U.S.C. § 7 [2001], 28 U.S.C. § 1738C [2001]). Moreover, as of 2008, 29 states had adopted state constitutional amendments that bar same-sex marriage, and of those states that did not adopt constitutional amendments, 15 adopted legislation similar to the federal DOMA which bars the state from recognizing a same-sex marriage celebrated in another state. See Human Rights Campaign, Statewide Marriage Laws (2008), available at http://www.hrc.org/documents/marriage_prohibitions.pdf (accessed Mar. 7, 2010).

3 See Introduction, pages 7–8.

4 See, for example, Richard Santorum, *It Takes a Family: Conservatism and the Common Good* (Wilmington, Del.: ISI Books, 2005); David Blankenhorn, *The Future of Marriage* (New York: Encounter Books, 2007); Council on Family Law, *The Future of Family Law: Law and the Marriage Crisis In North America* (New York: Institute for American Values, 2005); George W. Dent, Jr., "The Defense of Traditional Marriage," *Journal of Law and Politics, 15,* 581 (1999); William C. Duncan, "Domestic Partnership Laws in the United States: A Review and Critique," *Brigham Young Law Review* 961 (2001); Lynn D. Wardle, "Is Marriage Obsolete?," *Michigan Journal of Gender and Law, 10,* 189, 223–224 (2003).

5 See, e.g, William N. Eskridge, Jr., *The Case for Same-Sex Marriage* (New York: Free Press, 1996); Andrew Koppelman, "The Decline and Fall of the Case against Same-Sex Marriage," *University of St. Thomas Law Journal 2,* 5 (2004).

6 See, for example, American Law Institute, *Principles of the Law of Family Dissolution: Analysis and Recommendations,* §§ 6.01–6.06 (Newark: LexisNexis, 2002); Grace Ganz Blumberg, "Unmarried Partners and the Legacy of *Marvin v. Marvin*: The Regularization of Nonmarital Cohabitation: Rights and Responsibilities in the American Welfare State," *Notre Dame Law Review, 76,* 1265 (2001); Ira Mark Ellman, "'Contract Thinking' Was *Marvin's* Fatal Flaw," *Notre Dame Law Review, 76,* 1365 (2001); Martha Ertman, "The *ALI Principles'* Approach to Domestic Partnership," *Duke Journal of Gender Law and Policy, 8,* 107, 114 (2001).

7 See, for example, Nancy D. Polikoff, *Beyond (Straight and Gay) Marriage: Valuing All Families Under the Law* (Boston: Beacon Press 2008); Judith Stacey, "Toward Equal Regard For Marriage and Other Imperfect Intimate Affiliations," *Hofstra Law Review, 32,* 331, 340 (2003).

8 See, for example, Martha Albertson Fineman, *The Autonomy Myth: A Theory of Dependency* (Boston: The Free Press, 2004); Michael Warner, *The Trouble With Normal: Sex, Politics, and the Ethics of Queer Life* (Cambridge: Harvard University Press, 1999).

9 Santorum, *It Takes a Family,* 28 (emphasis in original). Santorum also says a number of things about the political left's position on families that can be dismissed out of hand, including that liberal elites do not support families because "the village elders *want* society to be individualistic, because a society composed only of individuals responds better to 'expert' command and control" (Ibid., 16–17). My discussion focuses on the parts of Santorum's argument that warrant more serious consideration.

10 See, for example, Dinitia Smith, "Love that Dares Not Squeak Its Name," *New York Times,* Feb. 7, 2004, B7.

11 Blankenhorn, *The Future of Marriage,* 23.

12 Blankenhorn cites a survey conducted by Norval Glenn in late 2003 and early 2004 in which respondents were asked which feature was more important to a good marriage: Thirteen percent of respondents chose "Promotes the happiness and well-being of the married individuals." Ten percent chose "Produces children who are well-adjusted and who will become good citizens." Roughly 74 percent of respondents, however, thought both these features were important and answered the survey "The two are about equally important" (Ibid., 226 [citing Norval Glenn, "National Fatherhood Initiative With This Ring…: A National Survey on Marriage in America," 30, 2005]).

13 Santorum, *It Takes a Family,* 21–22, 31; Blankenhorn, *The Future of Marriage,* 16.

14 Ibid., 16.

15 Ibid., 3, 105, 197, 201.

16 The 2000 Census found that 33 percent of the 293,000 same-sex female households had their own (biological, adopted, or step) children present in the household and that 22 percent of the 301,000 same-sex male households had their own (biological, adopted, or step) children present (Tavia Simmons and Martin O'Connell, "Census 2000 Special Reports: Married-Couple and Unmarried-Partner Household [2003]," available at http://www.census.gov/prod/2003pubs/censr-5.pdf [accessed June 20, 2009]). These numbers are likely overstated because of erroneous reporting by heterosexual couples. Ibid., n.4. Moreover, the children from a substantial percentage of these households are likely children born into past heterosexual relationships, but the Census data do not reveal this. Nevertheless, increasing numbers of lesbians and gay men are choosing to have children within the context of a same-sex relationship. In a Kaiser Family Foundation poll, 49 percent of gay men and lesbians who were not parents said they would like to have or adopt children of their own (Kaiser Family Foundation, "Inside-Out: A Report on the Experiences of Lesbians, Gays and Bisexuals in America and the Public's View on Issues and Policies Related to Sexual Orientation," [2001]). According to a 2007 Urban Institute and Williams Institute study, an estimated 65,000 adopted children live with a lesbian or gay parent, and an estimated 14,100 foster children live with a lesbian or gay parent (Gary J. Gates, M.V. Lee Badgett, Jennifer Ehrle Macomber, and Kate Chambers, The Williams Institute and The Urban Institute, "Adoption and Foster Care by Gay and Lesbian Parents in the United States," available at http://www.urban.org/UploadedPDF/411437_Adoption_Foster_Care.pdf [accessed June 20, 2009]).

17 In the year 2000, there were 10,801 children born through egg donations in the United States that were reported to the Center for Disease Control (Victoria Wright, Laura Schieve, Meredith Reynolds, and Gary Jeng, "Assisted Reproductive Technology Surveillance—United States, 2000," [Aug. 29, 2003], available at http://www.cdc.gov/mmwr/preview/mmwrhtml/ss5209a1.htm [accessed June 20, 2009]). Because sperm donation can be accomplished informally, the exact numbers of children born through it are unknown. One Washington Post article reports that donated sperm is used in 80,000 to 100,000 inseminations each year in the United

States; that in 2003, at least 15,000 in vitro fertilization procedures were performed with donated eggs; and that more than 1,000 babies are born each year through surrogacy (Liza Mundy, "It's All in the Genes, Except When It Isn't," *Washington Post*, Dec. 17, 2006, B1).

18 A recent analysis of a survey of same-sex couples married in Massachusetts found that nearly all (93%) of respondents agreed or somewhat agreed that their children are happier and better off as a result of their marriage. Respondents stated that their children felt more secure and protected; that they gained a sense of stability; and that marriage allowed children to see their families as validated by society or the government. In addition, 72 percent of respondents stated that they felt more committed to the relationship as a result of their marriage (Christopher Ramos, Naomi G. Goldberg, and M.V. Lee Badgett, "The Effects of Marriage Equality in Massachusetts: A Survey of the Experiences and Impact of Marriage on Same-Sex Couples," The Williams Institute [May 2009], available at http://www.law.ucla.edu/williamsinstitute/publications/Effects_FINAL.pdf [accessed March 14, 2010]).

19 Blankenhorn, *The Future of Marriage*, 105, 93. Blankenhorn later states, "To remove the male-female part from our public understanding of marriage would be to turn off marriage's single brightest and most unmistakable light" (Ibid., 150).

20 See, for example, *Bradwell v. Illinois*, 83 U.S. 130, 141 (1873).

21 *Orr v. Orr*, 440 U.S. 268, 283 (1979). See also *Frontiero v. Richardson*, 411 U.S. 677, 685–687 (1973).

22 This is the case for the Child Trends report, which Blankenhorn uses to argue that "research clearly demonstrates that…the family structure that helps children the most is a family headed by two biological parents in a low-conflict marriage" (Blankenhorn, *The Future of Marriage*, 123 [citing Kristin Anderson Moore, Susan M. Jekielek, and Carol Emig, "Marriage from a Child's Perspective: How Does Family Structure Affect Children, and What Can We Do about It?" (Washington, D.C.: Child Trends, Research Brief, June 2002) available at http://www.childtrends.org/Files//Child_Trends-2002_06_01_RB_ChildsViewMarriage.pdf [accessed March 14, 2010]). It is also the case for research by David Popenoe and Barbara Whitehead cited by Blankenhorn. (Blankenhorn, *The Future of Marriage*, 122–235 [citing David Popenoe and Barbara Dafoe Whitehead, "The State of Our Unions: The Social Health of Marriage in America, 2005," available at http://www.virginia.edu/marriageproject/pdfs/SOOU2005.pdf (accessed March 14, 2010)]).

23 Earlier studies that looked at children of gay parents often considered children born into heterosexual relationships that subsequently dissolved when a parent came out as gay or lesbian. These studies, therefore, could not separate out the effects on children of being raised by a gay parent from the effects of divorce. Charlotte Patterson summarizes the state of the research in "Children of Lesbian and Gay Parents," *Current Directions in Psychological Science, 15*(5), 241 (2006).

24 Gregory M. Herek, "Legal Recognition of Same-Sex Relationships in the United States: A Social Science Perspective," *American Psychologist, 61*(6), 607, 616–617 (2006).

25 Patterson, "Children of Lesbian and Gay Parents," 243.

26 Ibid., 242–243.
27 John Stuart Mill's harm principle, set out in his essay, *On Liberty*, is probably the most well-known liberal explication of the legitimate limits of the state (John Stuart Mill, *On Liberty and Other Essays*, John Gray (Ed.), [Oxford: Oxford University Press, 1st ed., 1991], 14). Likewise, Mills' defense of individuality and the benefits to society from allowing freedom and experimentation remain classic evocations of this cluster of values (Ibid. 74, 120–121, 128).
28 See Fineman, *The Autonomy Myth*, 7, 87–88.
29 See Ann Crittenden, *The Price of Motherhood* (New York: Metropolitan Books, 2001).
30 Stacey, "Toward Equal Regard for Marriage and Other Imperfect Intimate Affiliations," 344.
31 Warner, *The Trouble With Normal*, 91.
32 Ibid., 35.
33 Ibid., 36.
34 Warner argues:

> [T]his kind of social engineering is questionable. It brings the machinery of administration to bear on the realm of pleasures and intimate relations, aiming to stifle variety among ways of living. It authorizes the state to make one form of life—*already normative*—even more privileged. The state's administrative penetration into contemporary life may have numbed us to the deep coerciveness in this way of thinking. We take it for granted. Yet it is blind majoritarianism, armed not only with an impressive battery of prohibitions and punishments, but with an equally impressive battery of economistic incentives and disincentives, all designed to manipulate not just the economic choices of the populace, but people's substantive and normative vision of the good life (Ibid., 112) (emphasis in original).

35 Ibid., 36.
36 Fineman, *The Autonomy Myth*, 140–141.
37 Ibid., xix, 123.
38 See Mary Shanley, *Just Marriage* (New York: Oxford University Press, 2004), 16.
39 See *Goodridge,* 798 N.E.2d at 954–955 ("Civil marriage is at once a deeply personal commitment to another human being and a highly public celebration of the ideals of mutuality, companionship, intimacy, fidelity, and family. 'It is an association that promotes a way of life, not causes; a harmony in living, not political faiths; a bilateral loyalty, not commercial or social projects'" [quoting *Griswold v. Connecticut,* 381 U.S. 479, 486 (1965)]).
40 It might be argued, however, that although some individuals who enter into conjugal relationships may fare worse in the event of a breakup, if status-based marriages were eliminated, many other individuals would fare better because, in the absence of such recognition from the state, they would cease to enter into conjugal relationships altogether. Certainly Fineman and other commentators have suggested that women as a group would fare better if they avoided entering into marriage or marriage-like relationships with men (see Fineman, *The Autonomy Myth*, 135). Whether or not this is the case, my strong hunch is that ending civil recognition will have little effect on the numbers of people who enter into conjugal relationships—they will simply do so without the imprimatur of the state or its protections.

41 American Law Institute, *Principles of the Law of Family Dissolution*, §§ 6.01, 6.03–6.06.

42 See Elizabeth S. Scott, "Marriage, Cohabitation, and Collective Responsibility for Dependency," *University of Chicago Legal Forum*, 225 (2004).

43 See Marsha Garrison, "Is Consent Necessary?: An Evaluation of the Emerging Law of Cohabitant Obligation," *UCLA Law Review*, 52, 1 (2005).

44 Scott, "Marriage, Cohabitation, and Collective Responsibility for Dependency, 241–243.

45 As the Law Commission of Canada's important report, "Beyond Conjugality," argues, there are a broad range of relationships that could benefit from the stability and certainty provided by state formalization of their relationships (Law Commission of Canada, "Beyond Conjugality: Recognizing and Supporting Close Personal Adult Relationships [2002]," available at http://www.same-sexmarriage.ca/docs/beyond_conjugality.pdf [accessed June 20, 2009]). The report argues that the state should "provide an orderly framework in which people can express their commitment to each other and voluntarily assume a range of legal rights and obligations" (Ibid. 113). See also Bruce C. Hafen, "The Constitutional Status of Marriage, Kinship, and Sexual Privacy—Balancing the Individual and Social Interests," *University of Michigan Law Review, 81,* 463, 476–484 (1983).

46 This respect is incorporated into our jurisprudence. See, for example, *Lawrence v. Texas,* 539 U.S. 558, 562 (2003) ("In our tradition the State is not omnipresent in the home. And there are other spheres of our lives and existence, outside the home, where the State should not be a dominant presence. Freedom extends beyond spatial bounds. Liberty presumes an autonomy of self that includes freedom of thought, belief, expression, and certain intimate conduct."); Ibid., 567 ("This, as a general rule, should counsel against attempts by the State, or a court, to define the meaning of the relationship or to set its boundaries absent injury to a person or abuse of an institution the law protects. It suffices for us to acknowledge that adults may choose to enter upon this relationship in the confines of their homes and their own private lives and still retain their dignity as free persons. When sexuality finds overt expression in intimate conduct with another person, the conduct can be but one element in a personal bond that is more enduring. The liberty protected by the Constitution allows homosexual persons the right to make this choice.").

47 There are currently five states that retain such laws, although after *Lawrence v. Texas* their constitutionality is dubious: Florida, Michigan, Mississippi, Virginia, and West Virginia. (Fla. Stat. § 798.02 [2009]; Mich. Comp. Laws § 750.335 [2009]; Miss. Code Ann. § 97-29-1 [2009]; Va. Code Ann. § 18.2-345 [2009]; W. Va. Code § 61-8-4 [2009]).

48 Warner, *The Trouble With Normal,* 112.

49 There may be administrative rather than theoretical reasons to limit the number of persons that the state should recognize. There is, however, no reason that two persons should necessarily be the limit.

50 Distributing resources generally to families with children, however, accords with distributing based on need. As Elizabeth Warren and Amelia Warren Tyagi demonstrate, "having a child is now the single best predictor that a woman will end

up in financial collapse" (Elizabeth Warren and Amelia Warren Tyagi, *The Two-Income Trap: Why Middle-Class Mothers and Fathers are Going Broke* [New York: Basic Books, 2003] [emphasis omitted], 6). In their words, "married couples with children are more than twice as likely to file for bankruptcy as their childless counterparts" (Ibid.). They are also 75 percent more likely to be late in paying their credit card bills than a family with no children and far more likely to face foreclosure on their homes (Ibid., 6–7).

51 At common law, marriage was an institution premised on the hierarchical ordering of husband and wife. William Blackstone, who wrote an authoritative treatise on the laws of England, stated that, "By marriage,"

> the husband and wife are one person in law: that is, the very being or legal existence of the woman is suspended during the marriage, or at least is incorporated and consolidated into that of the husband: under whose wing, protection, and cover, she performs every thing.... Upon this principle, of a union of person in husband and wife, depend almost all the legal rights, duties, and disabilities, that either of them acquire by the marriage.... But, though our law in general considers man and wife as one person, yet there are some instances in which she is separately considered; as inferior to him, and acting by his compulsion.... The husband also, by the old law, might give his wife moderate correction. For, as he is to answer for her misbehaviour, the law thought it reasonable to intrust him with his power of restraining her, by domestic chastisement, in the same moderation that a man is allowed to correct his apprentices or children.
>
> (William Blackstone, *Commentaries on the Laws of England*, Vol. 1, [1765], 442–45). See also *Bradwell v. Illinois*, 83 U.S. 130, 141 (1873) (Bradley, J., concurring) ("So firmly fixed was this sentiment in the founders of the common law that it became a maxim of that system of jurisprudence that a woman had no legal existence separate from her husband, who was regarded as her head and representative in the social state....").
>
> Over time, this institution has gradually been stripped of this explicit hierarchical legal ordering, as well as of its gender-based legal duties. See, for example, *Stanton v. Stanton,* 421 U.S. 7, 10, 14-15 (1975) (rejecting the "notion" that "generally it is the man's primary responsibility to provide a home and its essentials" and noting that "[n]o longer is the female destined solely for the home and the rearing of the family, and only the male for the marketplace and the world of ideas") (citation omitted). Yet both the cultural resonance still attached to marriage and the failure to adjust societal norms that reward a single-minded attachment to the workplace so that workers require partners at home who will take care of their households continue to place women in heterosexual relationships at a disadvantage to men. In contrast to heterosexual relationships, same-sex relationships generally demonstrate greater equality between the partners (Gregory M. Herek, "Legal Recognition of Same-Sex Relationships in the United States: A Social Science Perspective," available at http://psychology.ucdavis.edu/rainbow/HTML/AP_06_pre.PDF [accessed June 20, 2009]).

52 See Introduction, pp. 6–7; Katharine T. Bartlett, "Brigitte M. Bodenheimer Memorial Lecture on the Family: Saving the Family from the Reformers," *University of California Davis Law Review, 31,* 809, 844–845 (1998).

53 For more discussion of this issue, see Chapter 3.

54 Susan Moller Okin, *Justice, Gender and the Family* (New York: Basic Books, 1989), 177 (quoting Anita Shreve, *Remaking Motherhood* [New York: Viking Press, 1987], 237).

55 See, generally, James S. Fishkin, *Justice, Equal Opportunity, and the Family* (New Haven: Yale University Press, 1983).

56 See Michael Walzer, *Spheres of Justice: A Defense of Pluralism and Equality* (New York: Basic Books, 1983), 127–128.

57 Ibid.

58 See Miller McPherson, Lynn Smith-Lovin, and Matthew E. Brashears, "Social Isolation in America: Changes in Core Discussion Networks Over Two Decades," *American Sociological Review, 71,* 353 (2006), which I discuss in the Introduction, p. 7.

59 Between 1960 and 2000, employment of married mothers nearly tripled overall, with the employment rates for mothers with children under six increasing the most rapidly (Janet C. Gornick and Marcia K. Meyers, *Families That Work: Policies for Reconciling Parenthood and Employment* [New York: Russell Sage Foundation Publications, 2003], 27–28). All told, women's participation in the labor market rose from 28 percent in 1940 to 60 percent in 2000 (Ibid., 27).

60 Michael Hout and Caroline Hanley, "The Overworked American Family: Trends and Nontrends in Working Hours 1968–2001," (2002), available at http://ucdata.berkeley.edu/rsfcensus/papers/Working_Hours_HoutHanley.pdf (accessed March 16, 2010). See also Jerry A. Jacobs and Kathleen Gerson, "Overworked Individuals or Overworked Families?," *Work and Occupations, 28,* 40 (2001).

61 According to the Census Bureau, United States workers spend an average of 25.5 minutes commuting to their job each way, or 51 minutes total on their commute (Bureau of the Census, 2008 American Community Survey, "Mean Travel Time to Work of Workers 16 Years and Over Who Did Not Work at Home (Minutes)," available at http://factfinder.census.gov/servlet/GRTTable?_bm=y&-geo_id=01000US&-_box_head_nbr=R0801&-ds_name=ACS_2008_1YR_G00_&-_lang=en&-redoLog=true&-format=US-30&-mt_name=ACS_20 [accessed March 16, 2010]).

62 See Suzanne Bianchi, John P. Robinson, and Melissa A. Milkie, *Changing Rhythms of American Family Life* (New York: Russell Sage Foundation Productions, 2007); see also Robert Pear, "Married and Single Parents Spending More Time With Children, Study Finds," *New York Times*, Oct. 17, 2006, A12.

63 See McPherson, Smith-Lovin and Brashears, "Social Isolation in America: Changes in Core Discussion."

64 Ibid.

65 See generally Robert Putnam, *Making Democracy Work: Civic Traditions in Modern Italy* (Princeton, NJ: Princeton University Press, 1994); *Bowling Alone: The Collapse and Revival of American Community* (New York: Simon & Schuster, 2000).

66 Policies that help families reconcile work and caretaking are discussed in more detail in Chapter 3.

67 See J. Thomas Oldham, "What Does the U.S. System Regarding Inheritance Rights of Children Reveal about American Families?," *Family Law Quarterly, 33,* 265, 269 (1999).

68 See Scott, "Marriage, Cohabitation, and Collective Responsibility for Dependency," 241–245.

69 Ibid.

70 Dina ElBoghdady, "For Love and Money: Amid Economic Sickness, Bridal Industry Radiates Health," *Washington Post,* May 25, 2003, F1.

71 See Judith Stacey, "The New Family Values Crusaders: Dan Quayle's Revenge," *The Nation, 259*(4), July 25, 1994, 119. See also Linda C. McClain, *The Place of Families: Fostering Capacity, Equality, and Responsibility* (Harvard University Press, 2006), 191–219.

72 See Iris Marion Young, "Reflections on Families in the Age of Murphy Brown: On Gender, Justice, and Sexuality," in Nancy J. Hirschmann and Christine Di Stefano (Eds.), *Revisioning the Political: Feminist Reconstructions of Traditional Concepts in Western Political Theory* (Boulder, CO: Westview Press, 1996), 251.

73 See Nancy Dowd, "Stigmatizing Single Parents," *Harvard Women's Law Journal, 18,* 19, 34–35 (1995).

74 Gary Painter and David I. Levine, "Family Structure and Youths' Outcomes: Which Correlations are Causal?," *Journal of Human Resources, 35*(3), 524 (2000).

75 Sara McLanahan and Gary Sandefur, *Growing Up in a Single-Parent Family: What Hurts, What Helps* (Cambridge: Harvard University Press, 1994); Thomas Deleire and Ariel Kalil, "Good Things Come in Threes: Single-Parent Multigenerational Family Structure and Adolescent Adjustment," *Demography, 39*(2), 393 (2002); Leslie N. Richards and Cynthia J. Schmiege, "Problems and Strengths of Single-Parent Families: Implication for Practice and Policy," *Family Relations, 42*(3), 277 (July 1993).

76 See Marian Wright Edelman, "Preventing Adolescent Pregnancy: A Role for Social Work Services," *Urban Education, 22*(4), 496 (1988) ("New analysis of national survey data…shows that minority and white birth rates are essentially the same if we control for income and basic skills deficits—'shortfalls that reduce teens' life options.'"); Kristen Luker, *Dubious Conceptions: The Politics of Teen Pregnancy* (Cambridge: Harvard University Press, 1997).

77 Covenant marriage laws, in which individuals getting married can choose whether or not heightened standards will apply at divorce, also pose less of a conflict among important goods (see Ariz. Rev. Stat. § 25–901 to 25–906 [2000 & Supp. 2004], Ark. Code Ann. § 9–11–801 to 9–11–811 [2002 & Supp. 2003], La. Rev. Stat. Ann. § 9:272 to 9:276 [2000 & Supp. 2005]). Given the small number of couples who choose to enter into covenant marriage where it is available, though, as well as the problems with requiring parties to remain in a marriage that one party wants to exit, the state would be wise to seek alternative policies. In Louisiana, 2 percent, in Arizona, 0.25 percent, and in Arkansas, only 71 out of approximately 38,000 marrying couples elected the covenant marriage option during the first year (2001–2002) of its availability. Scott Drewianka, "Civil Unions and Covenant Marriage: The Economics of Reforming Marital Institutions (2003)," available at http://www.uwm.edu/~sdrewian/MEApaper2003.pdf (accessed March 16, 2010).

78 See McClain, *The Place of Families*, 131–154.

79 See Bartlett, "Brigitte M. Bodenheimer Memorial Lecture on the Family," 842. Bartlett cites figures from a 1986 study that indicates that women initiate divorce in 62 to 67 percent of cases (Ibid., 842 n.135). A more recent study gives approximately the same result, placing the figure at slightly above two-thirds (Margaret F. Brinig and Douglas W. Allen, "These Boots Are Made for Walking: Why Most Divorce Filers Are Women," *American Law and Economic Review, 2,* 126, 127–128 [2000]). More recent data on the division of household responsibilities indicate that married mothers perform an average of 19.4 hours of housework per week, while married fathers perform an average of 9.7 (Bianchi, Robinson, and Milkie, *The Changing Rhythms of American Family Life*).

80 See June Carbone, *From Partners to Parents: The Second Revolution in Family Law* (New York: Columbia University Press, 2000).

81 See Clare Huntington, *Repairing Family Law*, 57 Duke L.J. 1245 (2008); Patrick Parkinson, "Family Law and the Indissolubility of Parenthood," *Family Law Quarterly, 40,* 237 (2006).

82 Isaiah Berlin, "Two Concepts of Liberty," in *Four Essays on Liberty* (Oxford: Oxford University Press, 1969), 168.

CHAPTER 5

1 See *Mozert v. Hawkins County Board of Education*, 827 F.2d 1058 (6th Cir. 1987).

2 See Chapter 1, pp. 23–26.

3 The term is Duncan Lindsey's (Duncan Lindsey, *The Welfare of Children* [New York: Oxford University Press, 2003]).

4 See Cynthia Andrews Scarcella, Roseana Bess, Erica S. Zielewski, and Rob Green, Urban Institute, "The Cost of Protecting Vulnerable Children IV," 6–10 (2004), available at http://www.urban.org/UploadedPDF/411115 VulnerableChildrenIV. pdf (accessed Sept. 18, 2009).

5 The Adoption and Safe Families Act of 1997, 42 U.S.C. 671(a)(15)(B).

6 Ibid.

7 See Scarcella, "The Cost of Protecting Vulnerable Children IV," 33–34 .

8 Ibid., 16, 19, 21.

9 Most family preservation programs limit services to 30, 60, or 90 days (Duncan Lindsey, *Preserving Families and Protecting Children: Finding the Balance* [1997], available at http://www.childwelfare.com/kids/fampres.htm [accessed March 15, 2010]). See also Mark E. Courtney, "Factors Associated with the Reunification of Foster Children with their Families," *Social Service Review, 68,* 1 (1994) (survey of children entering foster care between 1988 and 1991 found 70 percent received only emergency response services, 20 percent received no services, and only 10 percent received extensive services). Of families offered services to prevent a child from being taken away, many received counseling (42.7 percent). Only 26.2 percent received financial assistance; 16.7 percent received help with transportation; and 7.5 percent received employment assistance. Even fewer families received services once a child was removed: 35.2

184 Notes to pages 120–121

percent received counseling; 3.8 percent received employment assistance; 17.8 percent received financial assistance; and 8.1 percent received transportation (Lindsey, *The Welfare of Children*, 145).

10 U.S. Department of Health and Human Services, "The AFCARS Report: Preliminary FY 2010 estimates as of June 2011," available at www.acf.hhs.gov/sites/default/files/cb/afcarsreport18.pdf (hereinafter AFCARS Report) (accessed May 25, 2012). In total, 408,425 children were in the foster care system as of Sept. 30, 2010 (Ibid).

11 42 U.S.C. § 675(5)(E)(2006). The purpose of this provision is to create a clear "expectation...that the biological parents have a fixed period of time to improve.... Once that fixed period of time has been exceeded, the system should begin rapid movement toward placing the child with another family" (*Adoption and Support of Abused Children: Hearing before the Senate Committee on Finance*, 105th Congress [1997] [statement of Rep. Camp]).

12 42 U.S.C. § 671(a)(15)(F)(2006).

13 Compare, for example, Marsha Garrison, who recounts that "[r]eformers...alleged that out-of-home care was frequently imposed on parents who needed only day care or financial assistance. They argued that the provision of intensive, in-home services could frequently avert placement, at lower cost and with less harm.... There was little evidence to support any of these propositions. Worse, there was evidence that contradicted them" ("Reforming Child Protection: A Public Health Perspective," *Virginia Journal of Social Policy and the Law, 12,* 591, 597 [2005]); and Richard J. Gelles and Ira M. Schwartz, who argue that the state expends too much effort to keep biological families together ("Children and the Child Welfare System," *University of Pennsylvania Journal of Constitutional Law, 2,* 95 [1999]); with Martin Guggenheim, who points out that no more than ten percent of cases involve serious abuse, and comments that "if the remaining ninety percent of children in foster care are there for reasons other than serious abuse, we now appear to have lost sight of our first principles" ("The Foster Care Dilemma and What to Do About It: Is the Problem That Too Many Children Are Not Being Adopted Out of Foster Care or That Too Many Children Are Entering Foster Care?," *University of Pennsylvania Journal of Constitutional Law, 2,* 141, 147–148 [1999]); and Richard Wexler, who states that "ASFA was the culmination of an assault on safe, effective programs to keep families together that began in the 1990's.... In the name of child safety, it has made children less safe" ("Take the Child and Run: Tales from the Age of ASFA," *New England Law Review, 36,* 129, 130 [2001]).

14 See Joseph J. Doyle, Jr., "Child Protection and Child Outcomes: Measuring the Effects of Foster Care," *American Economic Review, 97,* 1583 (2007) (finding that children in Illinois in marginal situations for placement have better outcomes in terms of delinquency, teen birth rates for girls, and earnings, if they are left with their families).

15 Poor families are vastly overrepresented in the foster-care system. Between 68–71 percent of children entering foster care come from families that received either federal welfare benefits or Medicaid (U.S. Department of Health and Human Services, "Dynamics of Children's Movement Among the AFDC, Medicaid, and

Foster Care Programs Prior to Welfare Reform: 1995–1996," 9 tbl. 1 [2000]). See also note 41.

16 Children in foster care exhibit mental-health problems at two-and-a-half times the rate expected of children in the general population (June M. Clausen et al., "Mental Health Problems of Children in Foster Care," *Journal of Children and Family Studies, 7,* 283, 284 [1998]). Moreover, 75–80 percent of school-aged children in foster care score either in the clinical or borderline range on one or both of the behavioral and social competence domains (Molly Murphy Garwood and Wendy Close, "Identifying the Psychological Needs of Foster Children," *Child Psychiatry and Human Development, 32,* 125, 125 [2001]). Children in foster care also suffer developmental problems, including cognitive delays, at a much higher rate than the general population (Ibid., 126).

17 *Nicholson v. Williams,* 203 F. Supp. 2d 153, 199 (E.D.N.Y. 2002) (testimony of Dr. Peter Wolf), vacated in part and remanded by *Nicholson v. Scoppetta,* 116 Fed. Appx. 313 (2d Cir. 2004).

18 AFCARS Report.

19 The Pew Commission on Children in Foster Care reported that in 2002, 44 percent of children leaving foster care had lived in one home, 22 percent lived in two homes, 27 percent lived in three or more homes, and 10 percent lived in five or more homes. On average, children have three different foster-care placements (Pew Commission on Children, "Fostering the Future: Safety, Permanence and Well-Being for Children in Foster Care" [2004], 9, available at http://pewfoster-care.org/research/docs/FinalReport.pdf [accessed Mar. 19, 2010]). In addition, a study of Washington State's child-welfare system found that one-third of the children in foster care experienced between four and nine placements, and one-third experienced ten or more placements (Washington Department of Social and Health Services, Office of Children's Administration Research, Washington State Department of Social and Health Services, "Foster Youth Transition to Independence Study 4" [2003], available at http://www.thesociologycenter.com/GeneralBibliography/FYTRpt_2.pdf [accessed Mar. 20, 2010]).

20 See Mary I. Benedict et al., "Types and Frequency of Child Maltreatment by Family Foster Care Providers in an Urban Population," *Child Abuse & Neglect, 18,* 577, 581 (1994) (finding foster families were almost seven times as likely to be reported for physical abuse as other families, and four times as likely to be reported for sexual abuse; these families were also almost twice as likely to be reported for neglect).

21 See Barbara Bennett Woodhouse, "Ecogenerism: An Environmentalist Approach to Protecting Endangered Children," *Virginia Journal of Social Policy and the Law, 12,* 409, 417 n.47 (2005) (citing Congressional Record 143, S12,210 [daily ed. Nov. 8, 1997] [statement of Sen. Grassley]).

22 Press Release, Casey Family Programs, "Former Foster Children in Washington and Oregon Suffer Post Traumatic Stress Disorder at Twice the Rate of U.S. War Veterans, According to New Study," (Apr. 6, 2005), available at http://www.jim-caseyyouth.org/docs/nwa_release.pdf (accessed Mar. 19, 2010).

23 According to the AFCARS Report, 51 percent of children who enter foster care are returned to their biological parents (AFCARS Report).

24 Bernard Horowitz and Isabel Wolock, "Material Deprivation, Child Maltreatment and Agency Interventions Among Poor Families," in Leonard Pelton (Ed.), *The Social Context of Child Abuse and Neglect*, 137, 146 (New York: Human Sciences Press, 1985)

25 Jane Waldfogel, in a study of the Boston offices of the Massachusetts child protective services agency, found that 53 percent of reports of child maltreatment cases referred to children already known to the agency. About two-thirds of these children's cases had been closed by the time of the report; the remaining third were still open (Waldfogel, *The Future of Child Protection*, 15–16).

26 AFCARS Report.

27 ASFA requires that where a child has been in care for fifteen out of twenty-two months, absent certain exceptions, the burden shifts to the state to show why a petition to terminate parental rights should not be filed (42 U.S.C., 675[5][E]). The purpose of this provision is to create a clear "expectation...that the biological parents have a fixed period of time to improve.... Once that fixed period of time has been exceeded, the system should begin rapid movement toward placing the child with another family" ("Adoption and Support of Abused Children: Hearing before the Senate Committee on Finance," 105th Congress [1997] [statement of Rep. Camp]).

    ASFA further declares that in situations in which a court determines that "reasonable efforts" to reunify a family are not required, the state must hold a permanency hearing within 30 days, and must make "reasonable efforts to find another permanent placement for the child" (42 U.S.C. 671[a][15][E]). Further, permanency hearings must now be held annually (42 U.S.C. 675[5][C]).

28 The AFCARS Report states that the mean number of months of children in foster care waiting for adoption is 37.3 months, and the median wait is 28.3 months. A significant number of children, however, wait far longer. A full 16 percent of children, or 17,618, have been waiting for adoption for five years or more (AFCARS Report).

29 Ibid.

30 See Ada Schmidt-Tieszen and Thomas P. McDonald, "Children Who Wait: Long Term Foster Care or Adoption," *Children and Youth Services Review, 20*, 13, 15 (1998); Madelyn Freundlich, "Supply and Demand: The Forces Shaping the Future of Infant Adoption," *Adoption Quarterly, 2*, 13, 39 (1998). Grade school children are almost four times as likely as preschool-aged children to be slated for long-term foster care rather than adoption; that figure goes up to 33 times as likely for adolescents (Schmidt-Tieszen, "Children Who Wait," 23–24). Non-Caucasian children, meanwhile, are roughly three times more likely to end up in long-term foster care than white children, when other factors are held constant (Ibid., 23).

31 For example, a study by Chapin Hall Center for Children at the University of Chicago, which interviewed youths before leaving foster care and then between 12 and 18 months later, found that fewer than 25 percent were enrolled in college compared to 57 percent of 19-year-olds nationally. Only about 40 percent were employed at age 19, compared to about 60 percent of their peers, and more than 75 percent of these employed youths had earned less than $5,000 in the past year.

Fourteen percent of them were homeless at least once since leaving care. About one-third of them suffered from mental-health problems, including posttraumatic stress disorder, substance abuse problems, and depression. Nearly half of the women became pregnant by age 19, twice as many as their peers. About one-quarter of the young men and women reported having a child, twice as many as their peers, although they were less likely to be married or cohabiting. Moreover, a full 30 percent of the young men and 11 percent of the young women had been incarcerated between aging out of foster care and their subsequent interview with the researchers (Mark E. Courtney, Testimony before the Subcommittee on Income Security and Family Support, Committee on Ways and Means, United States House of Representatives "Children Who Age Out of the Foster Care System," [July 12, 2007], available at http://www.chapinhall.org/sites/default/files/old_reports/387.pdf [accessed Mar. 19, 2010]). A longer-range study by the General Accounting Office showed that by two-and-a-half to four years after youths left foster care, more than 60 percent of young women had given birth to a child (General Accounting Office, "Child Welfare, Complex Needs Strain Capacity to Provide Services" [1995], available at http://www.gao.gov/archive/1995/he95208.pdf [accessed Mar. 19, 2010], 14–15). See also Jim Moye and Roberta Rinker, "It's a Hard Knock Life: Does the Adoption and Safe Families Act of 1997 Adequately Address Problems in the Child Welfare System?," *Harvard Journal on Legislation,* 39, 375, 377 (2002).

32 This toll seems to have been almost completely overlooked by Congress in the passage of ASFA. Indeed, some members of Congress exhibited a bizarre belief that children could and should trade up families, much the same way that a driver trades up cars. See, for example, Adoption and Support of Abused Children: Hearing before the Senate Committee on Finance, 105th Congress (1997) ("Adoption is good for children. The reason is simple. Nearly every adopted child is put in the midst of the best child-rearing machine ever invented—the family. Children reared in families, especially two-parent families, grow up to do well on nearly every measure—marriage, employment, education, avoidance of crime, and independence from welfare.").

33 See note 15.

34 As of September 30, 2006, African-American children comprised 29 percent of the children in foster care although they were only 14 percent of the general population under age 18 (AFCARS Report; Annie E. Casey Foundation, "The Changing Child Population of the United States: Analysis of Data from the 2010 Census 7," available at http://www.aecf.org/~/media/Pubs/Initiatives/KIDS%20COUNT/T/TheChangingChildPopulationoftheUnitedStates/AECFChangingChildPopulationv8web.pdf [accessed May 25, 2012]). By contrast, white children comprised only 41 percent of the foster-care population, although they made up 54 percent of the country's children ("The AFCARS Report"; "Changing Child Population"). Latino and Native American children are also disproportionately overrepresented in this system (Ibid.).

35 See Naomi Cahn, "Children's Interests in a Familial Context: Poverty, Foster Care, and Adoption," *Ohio State Law Journal, 60,* 1189, 1198–1199 (1999) (discussing studies showing how poverty leads to foster care).

36 Scarcella et. al, "The Cost of Protecting Vulnerable Children IV," 6.

37 Ching-Tung Wang and John Holton, Prevent Child Abuse America, "Total Estimated Cost of Child Abuse and Neglect in the United States," (2007), available at http://www.preventchildabuse.org/about_us/media_releases/pcaa_pew_economic_impact_study_final.pdf (accessed March 20, 2010).

38 See note 16.

39 Poor children are more than twice as likely to repeat at least one grade or drop out of high school, and are nearly twice as likely to be economically inactive (neither employed or in school) at age 24 (Jeanne Brooks-Gunn and Greg J. Duncan, "The Effects of Poverty on Children," *The Future of Children, 7[2],* 58–59 [1997]).

40 See Lindsey, *The Welfare of Children*; Cahn, "Children's Interests In a Familial Context."

41 The Third National Incidence Study of Child Abuse and Neglect found that "[c]ompared to children whose families earned $30,000 per year or more, those in families with annual incomes below $15,000 per year were: more than 22 times more likely to experience some form of maltreatment under the Harm Standard and over 25 times more likely to suffer maltreatment of some type using the Endangerment Standard; almost 14 times more likely to be harmed by some variety of abuse and nearly 15 times more likely to be abused using the Endangerment Standard criteria; more than 44 times more likely to be neglected by either definitional standard; almost 16 times more likely to be a victim of physical abuse under the Harm Standard and nearly 12 times more likely to be a victim of physical abuse using the Endangerment Standard; almost 18 times more likely to be sexually abused by either definitional standard" (Andrea J. Sedlak and Diane Broadhurst, U.S. Department of Health and Human Services Administration for Children, Youth, and Families, Executive Summary of the Third National Incidence Study of Child Abuse and Neglect [1996]). It is not clear how much of the relationship between income and maltreatment is causal and could therefore be diminished by reducing poverty, and how much of this link results from correlation with some third factor such as mental illness that led to the family's poverty, which a poverty-prevention strategy would therefore not cure. Research supports the position that at least some significant amount of the link between poverty and child maltreatment is causal (see, for example, Christina Paxson and Jane Waldfogel, National Bureau of Economic Research, "Work, Welfare, and Child Maltreatment," Working Paper 7343, [1999], available at http://www.nber.org/papers/w7343 [accessed Mar. 19, 2010]).

42 See Janet Currie, "Early Childhood Intervention Programs: What Do We Know?" *Journal of Economic Perspectives, 15,* 213, 217–220 (2001), available at http://www.econ.ucla.edu/people/papers/Currie/Currie149.pdf (accessed Mar. 19, 2010). The High/Scope Educational Research Foundation found in a long-term study that individuals over 40 who as children had been in a preschool program for poor three-and four-year-olds were far more likely to be successful than those not in the program on a variety of measurements including education, employment, and

probability of having a criminal record (Promising Practices Network, "Lifetime Effects: The High/Scope Perry Research Study Through Age 40," [2009], available at http://www.promisingpractices.net/program.asp?programid=128 [accessed Mar. 19, 2010]).

43 See A.J. Reynolds and D.L. Robertson, "School-Based Early Intervention and Later Child Maltreatment in the Chicago Longitudinal Study," *Child Development, 74,* 3, 4 (2003); A.J. Reynolds et al., "School-Based Early Intervention and Child Well-Being in the Chicago Longitudinal Study," *Child Welfare, 82*(5), 633 (2003). Some large part of these programs' decrease in maltreatment rates appear related to the parental-involvement component of the programs (see Reynolds and Robertson, "School-Based Early Intervention," 17–18).

44 The U.S. Census Bureau estimates that 2.1 million children under 13 are without adult supervision before and after school (Lindsey, "Preserving Families and Protecting Children," 72). See also U.S. Department of Health and Human Services, "Executive Summary: Third National Incidence Study of Child Abuse and Neglect and Child Maltreatment 1997: Reports from the States," available at http://www.childwelfare.gov/pubs/statsinfo/nis3.cfm [accessed Mar. 19, 2010]).

45 See 42 U.S.C. 607 (2009) (setting out mandatory work requirements).

46 Gornick and Meyers, *Families That Work,* Chapter 7.

47 See, for example, Deborah S. Harburger and Ruth Anne White, "Reunifying Families, Cutting Costs: Housing—Child Welfare Partnerships for Permanent Supportive Housing," *Child Welfare, 83,* 500–501 (2004); see also Tamar Lewin, "Child Welfare Is Slow to Improve, Despite Court Order," *New York Times,* Dec. 30, 1995, A6 (receiver in charge of D.C. foster- care system estimates "that a third to a half of the District's foster children could rejoin their families if they had adequate housing.").

48 See note 24, and accompanying text.

49 See note 16.

50 See, for example, Chris Jenkins, "Mental Illness Sends Many to Foster Care: Medical Costs Overwhelm Va. Parents," *Washington Post,* Nov. 29, 2004, B1 ("Almost one of every four children in Virginia's foster care system is there because parents want the child to have mental health treatment, a report commissioned by the General Assembly states. The study—the result of a months-long examination of the state's foster care and mental health services—chronicles the difficult decisions that thousands of Virginia parents have made to relinquish custody of their children to the foster care system so they can get mental health services that are otherwise unavailable or unaffordable.").

51 "In a 1998 Robert Wood Johnson national household telephone survey, 11 percent of the population perceived a need for mental or addictive services, with about 25 percent of these reporting difficulties in obtaining needed care. Worry about costs was listed as the highest reason for not receiving care, with 83 percent of the uninsured and 55 percent of the privately insured listing this reason" (Surgeon General, U.S. Department of Health and Human Services, "Mental Health: A Report of the Surgeon General" [1999], available at http://www.surgeongeneral.gov/library/mentalhealth/chapter6/sec1.html#patterns [accessed Mar. 19, 2010]).

52 The supportive state would also ensure the availability of community-mental-health services in poor areas, so that parents and children have access to them (See Julian Chun-Chung Chow, Kim Jaffee, and Lonnie Snowden, "Racial/Ethnic Disparities in the Use of Mental Health Services in Poverty Areas," *American Journal of Public Health*, 93[5], 792 [2003]). This is a particular problem for minorities, who have poorer access to these services, are less likely to receive services at all, and, when they do receive such services, often receive lower quality care (Ibid.).

53 U.S. Department of Health and Human Services, "Blending Perspectives and Building Common Ground: A Report to Congress on Substance Abuse and Child Protection," Ch. 4 (1999), available at http://aspe.hhs.gov/hsp/subabuse99/subabuse.htm (accessed Sept. 15, 2009).

54 Arthur F. Miller, "A Critical Need: Substance Abuse Treatment for Women With Children," *Corrections Today*, 63, 88–95 (2001); Stephen Magura and Alexandre B. Laudet, "Parental Substance Abuse and Child Maltreatment: Review and Implications for Intervention," *Children and Youth Services Review*, 18(3), 193, 202 (1996).

55 A number of studies have demonstrated the negative effects of such high-poverty areas on the children who live in them. These include vulnerability to mental-health problems, behavioral problems, and signs of chronic stress caused by the poor living conditions and levels of violence in their neighborhoods (see, for example, Carol Aneshensel and Clea Sucoff, "The Neighborhood Context of Adolescent Medical Health," *Journal of Health and Social Behavior*, 37, 293[1996]; Hope Hill and Serge Madhere, "Exposure to Community Violence and African American Chidren: A Multidimensional Model of Risks and Resources," *Journal of Community Psychology*, 24, 26, 39 [1996]; Carl Bell and Esther Jenkins, "Community Violence and Children on Chicago's Southside," *Psychiatry*, 56, 46 [1993]).

56 See note 36, and accompanying text. As Marsha Garrison notes, the cost of foster care may rise as high as $50,000 per child per year. In comparison, an intensive preschool program, shown to reduce abuse, costs $ 6,692 per year (Marsha Garrison, "Reforming Child Protection: A Public Health Perspective," *Virginia Journal of Social Policy and Law*, 12, 590 612, 625 [2005]). Subsidizing housing by one estimate would cost $8,260 per family (rather than per individual child) each year (Child Welfare League of America, "Issue Statement on Family and Youth Homelessness" [Washington, D.C.: Child Welfare League of America, 2003]).

57 See Emily Buss, "Parents' Rights and Parents Wronged," *Ohio State Law Journal*, 57, 431 (1996).

58 See Chapter 2, pp. 66–69.

59 Indeed, as Frances Olsen points out, the state does even more to stack the deck in favor of parents than simply leave families to their own devices by supporting family privacy: It actively enforces parents' power over children. For example, laws require that the state return runaway minors to their parents, and that children obey their parents' authority subject to being locked up in juvenile facilities. Laws also grant parents a right to custody of their children; thus a next-door neighbor or friend cannot take the child to live with them without the parents' consent. Parental prerogatives are also enforced indirectly through

child-labor laws and other laws that prevent children from living independently, as well as through a system in which welfare and child custody payments go to parents rather than children (Frances Olsen, "The Myth of State Intervention in the Family," *University of Michigan Journal of Law Reform, 18*, 835, 837, 850 [1985]).

60 The term *children's rights* has been attached to a relatively wide variety of positions. I use the label here to refer to those scholars who argue that children's judgment and opinions should be given greater weight in the legal system, and adults' views (often the parents') of children's interests should be given concomitantly lesser weight when they conflict with children's views (see, for example, Katherine Hunt Federle, "Looking Ahead: An Empowerment Perspective on the Rights of Children," *Temple Law Review, 68,* 1585 (1995); Barbara Bennett Woodhouse, "Who Owns the Child? *Meyer* and *Pierce* and the Child as Property," *William and Mary Law Review, 33,* 995, 1001 [1992]; "The Dark Side of Family Privacy," *George Washington Law Review, 67,* 1247, 1253–1254, 1257–1259 [1999]; James G. Dwyer, "Parents' Religion and Children's Welfare: Debunking the Doctrine of Parents' Rights," *California Law Review, 82,* 1371, 1383–1390 [1994]). Excluded from my definition of *children's rights* are theorists who argue that children's welfare should be taken into account by adults, but who do not seek to empower children themselves to exercise rights (See, for example, Annette Appel, "Pursuing Equal Justice in the West: Uneasy Tensions between Children's Rights and Civil Rights," *Nevada Law Journal, 5,* 141, 150–51 [2004]).

61 Several scholars powerfully make this point. See, for example, Martin Guggenheim, *What's Wrong with Children's Rights* (Cambridge: Harvard University Press, 2005), 245–266; Elizabeth Scott and Robert Scott, "Parents as Fiduciaries," *Virginia Law Review, 81,* 2401, 2414–1248 (1995); Elizabeth S. Scott, "The Legal Construction of Adolescence," *Hofstra Law Review, 29,* 547, 559 (2000); Harry Brighouse, "Hearing Children's Voices: How Should Children Be Heard?" *Arizona Law Review, 45,* 691 (2003).

62 See Scott and Scott, "Parents as Fiduciaries," 2445.

63 See Chapter 2, p. 65.

64 Ian Shapiro, *Democratic Justice* (New Haven: Yale University Press, 2001), 91.

65 See Elizabeth Scott, "The Legal Construction of Adolescence."

66 Ibid., 548.

67 As Elizabeth Scott notes, this is not the case in all areas, most particularly in criminal law. There, the law's failure to take account of adolescence and its developmental processes produces substantial incongruities and injustices (Ibid.).

68 Ibid., 548–549.

69 See Brighouse, "Children's Voices," 703–704.

70 See Buss, "Allocating Developmental Control," 34–36.

71 See Brighouse, "Children's Voices," 703.

72 Scott, "The Legal Construction of Adolescence," 567–568.

73 The Supreme Court has said the same (*Bellotti v. Baird*, 443 U.S. 622, 643–644 [1979]).

74 See Susan Bordo, *Unbearable Weight: Feminism, Western Culture, and the Body* (Berkeley: University of California Press, 1993), 71–97.

75 *Bellotti*, 443 U.S. 642.

76 This is the position taken by 10 states that now require that pregnant teens notify one or both parents in order to obtain an abortion. For a list of current state parental notification and consent laws, see Guttmacher Institute, "State Policies in Brief: Parental Involvement in Minors' Abortions," (2010), available at http://www.guttmacher.org/statecenter/spibs/spib_PIMA.pdf (accessed Mar. 19, 2010).

77 See, for example, *Hodgson v. Minnesota,* 497 U.S. 417, 439 (1990) (noting that parental notification requirement raises difficulties in the distressingly large number of cases in which family violence is a serious problem); Scott, "The Legal Construction of Adolescence," 567–568.

78 Michael New, "Using Natural Experiments to Analyze the Impact of State Legislation on the Incidence of Abortion," (2006), available at http://www.heritage.org/Research/Reports/2006/01/Using-Natural-Experiments-to-Analyze-the-Impact-of-State-Legislation-on-the-Incidence-of-Abortion (accessed Mar. 15, 2010).

79 The Supreme Court has declared that the judicial bypass option must be available to pass constitutional scrutiny where states enact parental notification or consent requirements (*Bellotti,* 443 U.S. 622, 643).

80 Ibid.

81 Carol Sanger, "Regulating Teenage Abortion in the United States: Politics and Policy," *International Journal of Law, Policy, and the Family, 18*(3) 305. In fact, abortion opponents tout the effectiveness of using judicial bypass to reduce abortion rates (New, "Using Natural Experiments").

82 Sanger, "Regulating Teenage Abortion in the United States: Politics and Policy."

83 Ibid., 306. See also Scott, "The Legal Construction of Adolescence," 569–576.

84 A model somewhat similar to this is currently in place in Maine (see Consent to a Minor's Decision to Have an Abortion, 22 M.R.S. § 1597-A [2010]).

85 See, for example, William Galston, *Liberal Purposes: Goods, Virtues, and Diversity in the Liberal State* (New York: Cambridge University Press, 1991), 246–48.

86 Eamonn Callan, *Creating Citizens: Political Education and Liberal Democracy* (New York: Oxford University Press, 1997), 254; John Rawls, *Political Liberalism* (New York: Columbia University Press, 1993), 55.

87 Stephen G. Gilles, "On Educating Children: A Parentalist Manifesto," *University of Chicago Law Review, 63,* 937, 940–41 (1996).

88 See Nomi Maya Stolzenberg, "He Drew a Circle That Shut Me Out: Assimilation, Indoctrination, and the Paradox of a Liberal Education," *Harvard Law Review, 106,* 581 (1993).

89 Michael J. Sandel, *Democracy's Discontent: America in Search of a Public Philosophy* (Cambridge: Harvard University Press, 1996), 65.

90 Stephen Macedo, *Diversity and Distrust: Civic Education in a Multicultural Democracy* (Cambridge: Harvard University Press, 2000), 5

91 Ibid., 237; Amy Gutmann, *Democratic Education* (Princeton, NJ: Princeton University Press, 1999), 29. "It is one thing to recognize the right (and responsibility) of parents to educate their children as members of a family, quite another to claim that this right of familial education extends to a right of parents to insulate

their children from exposure to ways of life or thinking that conflict with their own" (Ibid.).

92 Jonathan Green (Ed.), *Morrow's International Dictionary of Contemporary Quotations* (New York: William Morrow and Company, 1982), 298.

93 Susan Moller Okin, "Political Liberalism, Justice, and Gender," *Ethics, 105,* 23, 26 (1994).

94 Nancy L. Rosenblum, "Democratic Families, 'The Logic of Congruence' and Political Identity," *Hofstra Law Review, 32,* 145, 156–157 (2003).

95 Ibid., 157.

96 Linda McClain, *The Place of Families* (Cambridge: Harvard University Press, 2006), 83.

97 See Chapter 2, pp. 66–69.

98 Will Kymlicka persuasively argues, "It is all too easy to reduce individual liberty to the freedom to pursue one's conception of the good. But in fact much of what is distinctive to a liberal state concerns the forming and revising of people's conceptions of the good, rather than the pursuit of those conceptions once chosen" (Will Kymlicka, *Multicultural Citizenship: A Liberal Theory of Minority Rights* [New York: Oxford University Press, 1996], 82).

99 Callan, *Creating Citizens*, 154–155.

100 Sandel, *Democracy's Discontent*, 112; Stolzenberg, "He Drew a Circle That Shut Me Out," 611. See also Callan, *Creating Citizens*, 147.

101 Ibid.

102 Ibid. See also Gutmann, *Democratic Education*, 30 ("The same principle that requires a state to grant adults personal and political freedom also commits it to assuring children an education that makes those freedoms both possible and meaningful in the future.").

103 Shelley Burtt, "Comprehensive Educations and the Liberal Understanding of Autonomy," in Kevin McDonough and Walter Feinberg (Eds.), *Citizenship and Education in Liberal Democratic Societies: Teaching for Cosmopolitan Values and Collective Identities* (New York: Oxford University Press, 2003), 184.

104 Callan, *Creating Citizens*, 132 (1997).

105 Ibid., 133.

106 Ibid.

107 Meira Levinson, *The Demands of Liberal Education* (New York: Oxford University Press, 2002), 65. On a similar note, Harry Brighouse argues that we need "to teach children the skills needed to make comparative evaluations between their parents' and others' ways of life in order to give them a real opportunity to live well" (Harry Brighouse, *School Choice and Social Justice* [New York: Oxford University Press, 2000], 72–73).

108 See Thomas A. Spragens, Jr., *Civic Liberalism: Reflections on Our Democratic Ideals* (New York: Rowman and Littlefield, 1999), 129–30.

109 Eamon Callan, "Autonomy, Child Rearing and Good Lives," in David Archard and Collin M. Macleod (Eds.), *The Moral and Political Status of Children* (New York: Oxford University Press, 2002), 137. See also David Archard, "Children, Multiculturalism, and Education," in *The Moral and Political Status of Children,* 158.

110 See Stephen Macedo, *Liberal Virtues: Citizenship, Virtue and Community in Liberal Constitutionalism* (New York: Oxford University Press, 1990), 278.

111 Although the language of these next few paragraphs is my own, I owe a great deal of the discussion of parents' interests in their children's education to Eamonn Callan's fine discussion of this issue in *Creating Citizens* (Callan, *Creating Citizens*, 138–45).

112 Rob Reich, *Bridging Liberalism and Multiculturalism in American Education*, (Chicago: University of Chicago Press, 2002), 283–84.

113 Ibid., 284.

114 Callan correctly argues that "[w]e should want a conception of parents' rights in education that will not license the oppression of children. But we should also want a conception that will do justice to the hopes that parents have and the sacrifices they make in rearing their children" (Callan, *Creating Citizens*, 145).

115 Burtt, "Comprehensive Educations and the Liberal Understanding of Autonomy," 200–201.

116 David Archard, "Children, Multiculturalism, and Education," in *The Moral and Political Status of Children* 150, 158.

117 Gutmann, *Democratic Education*, 43.

118 Shelley Burtt, "The Proper Scope of Parental Authority: Why We Don't Owe Children an 'Open Future,'" in Stephen Macedo and Iris Marion Young (Eds.), *Child, Family, and State: NOMOS* XLIV (New York: New York University Press, 2003), 243.

119 Ibid., 259.

120 Ibid., 266.

121 This is the case insofar as the state's duty pertains to encouraging children's autonomy for their own sake. It may be the case that the state could appropriately encourage a higher level of autonomy in children because of its important role as a civic virtue.

122 See Isaiah Berlin, "Two Concepts of Liberty," in *Four Essays on Liberty* (Oxford: Oxford University Press, 1969), 168.

INDEX

CPSIA information can be obtained at www.ICGtesting.com
Printed in the USA
BVOW061125211112

305842BV00012B/1/P